Paul Spicer was born in London, spent his childhood in Kenya and Jerusalem, and attended Eton and Sandhurst in the 1940s. He served in the Coldstream Guards, followed by a long career with Shell and then Lonrho, where he spent many years travelling the world, rising to Deputy Chairman. Paul divides his time between Dorset and Kenya. This is his first biography.

‘In Paul Spicer, the notorious American expatriate and radiant beauty Alice de Janzé has finally met her match. Like Byron, she was “mad, bad and dangerous to know”, one of those Pilgrim Daughters who travelled abroad and enriched the European aristocracy, becoming a social celebrity in Paris during the early 1920s.

With the dedication and zest of a private detective, Paul Spicer pursues her into the ironically named “Happy Valley” of equatorial East Africa, where her melodramatic life ended in violence and tragedy. She appears like one of those extreme characters from the pages of Evelyn Waugh and Scott Fitzgerald. But, as Paul Spicer shows, truth is again stranger than fiction.’

Michael Holroyd
(Sir Michael De Courcy Frazer Holroyd CBE)

The Temptress

THE SCANDALOUS LIFE OF ALICE, COUNTESS DE JANZÉ

PAUL SPICER

SIMON & SCHUSTER

London · New York · Sydney · Toronto

A CBS COMPANY

First published in Great Britain by Simon & Schuster UK Ltd, 2010
This paperback edition published by Simon & Schuster UK Ltd, 2011
A CBS COMPANY

1 3 5 7 9 10 8 6 4 2

Simon & Schuster UK Ltd
1st Floor
222 Gray's Inn Road
London WC1X 8HB

www.simonandschuster.co.uk

Simon & Schuster Australia
Sydney

A CIP catalogue record for this book
is available from the British Library.

ISBN: 978-1-47113-401-2

Typeset in Perpetua by M Rules
Printed and bound by CPI Group (UK) Ltd, Croydon, CR0 4YY

To June Elizabeth Cadogan Spicer, my wife,
and our two children Rupert and Venetia.

And to our two grandchildren,
Alexander and Tara Watson.

Contents

Part Two

Relatives of Alice Silverthorne

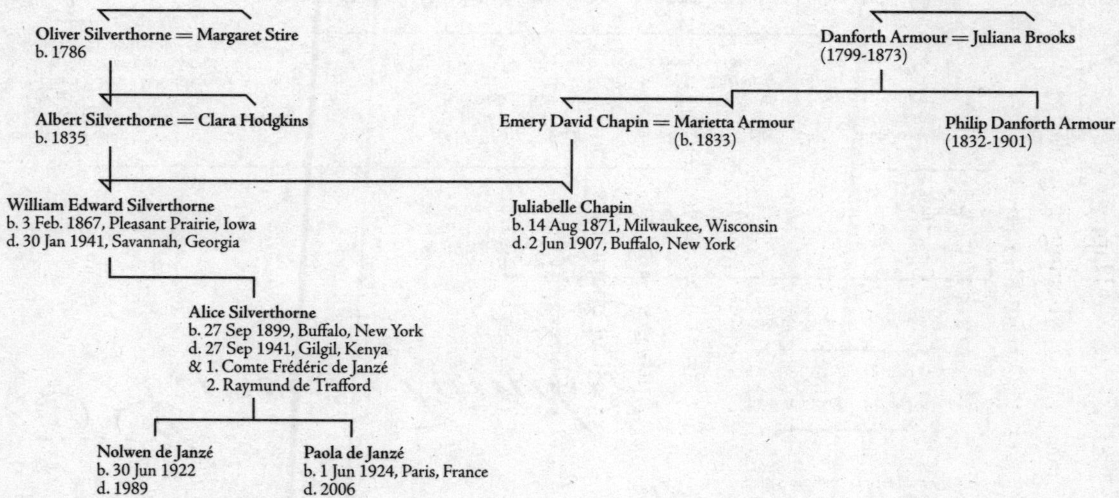

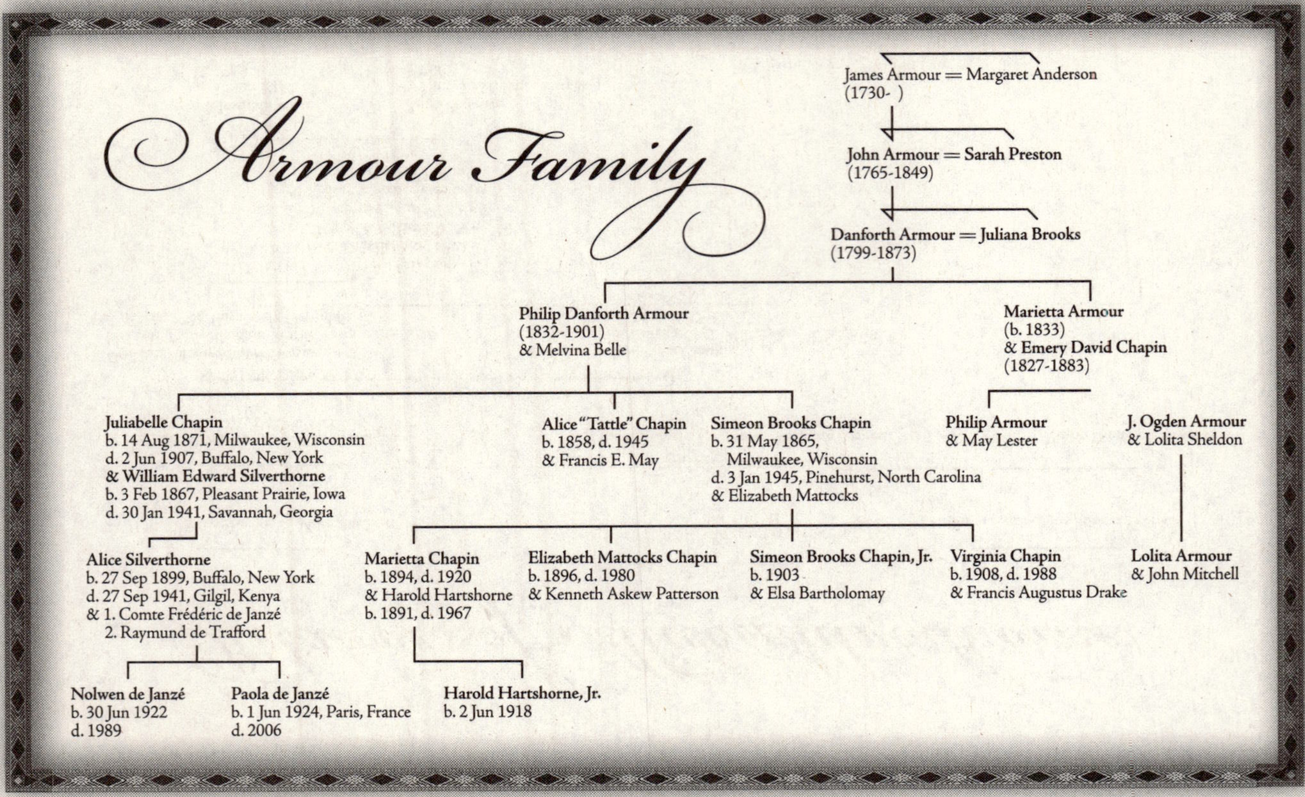
Armour Family
James Armour = Margaret Anderson
(1730-)
John Armour = Sarah Preston
(1765-1849)
Danforth Armour = Juliana Brooks
(1799-1873)
Philip Danforth Armour
(1832-1901)
& Melvina Belle
Marietta Armour
(b. 1833)
& Emery David Chapin
(1827-1883)
Juliabelle Chapin
b. 14 Aug 1871, Milwaukee, Wisconsin
d. 2 Jun 1907, Buffalo, New York
& William Edward Silverthorne
b. 3 Feb 1867, Pleasant Prairie, Iowa
d. 30 Jan 1941, Savannah, Georgia
Alice "Tattle" Chapin
b. 1858, d. 1945
& Francis E. May
Simeon Brooks Chapin
b. 31 May 1865,
Milwaukee, Wisconsin
d. 3 Jan 1945, Pinehurst, North Carolina
& Elizabeth Mattocks
Philip Armour
& May Lester
J. Ogden Armour
& Lolita Sheldon
Alice Silverthorne
b. 27 Sep 1899, Buffalo, New York
d. 27 Sep 1941, Gilgil, Kenya
& 1. Comte Frédéric de Janzé
2. Raymund de Trafford
Marietta Chapin
b. 1894, d. 1920
& Harold Hartshorne
b. 1891, d. 1967
Elizabeth Mattocks Chapin
b. 1896, d. 1980
& Kenneth Askew Patterson
Simeon Brooks Chapin, Jr.
b. 1903
& Elsa Bartholomay
Virginia Chapin
b. 1908, d. 1988
& Francis Augustus Drake
Lolita Armour
& John Mitchell
Nolwen de Janzé
b. 30 Jun 1922
d. 1989
Paola de Janzé
b. 1 Jun 1924, Paris, France
d. 2006
Harold Hartshorne, Jr.
b. 2 Jun 1918

De Trafford Family Tree

Sir Humphrey de Trafford 2nd Bt = **Lady Annette Mary Talbot**
b. 1 May 1808
d. 4 May 1886
(Lady Annette Mary Talbot) d. 1 Jul 1922

Mildred Mary Josephine de Trafford
b. 27 Mar 1856
d. 29 Dec 1934
& Sir Charles Bertram Bellew
3rd Baron Bellow Of Barmeath

Sir Humphrey de Trafford 3rd Bt
b. 3 Jul 1862
d. 10 Jan 1929
& Violet Alice Maud Franklin
d. 20 Jul 1925

Sicele Agnes de Trafford
b. 22 Feb 1867
d. 5 Feb 1948
& Charles William Clifford

Raymund Vincent de Trafford
b. 28 Jan 1900
d. 14 May 1971
& 1. Alice Silverthorne
& 2. Eve Drummond

Sir Humphrey Edmund de Trafford 4th Bt
b. 30 Nov 1891
d. 6 Oct 1971

Violet Mary de Trafford
b. 8 May 1893
d. 28 Feb 1968
& 1. Hon. Rupert Oswald Derek Keppel
& 2. Col. Keith Graham Menzies

Sir Rudolph Edgar Francis de Trafford 5th Bt, OBE
b. 31 Aug 1894
d. 16 Aug 1983
& 1. June Isobel Chaplin MBE
2. Katherine Lo Savio Balke

Sir Dermot Humphrey de Trafford 6th Bt
b. 19 Jan 1925
d. 22 Jan 2010
& 1. Patricia Mary Beeley
& 2. Xandra Carandini Lee

Prologue

It was around 3 a.m. on 24 January 1941 when the body of Josslyn Hay, Earl of Erroll, was discovered lying curled up and face down on the floor of his Buick car in Kenya, East Africa. The car had come to a rest over a gravel pit by the side of the Ngong road, eight miles from the capital of Nairobi. Joss, as he was known to all, had been shot at close range, the fatal bullet entering by the side of his left ear. Even in death, his otherwise unmarked face remained that of a very handsome man. At thirty-nine years old, Josslyn Victor Hay – twenty-second incumbent of the Erroll earldom, the hereditary High Constable of Scotland – was a lynchpin of Kenya's colonial community. Blond, clever, an ace card and polo player, Joss devoted a good deal of his considerable energies to seducing women, especially those who were already married. His very arrival in Africa in 1923 had taken place in scandalous circumstances – he had eloped with Lady Idina Gordon, an older divorcee and veteran of two marriages.

Much has been made of Joss and Idina and the famously decadent 'Happy Valley' crowd they gathered around them during the 1920s, although the truth is perhaps a little less exotic. The Errolls and their coterie were a small, tight-knit group of mainly British and aristocratic friends and farmers, attempting to forge a new existence in the Wanjohi Valley (a place that later acquired the epithet 'happy' due to the good spirits induced by its high altitude). Certainly, they found time to enjoy themselves there – house parties would begin at sundown and last until dawn, fuelled by alcohol and sexual intrigue. After his murder, it became clear that Joss – who had already been married, divorced, had remarried and was recently widowed at the time of his death – could have had any number of enemies. He had carried on numerous adulterous affairs throughout his life and had recently started a relationship with yet another married woman.

Although his death made newspaper headlines around the world, sympathy for the murdered earl did not always run deep. The American press, ever succinct, printed the immortal headline 'Passionate Peer Gets His'. There was, however, plenty of interest in who had committed the crime. After Joss's murder, the Kenyan Police, and the Attorney General in particular, decided the obvious culprit was Sir Henry 'Jock' Delves Broughton. Jock's new wife, the blonde and vivacious Diana, had become Joss's latest conquest, and the police reasoned that Jock had murdered Joss in revenge for stealing his bride. Jock was duly charged and then imprisoned. He went on trial on 26 May 1941, but was never convicted and after being acquitted on 1 July 1941, he was discharged. Although his name was cleared, Broughton never recovered from the ignominy of the trial, committing suicide the following year. To this date, the Erroll crime remains officially unsolved.

So who shot Lord Erroll? The question hangs in the air. Many possible answers have been given by a number of pre-eminent writers. The first to set his sights on the story was British journalist Cyril Connolly. A prominent contributor to the *New Statesman* in the 1930s, a critic for many years on the *Sunday Times* and literary editor of the *Observer* from 1942 to 1943, Connolly had been fascinated by the Erroll case from the beginning. In 1969, he joined forces with fellow journalist James Fox to undertake a complete investigation of the murder for the *Sunday Times* magazine. The result was published in that same year and was entitled 'Christmas at Karen', its content gleaned from dozens of interviews. With its accompanying photographs, including a picture of Erroll's head with its bullet wound, Connolly's article stopped short of naming a murderer, but even so, it reignited the controversy. Fox pursued the case even after Connolly's death, publishing his book about the murder, *White Mischief*, in 1982. It became a classic of crime reporting and was later made into a film starring Charles Dance and Greta Scacchi. In both book and film, a heavy shadow is cast over Broughton's self-proclaimed innocence: after all, Jock was the only person to stand trial for the murder. Many have taken his suicide to be tantamount to an admission of guilt.

Since the publication of *White Mischief*, there have been other authors who have either substantiated Fox's theory or disputed it. In 1997, Leda Farrant published her own version of events – *Diana, Lady Delamere and the Lord Erroll Murder* – in which she claimed that it was Diana herself who had committed the killing. According to Farrant, Diana was furious with Joss for refusing to marry her. In the 1999 memoir *Child of Happy Valley*, Juanita Carberry, who grew up in Kenya, relates that Broughton confessed his culpability to her three days after the murder when she was just fifteen years old. Most recently, the biographer Errol Trzebinski's biography of Lord Erroll, *The Life and Death of Lord Erroll* (2000), pins the blame on MI6 or another branch of British intelligence. The motive for assassinating Erroll, according to Trzebinski, was that Erroll had fascist leanings. The Oscar-winning screenwriter Julian Fellowes also revisited the facts of the case in his 2005 television special *A Most Mysterious Murder: The Case of the Earl of Erroll*, placing the blame squarely back on Broughton.

A peripheral character in all these narratives is Countess Alice de Janzé. Alice sustained an on-again-off-again affair with Joss for the best part of two decades and was probably still in love with him at the time of his murder. Born in Buffalo, New York in 1899, this transcendently beautiful American heiress became a French countess by marriage. After she arrived in Africa via Paris, attired in the latest French fashions, she quickly won over almost every man she encountered there, while still managing to befriend most of their wives. Alice was the very definition of a colourful character and, although hardly a well-known figure in our times, she achieved infamy during her own, making newspaper headlines around the world with her exploits. It is Alice's story that I will tell in this book.

For my part, I have been aware of Alice's name since childhood. Alice was a friend of my mother, Margaret Spicer. The two women met in Kenya when they were both newly arrived there in 1925 (my father, Roy Spicer, was serving as Commissioner of Kenya Police). At the time, Alice and her husband, Count Frédéric de Janzé, were staying with their friends Joss and Idina in the Wanjohi Valley. Margaret and Alice had much in common. Both were Americans abroad – Alice from Chicago, Illinois, and my mother born in Larkspur, Colorado. They were both fluent in French: Alice had arrived in Paris in 1920, chaperoned by her aunt; Margaret had been educated in Montreux, Switzerland. As new arrivals in Kenya they found themselves surrounded by a predominantly British expatriate crowd, so it is perhaps not surprising that they sought one another out. Alice and my mother were both musical, often entertaining the Happy Valley circle by singing popular American songs and spirituals from the Deep South, with Alice accompanying on the ukulele. My mother's friendship with Alice lasted until 1927, when she left Kenya to return to England.

Evidently, Alice exerted a considerable fascination for my mother – as she did for so many who knew her – because when my mother died in 1953, I came into the possession of her diaries and family papers and it was among these that I discovered numerous press cuttings and references to the glamorous countess. As well as the papers and cuttings, my mother left me her copy of *Vertical Land*, a book of sketches depicting life in Kenya in the mid-1920s written by Alice's husband, Frédéric. For most readers, the characters in Frédéric's *Vertical Land* appear to be fictional, since he changed the names of the real-life characters he described, but my mother had decoded these pen portraits, writing in pencil in the margins of her copy the true names of the characters.

In one story in *Vertical Land*, Alice appears as Delecia, a elegant American who is seen pulling up at Nairobi's exclusive Muthaiga Club in a low-slung Buick piled with luggage and a lion cub. Later in the book, in a portrait entitled 'Just Like a Gipsy' Frédéric describes another woman who can only be Alice, her ukulele transformed into a mandolin. The passage is characterized by the rather flowery Symbolist language fashionable in France at the time, and as such it gives us a highly stylized version of her person and presence:

> Wide eyes, so calm, short thick hair, full red lips, a body to desire. The powerful hands clutch and wave along the mandolin and the crooning somnolent melody breaks; her throat trembles and her gleaming shoulders droop.

> That weird soul of mixtures is at the door! her cruelty and lascivious thoughts clutched the thick lips on close white teeth.
>
> She holds us with her song, and her body sways towards ours. No man will touch her exclusive soul, shadowy with memories, unstable and suicidal.

Like most depictions of Alice, the portrait raises more questions than it answers, but there is no doubt that Frédéric was correct in his assessment of Alice as 'unstable and suicidal'. She was a woman who suffered throughout her life from the demons of melancholy, and who tried to take her own life on a number of occasions. Alongside this dark streak, however, was a vein of impetuous and often reckless daring. As a young heiress, she quickly tired of the Chicago debutante scene and began to explore the Jazz-Age nightclubs of the city, starting up an affair with a local mobster. After being banished to Paris by her family, she took a job at a French fashion house by day, cutting a swathe through the city's clubs and cafes by night. It was in France that she won her independence from her family when she married Frédéric, the sensitive, intellectual count who took her to Africa to help cure her of her unhappiness. After only a few months in Kenya, she decided to build a home there, leaving her two young children in France, too fearful of being a bad mother to grace them with more than the occasional visit. In Africa, her marriage to Frédéric fell apart after she started affairs with the two men who would become her great loves, Joss and her second husband, Raymund de Trafford.

As I began to research her life, the Alice I discovered was a lesson in contradictions. She could be bold and eccentric – she would go out riding alone amongst wild animals, kept a Nile crocodile in her bathtub in Paris, and launched herself with abandon into affairs with a string of dubious lovers. But her letters and other writings often reveal a sense of wrenching need and at times overwhelming unhappiness. In 1941, only eight months after Joss Erroll's murder, she finally succeeded in taking her own life at home in Kenya. She was forty-two. In virtually every depiction of the Erroll murder to date, Alice is described, suspected and cleared of suspicion. She is written about without any depth or explanation of her origins, her moods, her strengths and weaknesses. Her stunning beauty and great wealth is noted and then, in each instance, the author moves on. In Michael Radford's 1987 film of Fox's book, Alice was played by Sarah Miles, who portrayed her as an irresponsible and dizzy drug addict. The truth in such matters is, of course, always more complex and usually more interesting. Such was the case with Alice. (In fact, Alice never took drugs other than barbiturates for sleeping, relying on absinthe-spiked vodka cocktails for her highs.)

The more I read and investigated, the more I came to see that within the Alice legend were dozens of compelling anecdotes, inconclusive leads and half-told stories. Through my research, I discovered a woman who was in fact central – rather than peripheral – to the Erroll case. She seemed to me a figure worthy of further scrutiny, someone who needed to be placed in her full context. How did an American such as Alice end up in British colonial Africa? What was the nature of her affair with Joss? What hard evidence has ever been produced about the murder? What psychology has been deployed? According to anonymous letters sent to Jock Delves Broughton's defence counsel during his trial, the assassin was in fact a discarded mistress.

Part One

1

The Heiress

Alice de Janzé was born Alice Silverthorne, at home in Buffalo, New York on 28 September 1899. Home was an appropriately extravagant and elaborate setting for the arrival of this little heiress who would one day grow up to become a countess. The year before her birth, Alice's father, the Buffalo millionaire William Silverthorne, had bought a brand-new three-storey red-brick Georgian Revival mansion on Delaware Avenue, also known as Millionaire's Row. It was here that Alice was born and spent her early years. The house – designed by the pre-eminent Buffalo architects Esenwein and Johnson – was ostentatious, even by the standards of Millionaire's Row. There were large Doric pillars around the main doorways, a maze of vast and elegant rooms inside, and stables and servants' quarters at the bottom of a five-acre garden. William had made his fortune in the lumber trade and was eager to be counted amongst the most powerful in newly thriving Buffalo. His wife, Juliabelle Chapin, was a Chicago society beauty from one of the richest families in America, and she had brought to her marriage a considerable dowry and pedigree. The house was a monument to William's successes, both financial and social.

Alice was christened at the local Presbyterian church two weeks after her birth. Her parents had been married and childless for more than seven years prior to Alice's birth and they were overjoyed by the arrival of their much longed-for child. Such doting, wealthy parents ensured that their daughter's very early years were marked by an extraordinary degree of privilege. From the beginning, the attentions of an army of nurses and nannies were lavished upon Alice. William and Juliabelle were determined that their daughter would never want for anything in life and set about providing her with the very best that money could buy. Baby clothes were made specially in expensive fabrics imported from Paris. Juliabelle would take regular shopping trips to Chicago, New York and Boston, where she would purchase vast quantities of gifts and toys for her little girl. As Alice grew from infant to child, her parents supervised her education at home, employing private governesses who instructed her in French, German, reading, writing and basic arithmetic. For her seventh birthday, Alice was given her own pony and trap: there is a delightful photograph in existence of a 7-year-old Alice dressed in a short jacket and smock with a straw boater, sitting proudly in the wicker trap and holding the reins of the small black pony. By all accounts, the very young Alice was a carefree and affectionate child who adored her parents and was devoted to her pets.

Even so, the union between Alice's parents was far from easy. Juliabelle and William had always been something of a mismatch. William was robust, energetic, and careless. Juliabelle was more fragile, physically and emotionally, and prone to prolonged periods of sadness. What's more, they were both from very different social backgrounds. William was born in Pleasant Prairie, Iowa on 3 February 1867, the third of seven children born to Albert David Silverthorne and Clara Frances Hodgkins, a solidly 'merchant class' couple. William's father had made his money in the lumber business in the period after Chicago's Great Fire of 1871 when construction materials were at a premium. William himself had gone into the family business at a young age, working his way up through the ranks from the most menial of positions to the highest of managerial levels. He quickly proved himself to be a natural and talented businessman with a powerful drive for financial gain in this most socially and professionally mobile of cities. He was good-looking and popular, made friends easily and enjoyed socializing, carousing, playing cards and chasing girls.

Born on 14 August 1871, Juliabelle was the youngest daughter of the union between two of the most powerful Chicago families of the nineteenth century, the Armours and the Chapins. Her mother, Marietta Armour, was the sister of the famous Chicagoan Philip Danforth Armour, who is still listed as one of the forty richest American men of all time. Thanks to her father, Emery David Chapin, Juliabelle was related to the Springfield Chapins, founders and benefactors of Springfield, Massachusetts. Her paternal grandfather had made his money from investing in the railroads in Springfield, but the Chicago faction of the Chapin family was also associated with the meat-packing industry, much like their friends and colleagues, the Armours. When Juliabelle's parents married, the Chapins and the Armours were united by wedlock, and not for the first time. In fact, there had already been several Armour–Chapin weddings in Chicago and by the late nineteenth century the two families had become the city's equivalent of royalty: society columns were full of gossip about the family and their appearances at weddings, social events and debutante parties.

From birth, Juliabelle had been groomed to marry a wealthy and influential husband. Needless to say when William Silverthorne began to pursue Juliabelle, the Armour–Chapins were far from impressed. Despite William's quite significant wealth and promising career as an entrepreneur, the Armour–Chapins considered him a highly inappropriate match for one of the most eligible heiresses in Chicago. Even though William could trace his ancestors back to their arrival in Virginia from England in 1656, the Silverthornes had become comfortably affluent through business endeavours such as making felt and selling lumber and were therefore deemed socially inferior. Furthermore, the Armour–Chapins wholeheartedly disapproved of William's reputation as a drinker, gambler and ladies' man. Undeterred, William courted Juliabelle relentlessly, pursuing her with the same zest, determination and enthusiasm that he usually reserved for his business deals. Eventually, his good looks, charm and persistence won the day and he quite simply swept Juliabelle off her well-heeled feet. The undivided disapproval of her family notwithstanding, Juliabelle and William were married in Chicago on 8 January 1892. It was a modest affair by Armour–Chapin standards, with only close family in attendance. Shortly afterwards, the couple left for Buffalo where William and his brother Asa had recently purchased their own lumber yard.

At the time, Buffalo was the eighth largest city in the United States. By the early 1900s, it had a population of close to 400,000. Its proximity to Niagara Falls made it a popular tourist destination and a railway hub. It was an appealing and efficient centre of commerce for the many entrepreneurs – William and Asa included – who flocked to the city in the 1890s in the hope of making their fortunes there. Juliabelle began setting up home but William was doggedly determined to build up his business and was often away for long periods at a time, travelling across the country as far afield as Arkansas and Missouri in order to open new sawmills and set up plants. The seven years in which the couple failed to conceive a child were a period of enormous loneliness for Juliabelle, who found herself living far away from her home and family and with a husband who was frequently absent. Although the eventual birth of her daughter brought her a degree of fulfilment, it could not mend her fractured marriage.

In the years after Alice's birth, Juliabelle and William were unable to conceive another child, and although Juliabelle adored her only daughter, she continued to feel dissatisfied with her life in Buffalo. To make matters worse, her health was failing: she was weak and permanently tired. Meanwhile, William continued his regime of working and heavy socializing. He was drinking, gambling and spending more and more time in Chicago. There were rumours that he was having affairs, possibly even one with Juliabelle's cousin Louise Mattocks (a member of the Chapin clan). By the early part of 1907, Juliabelle was beside herself with unhappiness. She was now convinced that her husband and cousin were having a relationship. Gathering up her courage, she confronted William. What followed was a vicious argument that culminated in William locking Juliabelle out of the house at night in the middle of the icy Buffalo winter. Juliabelle was not readmitted until the morning. Shortly afterwards she was diagnosed with vascular laryngitis. She died six months later on 2 June 1907 at the age of only thirty-five. William had his wife embalmed with surprising speed and she was buried two days later on 4 June 1907.

William now found himself living alone with a young and very unhappy daughter. Juliabelle's death was a crushing blow to Alice who was deeply attached to both parents but who had always spent so much time with her mother. To a 7-year-old girl who woke up one morning to find her mother gone, it was little compensation that Juliabelle had willed an enormous inheritance to her daughter, placed in trust until she reached the age of eighteen. The trustees of the will were Juliabelle's father, her mother's elder brother Simeon B. Chapin (Uncle Sim) and her mother's elder sister, Alice (Mrs Francis May, known as Aunt Tattie). Meanwhile, in an effort to ease Alice's confusion and moderate his feelings of guilt, William redoubled his efforts to spoil his only daughter completely. He fawned on Alice, taking her with him everywhere he went. After Juliabelle's death, they travelled to Chicago together and on a whirlwind tour of Europe, with William continually showering his daughter with gifts and indulgences. A dangerous expectation was being established between father and daughter – one that would forever complicate Alice's relationships with men in the future. Whenever she wanted something from William, she was immediately and elaborately appeased.

There can be little doubt that William adored Alice, but it has to be said that he recovered from Juliabelle's death with remarkable ease. Barely a year later, he remarried. As it turned out, Juliabelle had been correct in her suspicions that William and her cousin were having an affair. His bride was none other than her cousin, Louise Mattocks. The wedding ceremony took place at the American Church on the quai d'Orsay in Paris on 8 July 1908 with Alice and two witnesses in attendance. It is likely that William proposed to Louise before he left for Europe, but that the engagement was kept secret in order to stifle the growing rumble of rumours back in Chicago. After the wedding, Alice accompanied her father and new stepmother on their lavish honeymoon around Europe. The Silverthornes travelled in the luxurious compartments of first-class train cars. They ate at the finest restaurants and stayed in the most well appointed of hotels. If William had set out to distract Alice from the death of her mother and to win over the heart of his new bride, this trip was certainly very successful, if fantastically costly.

For her part, Alice was developing an early and extensive knowledge of the great European cities. Before she was twelve, Alice had visited London, Paris, Nice, Monte Carlo and Rome. She was a precocious child, and it seems she appreciated both the sights and the culture on offer. Throughout her life, she would continue to travel, always feeling more at home when abroad. During the honeymoon, Alice charmed her stepmother, and the pair developed a genuine soft spot for one another. In this difficult period after her mother's death, the relationship with Louise must have been a welcome and stabilizing one. But William's latest conquest only served to redouble his problems with the Armour–Chapins. He had married into their ranks for a second time, an unforgivable outrage. The two families also believed, possibly with some justification, that William was an inadequate father. By parading Alice around the best hotels and restaurants in the world, they believed, he would damage her development and reputation. They were horrified by William's excesses and feared he would ultimately diminish Alice's chances of being accepted in society.

William, of course, carried on after his own fashion. On returning from Europe with his daughter and new bride, he set about looking for a new home. William and Louise decided to leave provincial Buffalo for New York City where William bought a house at 40 East 60th Street in Manhattan and a weekend retreat in Sharon, Connecticut. Over the coming years, Louise had several children by William, only two of whom survived to adulthood: Bill, born in May 1912, and Patricia, born in July 1915. Despite these new arrivals, Alice remained her father's particular favourite. At the age of twelve, she crossed the Atlantic in his company from New York to Cherbourg on the *Aquitania*, the magnificent Cunard liner. Alice liked to dress beyond her years and William did not deter her. Even at twelve she could pass for seventeen and she relished wearing silk dresses and make-up. Everyone she met on the *Aquitania* treated her as an adult. Word reached the Armour–Chapins that William would deliberately fail to introduce Alice as his daughter, with the result that many aboard the ship assumed that this beautiful young woman was his companion. Although it is likely that the relationship between Alice and her father remained innocent, Alice's relatives on her mother's side found William's approach to parenting distasteful and even outright obscene.

By 1913 William's fast lifestyle and ever-increasing expenditures were beginning to catch up with him. Some of his investments were failing, but despite this he continued to spend beyond his means. He had a reputation for extravagance and was determined to live up to it. In 1913 he bought himself a top of the line Stoddard Dayton motorcar with a six-cylinder, 8.6-litre Knight engine, hiring a uniformed chauffeur to drive him around town in it (his daughter would later inherit his taste for luxury

American cars). No expense was spared to feed his appetite for ostentation; it is suspected – although not proven – that William was dipping into Alice's trust fund in order to help with his business debts and to keep himself in the manner to which he had become accustomed. He was also drinking heavily and was almost certainly an alcoholic.

Then, in 1913, some kind of traumatic incident (or possibly an accident) involving William took place. Although we do not know the exact nature of the 'incident' we do know that it galvanized the Armour–Chapins. They became determined to act. That year, Juliabelle's brother, Uncle Sim, decided to take action against William Silverthorne, applying for Alice to be made a ward of the court. Uncle Sim was a Wall Street broker and a Chapin to boot. He could use his considerable influence and money to put forward the notion that William was an unfit father, that he had a reputation as a drinker and gambler, that he was failing to educate Alice properly and that he was embezzling funds from her inheritance. The court in New York ruled in Uncle Sim's favour. William lost custody of his daughter. Legal guardianship of Alice was awarded to Alice's Aunt Tattie. Juliabelle's family had achieved their intended revenge: they had taken from William his most precious possession, his daughter.

For Alice, this must have been a period of extraordinary heartbreak and confusion. She was a thirteen-year-old, on the brink of puberty, accustomed to her father's affection and indulgences. She would have been oblivious to the questionable morality of her relationship with William.

She only knew she adored this man who had been the one constant in her life since the loss of her mother. Now Alice was sent to live with relatives whom she barely knew, in unfamiliar surroundings. Although William was far from an ideal parent, the effect of this severance on Alice was dramatic and damaging. Alice went from being the object of her father's constant attention and care to being a complete exile from his presence and love. It's no wonder that as an adult Alice could react with astonishing violence when the men in her life threatened to leave her.

It was left to Aunt Tattie, Alice's legal guardian, to look after her, to arrange for her to be educated and to prepare her for adulthood. Aunt Tattie had no children of her own and no experience of childrearing. Although she was a kindly and well-meaning woman, she hoped to fashion her young charge into an obedient debutante, someone who would slip easily into Chicago's elite circles. Alice had other ideas. She was entirely accustomed to a life lived on her own terms and did not adapt well to the limits imposed on her by her aunt's vision. Doubtless exasperated, Aunt Tattie thought it best to send Alice away to boarding school. Alice was uprooted again, sent this time to Mount Vernon Seminary, a school for girls in Washington DC. A non-sectarian private school, it had been founded in 1875 by Elizabeth Somers. (The school has since been absorbed into George Washington University.) Alice stayed at Mount Vernon for the next four years. As a student, she excelled at English, and began to develop an interest in writing, publishing short stories and verses in the school's magazine. One of her poems, which appeared in the Mount Vernon Seminary magazine in 1917 – the year that the United States entered the First World War – gives us an insight into her state of mind at this time:

The Storm
by Alice Silverthorne

A chill light shines in the sullen sky
With an angry sulphurous glow.
And a sharp wind sifts
Through the mountain rifts,
And whirls the leaves in eddying drifts,
To die on the earth below.

The grim-voiced winds are approaching fast,
Lean clouds slink out of the sky.
And a terror reigns
Amid the hurricanes
That whip the trees with the lash of rains
As the storm goes sweeping by.

So when you come, like the great red storm,
My cares, like the clouds, flee too.
And my heart leaps high,
With a happy cry,
Toward the turbulent blue of the wind-streaked sky,
– Swept free of the clouds by you!

The poetry, although obviously amateur in nature, reveals a troubled sensibility and an intense longing in

Alice. By the age of sixteen she had undergone the death of her mother, separation from her father, and displacement on a number of occasions. It is hard to imagine that such a headstrong personality, who was used to being constantly appeased, would have adapted easily to the structured environment of a traditional girls' boarding school. In her poem, when she longs for the clouds to be 'swept free', it is easy to interpret this as a cry for help to her father, whose leniency she must have sorely missed.

In fact, the turbulent weather Alice described in her poem had a direct correlation in her emotional life. Around the time of 'The Storm', she attempted suicide. Patsy Chilton – the former wife of Dr Roger Bowles, who served as a part-time doctor to Alice in Kenya and who knew Alice well between 1938 and 1941 – remembers being told by an American friend that Alice had tried to slash her wrists as a young girl at school. The attempt may have been simply a cry for help, inspired by the hope that her father would come to her rescue. There is no doubt that Alice was lonely and missing William during this period of her life, but it is also likely that she was already suffering from cyclothymia, a strain of bipolar disorder or manic depression that would afflict her for the rest of her life. It is extremely common for sufferers of the disease to first experience its symptoms during adolescence, at which point stress or trauma can easily trigger its alternating periods of lows and highs. Although Alice's attempt to kill herself failed, it had an immediate impact on her life. Shortly afterwards, she was taken out of the school and went to live with Aunt Tattie in Chicago.

Alice was now seventeen years old, extremely pretty and advanced for her years. At Aunt Tattie's, she quickly made a new friend, her cousin, the debutante Lolita Armour. Two years older than Alice and already a minor celebrity in Chicago, a young woman whose every appearance was reported in the newspaper gossip columns, Lolita was immediately attracted to her troubled but highly attractive younger cousin. Lolita's mother, Mrs J. Ogden Armour, was a patron of music and the arts and spent the war raising money and helping to boost the morale of the troops. Alice was enlisted to help with the war effort by selling programmes at charity events, knitting hats and scarves for the soldiers, and serving tea and coffee at church functions. Lolita also began introducing Alice to Chicago's debutante circles, filling her in on all the latest gossip and goings-on amongst the most fashionable families in the city. Despite Alice's recent difficulties, she found she socialized easily and, thanks to her good looks, was an appealing new presence on the Chicago scene. She was given her own 'coming out' ball, after which she was quickly invited to all the good parties and social occasions, attracting the attentions of many of the city's well-to-do young men in the process. Alice was now a fully fledged member of the Chicago elite. She served as bridesmaid at many of the Armour–Chapin family weddings during this time and appears in formal photographs, an especially attractive girl with a pout. She soon began to outshine all the other debutantes, even her cousin Lolita.

A newspaper illustration from her debutante years shows

Alice's early beauty to great effect. In the picture, her distinctive wide-set, almond-shaped eyes are enhanced with mascara, kohl and shadow. Her lips – painted and defined – form a perfect bow. Her hair is bobbed and waved, worn to one side, giving her the look of a silent film star, a Clara Bow or a Louise Brooks. Even at such a young age, her gaze in the illustration is assured rather than demure (if perhaps a little sullen). Now in her late teens, Alice had already learned to use her eyes in a highly seductive way and she had no trouble getting the young men of Chicago to notice her: she would bow her head and look up, without diverting her gaze from the object of her attentions, allowing her suitor to talk, and continuing to look at him while inclining her head from side to side, giving herself an air of wonderment. This technique was highly effective and became a trademark with Alice. She was also shortsighted, but rarely wore glasses, which gave her grey eyes an especially dreamy expression. Another distinctive feature was her voice, which, by late adolescence, was already lowering in tone. She had a ready and captivating laugh, and threw her head back as she exercised it. The only aspect of her physical appearance with which she struggled was her hair: it was thick, curly and hard to control. She changed her hairstyle numerous times during her youth and adulthood, sometimes parting it down the middle, sometimes plaiting it into buns on either side of her head. The most glamorous effect came from straightening it with the help of a maid or hairdresser so that it was either sleek against her head or loose around her shoulders.

Initially, Alice enjoyed the attention she received at parties and in the press, but as she became more accustomed to the Chicago social whirl, she quickly began to tire of it. She possessed an adventurous spirit and hated to be placed in a box. Evidently, she was frustrated by the restrictions and unspoken codes of the debutante lifestyle where she could barely move without being spotted and recognized. This was a somewhat shallow world ruled by somewhat shallow people who placed enormous value on the 'right' make-up and clothes, and who cared most of all about whom you were seen with and where you had gone for dinner the previous night. No end of effort was made to look attractive. Chicago debutantes were known to take the train to New York just to have their faces, hair, eyebrows and lips made up by Elizabeth Arden on Fifth Avenue, before dashing back to Chicago in time to get dressed for the next ball. Alice, a natural beauty, had no such compulsion. She began to find the rounds of debutante parties unspeakably dull. It was at this point in her life that Alice began to explore Chicago's seamier sides.

The novelist F. Scott Fitzgerald dubbed the decade to follow the 'Jazz Age' but Chicago was ahead of the game. In 1918 and 1919, when Alice began to frequent Chicago's nightclubs, jazz was helping to create a new atmosphere of post-war optimism and liberation that crossed racial and class boundaries. Partygoers were unhindered by the Prohibition that would begin in 1920 – Alice learned to take her drink and loved to dance until the early hours. She was moving away from her elite circle and beginning to explore her identity outside her family and their expectations for her. She was also meeting some decidedly shady characters. Organized crime was rife in Chicago. James 'Big Jim' Colosimo, the most powerful mobster in the city, ran 'The Outfit', as it was known. His gang of Irish, Italian, Jewish and Greek cohorts controlled the fourteen gangland districts of the city and all of the vice, gambling and labour racketeering. When Al Capone fled Brooklyn in 1919 and came to Chicago, it was to join Colosimo's ranks. Jazz clubs like the Green Mill, where Alice was a regular, were the places where the leading mobsters went to socialize and operate.

Around this time, rumours began to circulate that Alice was stepping out with a good-looking man of Italian descent with a doubtful reputation. The mobster in question has never been named but later in life Alice spoke of him to her friend Margaret Spicer. This unnamed character couldn't have been Al Capone, because he arrived for the first time in Chicago in 1919 (at which point he was newly married to an Irish girl baptized Mary, known as Mae) but there were plenty of other candidates. Whatever the exact identity of this new boyfriend, Uncle Sim and Aunt Tattie were quite naturally alarmed. It was feared that the gang member in question might begin to exert pressure on the wealthy Armour–Chapins. Worse, the sensitive Alice could be dragged into a mire of criminality. Alice was popular with all her relations who felt, quite rightly, that she was vulnerable. What's more, she had recently come into her inheritance and although the exact degree of her wealth is unknown, it is assumed she was worth several million dollars. In order to put some distance between

Alice and the growing scandal, Uncle Sim and Aunt Tattie thought the best course of action was to remove Alice from Chicago for a time. Aunt Tattie had an apartment in Paris so it was decided that Alice should be taken there immediately.

Alice arrived in Paris with Aunt Tattie early in 1920, a few months before her twenty-first birthday. The two women installed themselves in Aunt Tattie's apartment, close to the Bois de Boulogne, at 115 rue de la Pompe, from which Alice could explore the city. Paris had rebounded from the First World War in spectacular style. The cafes of Montparnasse were awash with artists, composers, poets and writers. In the city's bals musettes and nightclubs the strains of the same jazz music that Alice had loved in Chicago could be heard. Alice took to the city immediately. She was young and adventurous, keen to assert herself beyond the limited role established for her by her family. Aunt Tattie had friends who ran a small fashion house called Arnot in rue Saint-Florentin near the place de la Concorde. Alice had always loved dresses and was already showing an excellent eye for fashion, and so Monsieur Arnot employed her as his head manageress in the shop and enlisted her help on buying trips. This was Alice's first job and her first taste of an identity for herself as a woman with her own career and interests. The 1920s were an exciting time to be involved in dress design: these were the inter-war years, a time of regeneration and abundance, and those in the fashion industry were taking full advantage of the new and exuberant mood. Waistlines were dropping, hems were rising, and corsets were being cast off. Alice thoroughly enjoyed the time she spent working at Arnot. During the day she worked, but in the evenings she socialized, eating in the best restaurants, mixing with artists and local celebrities, visiting nightclubs and late-night bars, always dressed exquisitely.

Then, just as Alice began to take flight, she was brought quickly back down to earth. She was about to meet the man she was going to marry.

2

The Countess

In May of 1921, Alice Silverthorne was introduced to Count Frédéric de Janzé in a Paris antique shop. She was nearly twenty-two. Frédéric was twenty-five. The count was tall and good-looking with acutely blue eyes. A sensitive man and an intellectual, he read voraciously, wrote a daily journal, and later published autobiographical works in the guise of fiction. Alice's obvious sense of style and her American manners and accent immediately set her apart from the other women of Frédéric's acquaintance. It is possible that even from their first meeting he detected in her a rare combination of fragility and brazenness that appealed to his romantic nature.

Frédéric was born on 28 February 1896 in Paris, the eldest son of Count François Louis Léon de Janzé and Moya de Janzé, née Hennessy. The family's nobility originated in 1815 when the first Count de Janzé, a lawyer from Brittany, was given his title by Louis XVIII after he helped the Duke de Rohan safeguard his considerable power and wealth in the aftermath of the 1789 revolution. The title was passed down to Frédéric via his uncle, Count Albert de Janzé. Frédéric also had strong American connections on his maternal side. His mother, born Moya Hennessy, was from a well-connected Irish-American family in Connecticut – her own mother was Charlotte Mather, a descendant of Increase Mather, the early American Puritan minister and father of the influential author and minister Cotton Mather. The young Moya had met Count de Janzé on a trip to France and after their marriage the couple settled at the de Janzé ancestral estate, Château Parfondeval, in Normandy. Their two sons, Frédéric and Henri, both inherited the title of Viscount at birth, and after the death of their father in 1921, Frédéric, being the eldest, took on the title of Count.

Frédéric grew up in Paris but attended Cambridge University where he read English literature and discovered a proclivity for writing prose and poetry in English. Thanks to his time as a student, he spoke English with barely a hint of a French accent. He left Cambridge in the early part of the First World War to serve as an officer in the French Air Force. By 1917, he had been appointed aide-de-camp to Maréchal Lyautey in Morocco but after contracting malaria he was sent back to Paris to convalesce. On his return, Frédéric continued to pursue his interests. He frequented literary circles, and developed close friendships with Marcel Proust, Maurice Barrès and Anna de Noailles. He also became romantically involved with an American girl named Ruth Fiske. On 31 March 1918, the *New York Times* reported his engagement to this 23-year-old nurse from New Jersey whom he had met during his stay at the Astoria Hospital in Paris. After much pressure from his mother, who believed that a 'mere' nurse was an unsuitable bride for the viscount, he was persuaded to call off the engagement. Moya de Janzé had clear ambitions for her son. She wanted him to marry well, preferably a wealthy heiress who could help restore the de Janzés' crumbling estate and fortunes.

Moya liked Alice from their first meeting, not only for her money, but also for her style and liveliness. An immediate bond was formed between these two women who spoke the same language and came from the same part of the world. Moya vigorously encouraged Frédéric's courtship of Alice Silverthorne, although it was doubtful that he needed too much persuasion. Frédéric was already smitten with the beautiful American heiress. Alice's enthusiasm for the count was more muted, but she was intrigued. Frédéric was likeable, shy and unassuming but also clever and charming. The new couple complemented one another. She was the poor little rich girl from Chicago; he was the elegant, sophisticated aristocrat from Europe. He was timid, she was bold. She lacked constancy, he provided stability. Both parties were aware that the outside world deemed this to be a 'good match'. He would bring aristocratic credibility to the marriage, while she would provide him with her considerable wealth. But although there was a degree of affinity between the two – and certainly a good deal of eagerness on the part of Frédéric – it seems passion was never a major feature in their relationship. They were, from the beginning, excellent friends.

With Moya's encouragement, Frédéric pursued Alice in earnest. He escorted her to restaurants and nightclubs. He introduced her to members of his aristocratic and literary French set and met her wealthy American expatriate crowd in return. During the summer of 1921, Alice accepted an invitation by her old friends from Chicago, the Spauldings, to go on a motoring tour in the South of France. By the time they had reached Biarritz a fortnight later, Frédéric was waiting there with a marriage proposal. Alice accepted and wired Aunt Tattie in Chicago with the news. Alice's aunt was delighted. Like Moya, she agreed that Frédéric and Alice were an excellent match, evidently approving of the count's aristocratic credentials. The engagement was announced on 10 August 1921 in the *Chicago Daily Tribune*. 'Interest in the announcement is not lessened by the fact that it has been expected daily,' it was reported, 'rumours of the young Viscomte's attachment to Miss Silverthorne having reached Chicago society some time ago.'

Aunt Tattie hurried to arrange the wedding, which she insisted should take place in Chicago. For her part, Alice was stipulating that she wanted to be married by the end of September, in only a few weeks' time. It appears that Alice's haste to marry had less to do with her eagerness to become Countess de Janzé and more to do with her fear that she would change her mind. On the one hand she wanted to marry Frédéric as this was her chance to escape from Aunt Tattie and her family. On the other hand, she wasn't in love with Frédéric and she knew it. It is possible that Alice's reaction also had to do with fear of her wedding night. She was most probably a virgin: young girls of Alice's background and upbringing were allowed to be flirtatious and sexy to the point where kissing and heavy petting were permitted, but it went no further. Virginity was prized and essential for marriage, which meant that Alice was almost certainly completely inexperienced. The thought of going to bed with Frédéric may have been extremely alarming to her, especially as she did not find him particularly attractive. On two separate occasions she told Aunt Tattie that she wanted to pull out. Pat Silverthorne, Alice's half sister, remembers Alice's tantrums during this period and poor Aunt Tattie's exasperation as a result.

Alice's trepidation and ambivalence continued, but the engine of the wedding had been set in motion and could not be stopped. In order for Alice – who was Presbyterian – to marry in a Catholic church to a Catholic man, she had to be given Catholic instruction. Father Casey and Father Shannon of East Lakeview, a section of Chicago, carried this out in some haste. Father Casey informed Alice that any children of the union were to become Catholic and they must be baptized as Catholics. By now, the invitations and guest list had been agreed upon, the church was booked and Frédéric and his family were already in New York preparing for their journey to

Chicago. On their arrival, even the aristocratic de Janzés would have been impressed by the vast means of the Armour–Chapins, and by Aunt Tattie's lavishly well-appointed home.

The wedding took place as planned on 21 September 1921 at five in the afternoon at the Church of Our Lady of Mount Carmel in East Lakeview. It was a small but elegant affair. Guests included various Armour–Chapin family members as well as some notable society friends. Alice looked the picture of sophistication in a white satin gown with a court train and bouquet of lilies. Her floor-length veil was made from lace that had been her mother's and was held in place with a band of medieval pearls. The matron of honour was Alice's cousin Lolita Armour, who wore a simple beige gown of satin and a hat of brown velvet. Her two bridesmaids were her cousin Elizabeth Chapin and a friend, Mary Baker. Following the ceremony there was a small reception at Aunt Tattie's lakeside Chicago apartment on Sheridan Road. The event was reported in the *Chicago Daily Tribune* alongside a photograph of the newlyweds. Although Alice looks stunning in her long gown and veil, there is little evidence of the exuberance or radiance that is normally associated with a bride on her wedding day. In fact, Alice looks positively morose.

Although Alice's stepmother, Louise, travelled to Chicago for the occasion, William Silverthorne was not invited to his daughter's wedding. In her father's absence, it was left to Uncle Sim to give Alice away. Did Alice appeal to her Armour–Chapin relatives to allow William to attend? She had long since come of age, and was about to become a newly married women, therefore possessing a newfound degree of independence. She could have requested that he be invited. In fact, there is every possibility that she simply did not want William there. In the coming years, Alice did not attempt a reconciliation with her errant father and it seems that, for whatever reason, William was disinclined to play an active part in his daughter's life. Since his separation from Alice, he had continued with his business interests, experimenting in patenting various inventions including new pour-outs for bottles and ways of treating paper to make it waterproof; he was also instrumental in developing several mining prospects in Canada. Alice and William certainly corresponded during the ensuing years, but they would rarely meet. Their estrangement, if not complete, was effective.

After the wedding Alice and Frédéric spent two weeks at the Armour house on Long Island. There is a photograph of Alice from this time that can still be found in the de Janzé family albums at their ancestral estate, Château Parfondeval, in Normandy. She is sitting cross-legged on a rumpled bed at the house on Long Island wearing nothing but her nightdress, big windowpane reading glasses on her nose. On her face is a look of wry bemusement, an expression that seems to be saying, 'Is that all? What a big fuss over nothing!' If Alice had been at all nervous about marriage and the necessity of entering into a sexual relationship with Frédéric, then her timidity soon turned to disappointment. While Frédéric was clearly very attracted to Alice, his new wife could not return the compliment and in all likelihood, the consummation of their marriage was a tepid affair. Frédéric was an instinctive gentleman, only a little more experienced than his new wife, someone who would never be able to match the powerful masculinity and sexual chemistry Alice later enjoyed with subsequent lovers.

Nonetheless, the newlyweds were about to become very happy travelling companions. They set sail for France on 5 October 1921, en route to Morocco, where they would spend most of the winter. Frédéric had been stationed in North Africa during the war and was keen to show his new wife around. Since the cessation of hostilities, Morocco had begun to be a popular tourist destination and the de Janzés stayed in five-star hotels, visiting the cities of Agadir, Casablanca and Rabat, as well as smaller outlying townships. They wandered through the rabbit-warren streets of the Marrakesh souk, absorbing the sights and smells of saffron, orange flower, almonds, dates, olives, bargaining with the vendors for leather goods, carpets and ceramics. They marvelled at the colourful medieval city of Fez and the historical wonders of Tangiers. They visited the Sarhro Mountains and took a short drive through the Sahara Desert to see the sand dunes in Merzouga where Alice drank mint tea and ate some of the best olives, dates and nuts she had ever tasted. Significantly, Morocco provided Alice with her first experience of Africa: it was during her honeymoon that she first became intoxicated by this vast and diverse continent, its raw energy and the untamed spectacle of its landscapes. The Moroccan trip marked the beginning of a love affair with the continent, a place that was to play both blessed saviour and cruel destroyer in her life.

Upon their return to Paris, Alice discovered that she was pregnant. Both the de Janzés and the Armour–Chapins were delighted with this news, as was Frédéric. It is likely that Alice was more circumspect. She was a young woman with a penchant for freedom and it's highly possible just the idea of motherhood would have made her feel weighted down. There is no doubt that this woman who adored French fashions found the physical changes of pregnancy to be both unpleasant and unbecoming. What's more, she was someone whose own mother had died at an early age. The process of becoming a parent was fraught with unresolved emotion and feelings of loss for Alice. While her new husband and relatives happily made plans for the baby's arrival, Alice retreated, cutting herself off from those around her and from the inevitability of what was about to take place.

For the time being, at least she could distract herself with the matter of where she was going to live. Aunt Tattie had invited the newlyweds to move into her apartment in rue de la Pompe in the fashionable and elegant 16th district. Frédéric's mother, Moya Hennessy, urged them to come to Parfondeval, the de Janzés' country home in Normandy. But Alice and Frédéric were keen to maintain a modicum of autonomy. With Aunt Tattie's help, they opted to pool their resources and buy an apartment of their own in the rue Spontini, not far from the rue de la Pompe. For Alice, Paris was unquestionably the preferred option to Normandy. She had many friends in Paris, knew her way around, there were parties to attend, places to go shopping and a lifestyle to maintain. Despite the fact that she was expecting a baby, she was not yet ready to give up her urban existence for the isolation of the northern French countryside.

Alice's first child, Nolwen Louise Marie Alice, was born in Paris on 20 June 1922. Mother and baby both recovered quickly from the birth. A suitable nanny was found and after only a few weeks of respite, Alice went on with social life in much the same way as she had before Nolwen's arrival. From the beginning, Alice found it difficult to bond with her daughter. After the baby's birth, the dark moods that had first plagued Alice in adolescence returned and she may have blamed motherhood for their re-emergence. No wonder she was keen to step out of her new maternal role, continuing to define herself as a social and independent creature. For Frédéric's part, although he had long suspected that Alice might be somewhat unstable, he had secretly hoped that a child might cure her of her sadnesses. He loved Alice and was determined to support her in whatever she wanted to do, but he was also disappointed to discover that the birth of their first child had failed to revive her spirits. On the contrary, the arrival of Nolwen seemed to have made her more prone to withdrawal, and her estrangement from the baby disappointed him greatly.

As Alice instinctively moved away from the demands of her husband and child, she began spending a great deal of time with her new friend Paula Gellibrand. Born in London in 1898, Paula was a famous society model, described by many of her contemporaries as the most beautiful woman in Europe. Later, Paula became a favourite model for Cecil Beaton, who photographed her many times, emphasizing her Modigliani features and exquisitely slender hands. She was also a muse to the novelist Enid Bagnold, who used her as an inspiration for the eponymous heroine of her novel *Serena Blandish* (1924). Alice first met Paula in Paris in 1921, when Paula had recently become engaged to Cuban-Castilian count Pedro José Isidiro Manuel Ricardo Mones Maury, the Marquis de Casa Maury, otherwise known as Bobby or, less flatteringly, the Cuban Heel. This Bugatti-driving Grand Prix winner lost his fortune during the Wall Street crash, and then later remade it running the Curzon cinema in London. Although no one could quite understand why Paula was marrying the marquis – it seems he had few redeeming qualities – the newly engaged Paula was in Paris to visit friends and to organize her wedding, which ultimately took place in 1923 at St James's Church, Spanish Place, in London.

Paula and Alice quickly became close friends and allies, attending soirées, going to the opera and ballet together, frequenting the best art exhibitions and fashion shows. They were both fun-seekers, naturally adventurous, with a shared tendency for daring and a love of haute couture (Paula went on to become a fashion designer). Both were brunettes, extremely beautiful into the bargain, and their attraction to one another may also have had something to do with the fact that they sensed neither one would ever become jealous of the other. Of all the women in Alice's life, it was Paula who came closest to providing her with a soulmate. Alice attributed much of her recovery after the birth of her daughter to the fact that she could spend so much time with Paula, and so when Paula left Paris for London in January 1923, Alice was bereft.

There was nobody in her immediate group of friends who could replace Paula. For Alice, already ill-at-ease with the roles of countess and mother, Paula's departure triggered another bout of depression. Although the upper echelons of aristocratic Paris might have seemed glamorous at first, such society soon revealed itself to be stultifying in its elitism and formalities. Alice remained close to Frédéric's mother, Moya, but found the rest of her husband's extended family and friends to be cold, forbidding and snobbish. There were rules that had to be followed for the simplest of actions and every social interaction was a complex affair. Alice's French was good, but even so, she spoke with an American accent and was intelligent enough to know when she was being looked down upon. As she struggled to improve her language skills and her knowledge of 'comme il faut', she would have found it exhausting and tedious work.

It was under these circumstances that Frédéric was able to persuade Alice that a spell in the countryside at Parfondeval with her daughter might do her some good. Situated in the heart of Normandy, near the small town of Londinières, the château at Parfondeval had been in the de Janzé family since the mid-seventeenth century (in fact, the house is still in the possession of the de Janzé family). It is spacious and sprawling, with three separate living quarters. The central apartment, where Moya lived, consisted of a series of wide floors connected by a steep staircase. The right pavilion or east wing belonged to Frédéric's brother, and the left pavilion or west wing was Frédéric's birthright and where he kept a small library.

In Normandy Alice found herself at a healthy distance from her social life in Paris and in sympathetic company, at least for the most part. Aunt Tattie had arranged for Edward, her faithful African American butler from Chicago, to go to France and join the staff at Parfondeval. Alice had grown very fond of Edward when she lived with Aunt Tattie as a teenager. He had a quick sense of humour and was a talented magician who frequently performed little conjuring tricks to entertain her. He was also an accomplished photographer and was given his own dark-room at Parfondeval. In later years Edward proved to be a close friend to Alice's two children, both of whom gravitated to him.

Moya de Janzé, the mistress of the house, was a kindly woman who was proving to be an adoring grandmother to Nolwen. Alice had always felt comfortable in the company of her mother-in-law who understood Alice's struggles to adjust to France and the French way of life. As a fellow American who had become a French countess, Moya could help explain exactly what was expected of Alice when it came to etiquette and protocol. Even in this isolated corner of Normandy, manners and traditions were an integral part of daily life and to ignore them would only have caused consternation amongst the staff and neighbours. At Moya's urging, Alice agreed to stop riding her horse astride, as she had done in America, and to ride sidesaddle, on the left side, as was the local custom. Any other method was considered inelegant and unbecoming for a French woman of Alice's status. Alice had been trained from early girlhood to ride sidesaddle and had left and right sidesaddles in her trousseau. She was an able horsewoman and quickly accommodated to European tackle, bridles and riding style.

Riding and hunting were among Alice's greatest pleasures during her stay at Parfondeval. At her husband's estate she was surrounded by miles and miles of open countryside and forests, mostly full of deer and wild boar. When riding, Alice experienced the kind of freedom from her responsibilities that she craved. As a woman with a strong visual sense, she also appreciated the spectacle of the Parfondeval hunts: as many as six elegantly attired huntsmen would ride out equipped with large curling hunting horns and high domed hunting hats. Isolated for the most part from those around her, Alice often found a more natural and satisfying interaction with animals and nature. Throughout her life, she loved to ride and always kept pets. At Parfondeval, she surrounded herself with her four beloved Alsatian dogs. In a photo of the young countess taken in Normandy, she is gazing lovingly and intently at these large and wolf-like creatures. Even with her animals for solace, however, Alice soon grew restless in the countryside. After three years in France, Alice still spoke with a heavy accent and often complained to Moya and Frédéric that the servants at Parfondeval were laughing at her behind her back.

What's more, Alice had a new sister-in-law with whom to contend. Shortly after Nolwen's birth in June of 1922,

Frédéric's younger brother, Henri de Janzé, had married an English beauty called Phyllis Boyd. Unable to afford a place of their own in Paris or London, the newlyweds had since taken up residence at Parfondeval, occupying the east wing of the château, sharing the grounds with the other members of the household. Henri was twenty at the time of the wedding and Phyllis was twenty-eight. Born in London in 1894, Phyllis was the daughter of Lady Lilian Boyd and the granddaughter of the second Earl of Munster on her mother's side. Her father, W.A.E. Boyd, had been a captain in the Life Guards. Phyllis could also boast that she was the great-great-granddaughter of the beautiful Dorothea Bland (better known by her stage name Mrs Jordan), the long-time mistress of King William IV. In other words, Phyllis possessed the exact kind of aristocratic pedigree that Alice, as an American, lacked. There is no doubt that Alice perceived Phyllis's appearance at Parfondeval as a threat. Phyllis was five years older than Alice. She was intellectual and cultivated, having studied art at the Slade School in London, where she had shown impressive talent. The writer Osbert Sitwell later commented on Phyllis's 'artistic ability' and 'unusual personal charm and distinction'. The novelist Barbara Cartland, who witnessed her dancing at London's Embassy Club in the early 1920s, noted her 'mysterious, haunting beauty', her 'high cheekbones and pale aquamarine eyes' as well as her 'violent temper'. The artist Dora Carrington, who fell in love with Phyllis during her time at the Slade – and who visited her at Parfondeval towards the end of 1922 – found her 'dazzling', 'like a grand Persian whore with a scarlet mouth'.

In other words, Alice's place in the de Janzé family had been somewhat usurped by this impressive new arrival from England and inevitably there was some competition and tension between the sisters-in-law. Alice was ahead of the game slightly because she had produced a child by the middle of 1922, and this placed her in good stead with the family-conscious de Janzés. But in the background, there was a rumble of sniping from Phyllis's side. It seems that Phyllis found Alice to be intellectually bereft and childishly moody. It is true that Alice would rather be outdoors than in a library, but it is still worth noting that throughout her life she managed to hold her own with a string of intellectual men and women. As for her moods, these were by no means predictable, and so it is no surprise that Phyllis, who was from a more reserved English background, would have found them unseemly. Above all, Phyllis was bold, confident and upper class, therefore much more at home in the gentrified world of the de Janzés. Phyllis regularly sneered at Alice's 'gauche' and 'American' behaviour and frequently joined in mocking her French and her refusal to learn the codes of conduct befitting a countess. It was at this time that Phyllis and Henri began referring to Alice as 'La Negresse'. This strange tease may have had something to do with Alice's hair, which was naturally very curly. Or it may have originated from the haughty European assumption that all old white American families had once employed slaves and therefore were likely to have African ancestors somewhere along the line. The rumour that Alice had black blood – as propagated by Henri and Phyllis – was one that stuck. Years later, Alice's grandson,

Guillaume de Rougemont, remembers that Henri de Janzé's daughter Solange believed that Alice was a 'negresse', and that consequently her cousin Guillaume de Rougemont must have 'a touch of the tar brush'.

For some months during Alice's stay at Parfondeval, there was much backstabbing between the two women. Finally, a truce was reached after it became apparent that they shared a passion for haute couture. Alice and Phyllis even put aside their animosity for long enough to talk about the idea of going into business together. They spoke of starting a little boutique in Paris, recognizing in one another the qualities that would be needed for a successful business venture – Phyllis had the flair while Alice had the contacts and money to make it work. The boutique never materialized and so we can only imagine what owning a business might have done for Alice's sense of worth and independence during this period of her life. She had loved working for Arnot as a young woman in Paris and had benefited greatly from the feelings of usefulness and satisfaction an occupation can bring. Now, Alice found herself in Parfondeval, far from Paris, without direction, bored and unfulfilled. It was in this frame of mind that she allowed Frédéric to persuade her that a second child might be the answer to her problems.

Alice named the new baby Paola, after her friend Paula, whom she still missed terribly. Paola Marie Jeanne was born on 1 June 1924. Once again, Alice fell into an prolonged depression soon after the birth. This was not an easy time for Alice and there was little anybody could do to help. For his part, Frédéric had learned to forgive his wife's bouts of sadness and inertia, especially as these were followed by bursts of marked vivacity, giving him the impression that she had completely recovered. But then the dark moods would return again. It is likely that members of Frédéric's family regularly wished that Alice would simply snap out of her introspection, assuming she was simply lazy, selfish, or even heartless, particularly when she failed to bond with her daughters. Certainly, her relationship with Frédéric suffered as a result of her shifting moods. While Frédéric pursued his intellectual life, confining himself to his books, his library and his literary friends, Alice was lonely. Motherhood simply held no real interest for her. Instead of bringing her a degree of fulfilment, her duties to her two daughters only made her feel trapped in a role for which she felt unsuited.

The cyclothymia, which Alice almost certainly suffered from, is a strain of bipolar syndrome that can often develop into full-blown manic depression later in life. Her moods and frequently erratic behaviour reflected the classic symptoms of the disease: sufferers undergo periods of mild but often debilitating depression alternating with periods of high spirits and irritability. It is estimated that a quarter of those afflicted attempt suicide at some point in their lives, as Alice had done as a teenager. The term 'cyclothymia' was coined as early as 1877, but it was only much later, in the latter part of the twentieth century, that effective medications for stabilizing its symptoms were developed. It is highly likely that if Alice had lived in the present day, she would have been given the drugs she needed to alleviate her moods, thereby drastically altering the shape of her life. However, in 1925, no such treatments existed. To make matters worse, in the course of her time at Parfondeval, Alice had begun having frequent bronchial attacks brought on by lingering consumption, a condition with which her mother had also struggled.

Ever dutiful, Frédéric remained hopeful that another change of scene would help. He began to make plans to take Alice away, to Africa, a place that he hoped would lift her spirits completely.

3

Kenya

By the autumn of 1925, Alice was suffering from both physical and emotional problems: she was plagued by her bronchitis and what can best be described as an ingrained depression. In an effort to cure his wife of her difficulties, Frédéric decided to take Alice to Kenya in what was then British Colonial East Africa, where he hoped the balmy climate and high altitudes would help alleviate Alice's troubles. The African trip was to be a mutually beneficial arrangement. Frédéric was an avid traveller and hunter. In Kenya he would have ample opportunity to satisfy his interest in exotic locations and passion for shooting. Alice, meanwhile, could look forward to discovering another corner of the fascinating continent she had first encountered during her honeymoon in

Morocco. In Kenya, Frédéric reminded her, she would be able to ride for miles under wide-open skies, surrounded by herds of wild and exotic animals.

What's more, the de Janzés would be staying with friends who would provide the perfect antidote to the stuffy confines of French society. Frédéric and Alice had an invitation to visit Josslyn Hay, the future Lord Erroll, and his new wife Lady Idina, at their home in Kenya's Wanjohi Valley. Joss and Idina had first met the de Janzés in Paris in 1923, at which time both couples were only recently married. The Hays were a striking pair, two people whose reputations preceded them. Joss was an Etonian who had been expelled from the school, and whose diplomat father had taken him away to Berlin as an honorary attaché, in the hope that his son might still enter the Foreign Office. Although stationed in Berlin, Joss found London and Paris far more amusing and often neglected his duties in a continuing quest for fun and women. It was in Paris that he met Frédéric and Alice. Joss was tall and attractive with pale-blond hair and an air of swagger about him which came, in part, from an innate belief in his own superiority: his ancestors could be traced to the fourteenth century and, as the heir to the earldom of Erroll, he would also inherit the hereditary title of High Constable of Scotland. Despite his illustrious heritage, however, there was a wildness to Joss: he was a natural womanizer, without respect for rules, regulations, or husbands in particular.

When Joss first met Lady Idina (née Sackville) in London in 1922, she was still married to her second husband, Charles Gordon. The daughter of the eighth Earl de la Warr, she was something of a femme fatale, even by present-day standards. She had married her first husband, Euan Wallace, in 1913, an arrangement that didn't prevent her from carrying on numerous affairs. Attractive, witty and liberated – with the kind of slender frame that suited 1920s fashions for loose, sheath-like silk dresses – Idina was renowned for her skills at seducing (and then often abandoning) men. When Nancy Mitford came to write her satire of the British upper classes, *The Pursuit of Love* (1945), it was Lady Idina who served as the model for the heroine's mother, a woman who 'ran away so often, and with so many different people, that she became known to her family and friends as the Bolter'. Joss and Idina's union sparked a cause célèbre in London – the already disreputable Lady marrying a much younger soon-to-be Lord. In a photograph published on the cover of the *Tatler*, they are the picture of louche happiness, Idina in a flowing Grecian shift and barefoot, and Joss in snazzily patterned pyjamas.

Although there was doubtless a frisson of attraction between Alice and Joss upon first meeting, for the time being, it went no further. Alice was newly married and either pregnant or recovering from her pregnancies during the period of their first meetings. By early 1924, Joss and Idina recognized that they were on the verge of becoming society outcasts due to their scandalous union, so they decided to leave for Kenya, where Idina had lived for a time with husband number two. In the spring of 1924, they took up residence in the Wanjohi Valley, in the Kenyan highlands. Such a highly sociable couple might have felt isolated in the wilds of East Africa, but in fact the opposite was true. As soon as they arrived, they began sending out invitations to friends from Europe to come and visit. The de Janzés were high on the list of invitees.

In the early part of 1925, Frédéric started to make plans for the trip. He made enquiries as to how best to travel; on which boat line and by which route; he bought clothes, licences, weapons for shooting expeditions, and arranged for the necessary typhoid injections. The de Janzés decided to leave their daughters Nolwen and Paola in the safe hands of Frédéric's mother, Moya, ably assisted by Alice's Aunt Tattie. Paola was just fifteen months old; Nolwen was three years old. At such tender ages, they could not have understood that their mother was being taken away for the sake of her health or that both parents would be gone for such a long period of time. Alice and Frédéric planned to stay in Kenya for two months, with another two months factored in for travel there and back. If Alice was sad to bid farewell to her daughters, she also knew she had been given a reprieve. Here was her chance to escape from her responsibilities as a mother and as a countess. Together with Frédéric, she was eager to begin this new adventure.

In 1925, the journey from Paris to Mombasa took a little over a month. The de Janzés flew from Le Bourget airport in Paris to Marseilles in September 1925, having sent their cabin trunks ahead by rail. On the 17th of September, they set sail from Marseilles on the SS *Gascon*, a 28-year-old, single-funnelled vessel of the French Messageries Maritimes line. The ship housed seventy-eight first-class cabins, two of which were of a superior variety. The de Janzés had one of these; it was located on the preferred port (left) side, where passengers could gaze out on the coasts of France and then Italy. In her teenage years before the Great War, Alice had crossed the Atlantic from New York to Cherbourg on the *Aquitania*, the magnificent Cunard luxury liner popular with wealthy Americans making their way to France. By contrast, a working vessel like the SS *Gascon* must have come as something of a shock. Although the de Janzés dined at the captain's table, they would have felt they had little in common with their fellow passengers.

The ship passed Monaco, then San Remo at breakfast time. At Genoa there was time to go ashore for a drive before returning to dine on board. By the evening of the fifth day, the captain steered to the port side so that the more privileged passengers could see from their cabins the island of Stromboli, with its active volcano sending luminous red sparks of lava into the night skies. The *Gascon* navigated the Straits of Messina where temperatures began to rise. In the evenings, a small band played on board and Alice danced. Three days after leaving the Straits of Messina, they arrived at Port Said, where Egyptian 'Gully Gully' men, or conjurors, came on board to entertain the passengers. After the ship docked at Port Said, Alice and Frédéric went ashore to shop at Simon Artz, the famous department store, and to take tea at the Casino Hotel, re-embarking in time to leave at midnight en route for the Suez Canal. At Suez, the *Gascon* stopped for a half-day in order to off-load cargo. Alice and Frédéric would have looked down at the docks to see legions of completely naked ebony-skinned Sudanese labourers with massive halos of curly black hair ('Fuzzy Wuzzies' in the colonial lingo of the time). The passage through the canal took eight hours and was eerily calm after so many days at sea. Passengers aboard the *Gascon* would have appreciated the respite from the rolling of the ship as they contemplated Ferdinand de Lesseps's miracle of engineering. By now it was hot, with temperatures reaching 90 degrees Fahrenheit. In a time before air-conditioning, everyone cooled themselves with cabin fans. Games were organized on deck. Four days after Suez, the Gascon arrived at Aden. Most people preferred to stay on board since the only place to visit was the neighbouring port of Crater, a prospect which seemed daunting due to the heat. One more dress dinner and dance and five more days later they were through to the Indian Ocean.

The *Gascon* was bound for Mombasa. This lush island, connected to the mainland of Africa by a precarious-looking causeway, has its main port at Kilindini. As the ship approached its final destination, the view of Kilindini harbour would have been stunning: an ancient Portuguese fort, clusters of palm trees, hundreds of black porters, some in red fez hats, and Thomas Cook agents in sharp peaked caps thronging the harbour. After disembarking, Alice and Frédéric were reunited with their luggage and taken by rickshaw to the main railway station only half a mile away. The Mombasa railway station of 1925 was a basic construction: a simple facade with the station sign; then another notice indicated 'upper class passengers and luggage'. Just inside the station gates there were lists posted with each carriage number and the names of the occupants. The de Janzés' train left Mombasa station at four thirty in the afternoon to the sounds of applause and cheers from the platform and carriages. The engine pulled out across the causeway heading towards the mainland, then moved uphill through coconut plantations and mango trees, the elevation increasing incrementally with each mile.

This was the famous 'Lunatic Line' – the legendary railway built between 1895 (the first year of British rule in the Kenyan Protectorate) and 1901. Stretching from Mombasa on the east coast across nearly 600 miles to the shores of Lake Victoria in the west, the railway had first been proposed by the Imperial British East Africa Company but had been bedevilled by political controversy from the start. Back in London, there were questions about its cost (£5 million, about £450 million in today's money) and if there was actually any real need for it. Those in favour argued that the line would be a strategic move for the new British colony, a counterbalance to the imperial expansion being undertaken by the Germans in East Africa. Opponents argued that the line was a folly, built to prove the extent of British might and engineering ability rather than in response to a measurable need. The British radical politician Henry Labouchère dubbed the project the 'Lunatic Line', insisting that the railway was completely without purpose. The crux of his argument was that it crossed many hundreds of miles of completely empty and unoccupied lands en route to nowhere. His scathing poem about the project goes as follows:

What will it cost no words can express
What is its object no brain can suppose
Where it will start from no-one can guess
Where it is going to nobody knows.

What is the use of it none can conjecture
What it will carry there's none can define
And in spite of George Curzon's superior lecture
It is clearly naught but a lunatic line

The majority disagreed with Labouchère and building went ahead, continuing apace over a period of five and a half years. In the words of Albert Thomas Matson, who went on to become the health inspector for the Colonial Service in Kenya, this was 'the most courageous railway in the world' and along with the Orient Express and the Trans-Siberian Express, the Lunatic Line provided one of the world's great train journeys. Never before had a railway crossed such varied and often perilous terrain, spanning jungle, desert, mountains, plains, forest and swamplands, climbing from the coast to around 8,000 feet above sea level. Thirty-two thousand Indian workers were shipped in from the Subcontinent to lay its tracks, many of whom died of heatstroke and tropical diseases or were devoured by man-eating lions during construction. The track itself was only one metre wide and mostly single track to help facilitate the steepness of the climb. Thirty-five viaducts and one hundred and twenty bridges and culverts had to be built before it reached its end.

Wood-burning steam engines were British-made UR

35s, the type also used in India: they belched black smoke and frequent stops were required in order to refill their boilers with water. Despite this, well-to-do first-class passengers who boarded such trains in 1925 were treated with ample care. Alice and Frédéric dined in a grass-roofed hut after disembarking at Voi, some 150 miles uphill from Mombasa. Waiters were white-clad stewards from Goa, in India, who served up a menu of tinned salmon, meatballs, fruit and custard, and, for the first course, brown Windsor soup. (This beef and vegetable broth was very popular in Victorian and Edwardian times, especially on the railways, and was often said to have built the British Empire.) During dinner, attendants would carry the bedding into the carriages in order to make up the beds. On rejoining their carriage, Alice and Frédéric would have gone to their berth, closed their mosquito nets and opened their windows so as to enjoy the cool air coming in from the plains. First-class berths were comfortable, in the circumstances, and designed to accommodate two people, with private WCs and a small basin. Second-class berths were large, open affairs and could sleep four. Third-class carriages had simple slatted wooden benches and no beds at all. In 1925, the axles of the passenger carriages would have been badly sprung, causing an immense jolt each time the train's wheels hit a gap in the rail. The joke went that couples honeymooning in Kenya would never forget their time in one of the berths of the Lunatic Line.

During such a bumpy ride, sleep would have come fitfully if at all. Alice and Frédéric may have deliberately tried to stay awake, eager to see signs of wildlife from the window. Even so, the almost total blackness of the African night would have prevented any sightings. As the passengers dozed in their berths and seats, the train climbed through forest and red rock to the great plain that slopes from 1,000 feet above sea level to 6,000 feet at the foot of the Kenyan highlands. At Makindu, Alice and Frédéric joined their fellow passengers in an outdoor refreshment room for breakfast. Porridge, eggs and bacon and tea were the standard fare. By the time they returned to the train, dawn was breaking and the engine resumed its pace towards the Athi River. At six in the morning when the sun rose, Alice and Frédéric would have shared the delight of witnessing herds of giraffe, antelope, zebra and perhaps even elephants moving across the vast plains. At twelve thirty in the afternoon the train arrived at Nairobi Station, some 329 miles from Mombasa. Looking down at their clothes, Alice and Frédéric saw they were covered in a thin layer of red dust blown from the burnished rocks en route. They would have felt immensely weary from the journey and the thin air at such an altitude would have only added to their tiredness. By arrangement, no one was there to meet them. They knew that their friend Joss Hay would contact them later in the day at Nairobi's Norfolk Hotel, a favourite meeting place for Kenya's expatriate settlers and visitors. So they took two rickshaws and went to the Norfolk for hot baths. The Lunatic Line had delivered them to Nairobi twenty-four hours after their departure from Mombasa.

In 1907, after Winston Churchill returned from his visit to East Africa as Undersecretary of State for the Colonies, he brought back news of the line. He was impressed by it, describing it as 'one of the most romantic and wonderful railways in the world', and adding, 'The railway is already doing what it was never expected within any reasonable period to do, it is paying its way.' Indeed, by the time of Churchill's visit, the railway *had* begun to pay for itself. In a bid to justify the line's existence, the Commissioner for East Africa, Sir Charles Eliot, had invited settlers from the British colonies to farm the land surrounding the newly founded railway town of Nairobi. In this way, it would be possible to say the railway was serving the purpose of connecting these farmers and their goods with the coast, thereby silencing those critics who questioned the line's practical purpose. In other words, the British had built the line and then come up with a reason for its existence. Recruitment of farmers began in 1901 and the first pioneers started to arrive in 1903. They came from as far away as Canada and New Zealand, as well as from Great Britain, and although many from the British contingent were aristocrats, the majority were middle-class men and women who faced the enormous odds of farming this uncharted territory with little capital but great tenacity.

After the end of the First World War, a second wave of European settlers – made up mostly of ex-servicemen – arrived to farm the land and to help swell the numbers of whites in the area. The colony's foothold seemed assured and by the early 1920s, the settlers had established their own Parliament and Legislative Council. It was at this juncture that the early pioneers started to sit back and enjoy the fruits of their labours. They began to build large stone houses for themselves, with verdant lawned gardens and airy verandahs. They employed local servants to tend to their properties and staff their kitchens. This was the era of the 'English squires established on the equator', as Evelyn Waugh described them, and these moneyed residents were determined to translate the English way of life to Africa. Servants were taught how to be 'proper' butlers and chambermaids, how to lay tables with polished silver in the correct manner, and to serve and cook imitations of English cuisine. Meanwhile, their masters played polo, tennis and croquet, and held luncheons and tea parties. There was now an impressive level of comfort to the lives of the colonial settlers in Kenya.

Wealthy socialite travellers had begun to come to Kenya for adventure, romance and safaris, and many of them decided to stay. The undisputed ringleaders of this small but decadent new circle were the de Janzés' friends, Joss and Idina. As part of Idina's divorce settlement with her former husband, she had inherited 2,500 acres of farmland in the Wanjohi Valley north of Gilgil. The Hays had built a house on the land, calling it Slains after the Erroll family home in Scotland (sold by Joss's predecessor, the profligate nineteenth Earl of Erroll). Here, Idina began to throw house parties for visiting friends and local socialites. The flow of cocktails only served to fuel natural highs brought on by the extreme altitude of the highlands. Far from home, the Hays and their clique of friends found themselves freed from the restrictions of their families and society. Repressions were cast aside with abandon. Idina's parties would often last for days at a time and it was even rumoured that – at the hostess's insistence – every guest would have to sleep with someone other than the person they had arrived with before the party could finish. This liberated atmosphere was to give rise to the name 'Happy Valley'. It was also the heady realm which Alice and Frédéric were about to enter.

Joss arrived to meet his guests at the Norfolk Hotel on 25 October 1925. The three friends were reunited at the hotel's door, excited to be meeting again so far away from Paris. They would have spoken in a mixture of French and English. Joss explained he had left Idina behind at their home for a very good reason. She was pregnant and the journey to Nairobi was bumpy and arduous. Joss was driving his brand-new, 1922 model, long-bodied, open-top Hispano Suiza, a wedding present from Idina. It was a car of enormous power with an engine having six cylinders in line, a single overhead cam, and over 6 litres in capacity. The car's massive, semi-elliptic front and rear suspension had been designed to cope with rough Spanish roads, making the car ideal for the challenges of the steep and rutted Kenyan byways. Practicalities aside, there would have been few cars more glamorous than Joss's in 1920s Nairobi, its bonnet topped by a flying stork, 'La Cigogne Volante'. The man behind the wheel of the Suiza would have been just as imposing, his blond hair ruffled from the drive, his skin tanned from the Africa sun, and his body clad in a well-cut safari suit.

Joss had brought with him a Ford box-body car, a back-up to the Suiza, driven by a Somali driver who carried a spear. The following morning after an early breakfast,

Joss's servant loaded up the two cabin trunks on the Ford. Joss, Frédéric and Alice climbed into the front bench seat of the Suiza. It would have been characteristic for Joss to insist that Alice sat in the middle between the two men, ensuring she was thigh to thigh with him for the journey to Wanjohi. The gear handle and handbrake of the car were to the right of the driver (who also sat on the right), so there was nothing to come between Alice and her attentive host. Joss set off at high speed, his preferred tempo. The roads leading out of Nairobi at this time were made of murram, a degraded stone gravel dug from nearby quarries that was crushed, then spread and rolled, making for a dusty ride, especially when going so fast. The Suiza quickly scaled the Kikuyu Escarpment, some 6,000 feet up and 20 miles from the city. Here, a heart-stopping sight awaited the travellers. Looking down from the precipice, Alice and Frédéric could see below them the sheer drop of the Great Rift Valley. This continental divide, a literal rift through the heart of Africa, stretches 4,000 miles from Mozambique to Northern Syria, and is one of the true marvels of the world. Herds of wild game roam the valley floor which is dotted with defunct miniature volcanoes, including Longanot or Mount Margaret and the double-headed Suswa (described by H. Rider Haggard in *King Solomon's Mines* as the 'Twin Bosoms of Cleopatra'). It would have been an exhilarating prospect for Alice and Frédéric, who had only recently left behind them the tightly gridded streets and boulevards of Paris.

Next the Suiza began the descent to the bottom of the valley. Driving downhill at such an incline was enough to put an enormous strain on any car. The Suiza's brakes, although powerful, would have burned out had Joss not shifted into second gear to brake his descent. The engine grew hot, and at the bottom of the decline, Joss refilled the radiator with water from the stream that crossed the road, fed by a shaded spring. Next, he raced across the road heading to the right turn that would take them back uphill towards Gilgil and the Wanjohi Valley. Again, the climb was steep on a road that was rougher and dustier than the rest, so that by the end of the drive, a fine layer of red murram dust covered all three passengers. Alice wore a hat, but even so, her hair was thick with red specks. Joss, ever attentive and gracious to women, especially a woman as wealthy and beautiful as Alice, reassured his guest that Idina had brought a French lady's maid to Kenya and that she would wash and dress Alice's hair for dinner that evening.

Everything was conspiring to intoxicate Alice: the hot sun, the high altitude, the breathtaking views, the glamour of riding in the Suiza next to this attractive and confident Englishman. The two cars sped down the private road to Kipipiri, overlooked on the left by the Aberdare Mountains, before sweeping into the drive of Joss and Idina's farm. Idina was waiting for them, dressed casually yet elegantly in trousers and a blouse, her preferred outfit while in Kenya. The whole household had turned out to meet the new houseguests: the No. 1 houseman, a cook, a kitchen 'toto' (Swahili for child) and a 'dhobi' (washerman), as well as the French maid Marie, who immediately took to Alice when she heard her speak

French. The house, which had been built to Idina's specification in 1923, had four bedrooms with bathrooms, an elegant drawing room with a large raised fireplace, a dining room and an office. The rooms were fitted out with imported antique English furniture, old silver, leather-bound books and grand family portraits of Idina's and Joss's mothers.

But the feature that would have impressed Alice the most would have been Idina's bathroom, which was adjacent to the master bedroom. It was ten feet by eight feet and made of green travertine marble. Hot water was piped in from three 44-gallon drums heated by a log fire outside the bathroom. The water was somewhat discoloured by the local iron and murram sediment, but it was refreshing and stimulating. Idina was in the habit of taking a bath before dinner, wallowing in steaming water with a cocktail in hand while holding forth for dinner guests who were invited to join her as she bathed, in the nude, of course. The bath ceremony was just one of the many unconventional rituals at Slains. Another custom was that of dining in pyjamas and a dressing gown. Alice had no pyjamas, but she found a pair laid out neatly on her bedroom pillow by Marie. Dinner was usually late – around eleven at night – but in deference to Alice and Frédéric's long journey it is likely that it was served earlier that first evening. The African cook had been well taught by Marie and could manage cheese soufflé and *oeuf en cocotte* and there was champagne to celebrate the de Janzés' arrival. Despite the prevalence of French wine and food, Alice would have felt herself as far away as possible from the formalities of Parfondeval and Paris.

The following day, Alice and Frédéric had their first sighting by daylight of Slains and its surrounding landscape. It has often been observed that the Kenyan highlands are reminiscent of the English and Scottish countryside – albeit on an epic scale. When the one-time editor of the *East African Standard*, George Kinnear, later visited Wanjohi, he, like so many visitors before and since, found himself in thrall to the landscape. His description of the valley gives an idea of the sight of the Aberdare Mountains that awaited Alice and Frédéric when they awoke that morning:

> Every morning it takes the sun well nigh two hours to climb over the Aberdares and paint this valley with its rays and chase away the dew that cheats the drought. Many times I have stood shivering at dawn and watched the grey curtain of fading night lifted from the valley. The Aberdares stand like black bastions against the sun. Pockets of grey mist hide and reveal in turn. Here and there wisps of blue smoke rise lazily from hut and homestead. A silvery light steals down from the sky, but away over the Rift Valley the sky is already orange and yellow and a little pink. Suddenly the orchestra of the countryside plays the song of dawn and a dark hilltop is lit by a shaft of light. Even the streams run more noisily, chasing over the stones and leaping recklessly down the mountainside. Weirdly the light changes from silver to soft gold as the sun relentlessly climbs up the mountain; and then soars over the mountain ridge and restores

> all the colour to the flowers and the trees and to every living thing. Here is a lovely garden radiant with masses of flowers: there are several ponds and water always running back to the mountain stream from whence man had led it higher up the valley.

That morning, Alice and Frédéric were indeed treated to views of rolling hills layered in early-morning mists, the mountain peak of Kipipiri rising from the clouds, a great waterfall in the distance, and dense forests of cedar. Breakfast would have included porridge and fresh cream from a nearby dairy. Joss and Idina were intent on owning their own dairy, and were breeding Guernsey cattle to enable them to do so. After breakfast, Alice and Frédéric participated in another Slains ritual – the early-morning ride. Together with Joss, they rode out on three Somali ponies, with Idina staying at home due to her pregnancy. Although in France Alice had been forced to ride on the left side, in Kenya she was free to ride astride. These early-morning rides would have thrilled her: the beauty of the vistas, the unpopulated landscape, the sense of breadth and possibility, and above all the chance to see wild animals at close proximity. When she spied monkeys gambolling in the trees, she expressed a longing to own one as a pet. Joss and Frédéric duly obtained a tame monkey and gave it to her. Alice christened him Roderigo and he seldom left her side; she carried him shoulder high everywhere she went.

Alice would have cut a striking figure in Kenya, monkey at her ear. True to form, she had brought with her a sophisticated collection of Paris fashions and shoes, which she continued to wear, especially whenever she visited Nairobi. At Slains, however, she began to sport the cord trousers and loose blouses preferred by Idina. Like Coco Chanel, who had already shocked French society by wearing men's clothes, Idina and Alice carried off their masculine look with immense elegance. Alice also had several sets of khaki safari outfits made for her by Ahmed the tailor in Nairobi to her own design, complete with wide-brimmed hats and calf-high leather mosquito boots to protect her ankles from bites. Alice probably wore her boots only when visiting lower altitudes, however, as mosquitos generally cannot survive Wanjohi Valley's cold nights and high altitudes.

During their stay, Idina would take Frédéric and Alice by car to the nearby town of Gilgil to collect their mail. Letters from Aunt Tattie and Frédéric's mother, Moya, were soon arriving care of the Post Office filled with news about the children. Alice would write back, regaling the children with tales of her morning rides and the beauty of the African countryside. She described for them the scurrying warthogs and how they would suddenly stop, their tails sticking straight up in the air. She told them about the sweet little dik-dik (tiny antelope with cloven feet) and about the monkeys, especially Roderigo. But despite her eagerness to communicate with her family in France, the truth was that Alice was relieved to be away. She had never been comfortable in her role as a mother. As a child, she had been abandoned, once as a result of her mother's death, and again when she was removed from her father.

On some level, she must have been very comfortable with the idea of her children being cared for by Aunt Tattie – after all, this had been her own experience as a child.

The de Janzés remained in Kenya for three months, a month longer than originally planned. During that time they met most of the key players in Kenya's white settler community. Alice's charm and good looks captivated many. One of her most important social conquests was Hugh Cholmondeley, third Baron Delamere, known to everyone as 'D'. Thirty years her senior, the baron took a shine to Alice's beauty and her deep-voiced, American drawl. He also liked the fact that she was able to hold her drink, quaffing brandy and soda or pink gin with ease. Acceptance by D counted for a lot in the colonial community of the 1920s. Lord Delamere was the undisputed leader of the Kenyan settlers. He had arrived in Kenya in 1901, plunging his considerable personal wealth and energies into 100,000 acres of land near Njoro and encouraging his aristocratic friends in England to join him. Delamere, like his fellow settlers of all classes, had many setbacks in the beginning, particularly with the cattle he had imported, which quickly caught diseases and died. Over time, he learned to dip his herds to protect them from flies. He also mastered the art of growing wheat, employing a horticulturalist to develop a new variety of grain that would withstand local conditions. He began ranging his sheep on the edge of the Kinangop (a lower ridge of the plateau en route to the Wanjohi Valley) where conditions were clement and where his flocks soon thrived. D's tireless experimentation in farming often brought him to the brink of bankruptcy, but the wisdom of his experiences, which he shared with the other farmers in the area, is the reason that a colony flourished in the highlands at all. Later, when the settlers needed to defend themselves against the restrictive regulations of colonial officialdom, it was D who led the charge.

So much has been written about the Happy Valley crowd and their penchant for parties that it can come as something of a surprise to discover that most of its members were actually extremely diligent farmers, Joss and Idina included. At the time of Alice's arrival in Africa, Joss was meeting regularly with leading ranchers and farmers, such as D and Sir Francis Scott, seeking to learn from their long experience. Scott, the second son of the Duke of Buccleuch, was another Englishman who was instrumental in establishing effective farming techniques in the highlands. A former Coldstream Guards officer, he had arrived in Kenya with the wave of ex-servicemen settlers after the war, building himself a magnificent home called Deloraine near Nanyuki. Together with D, he was only too delighted to help a fellow old Etonian such as Joss establish himself in the valley.

Alice got to know the other farmers in the area. On her morning rides she came upon a Tudor-style house, Satima Farm, named after one of the Aberdare peaks, just to the south of Slains. The house belonged to Geoffrey Buxton, who farmed the surrounding 2,500 acres. Geoffrey Charles Buxton had been born in Thorpe, Norwich in 1879. He was a close friend of Denys Finch Hatton, the adventurer who was immortalized by Karen Blixen in *Out of Africa* (1937). Both Buxton and Finch Hatton had attended Eton, like so many of the settlers, Delamere and Joss included. Buxton had first arrived in Kenya in 1910 but when the Great War commenced, he returned to the UK and obtained a commission in the Coldstream Guards in 1916 and was awarded a territorial decoration after being mentioned in dispatches. On his return to Kenya, he devoted himself to farming. In fact, it was Buxton who had first lured Finch Hatton to the area, telling his friend that he had discovered 'Shangri La on the equator'. Unlike Idina, who entertained in pyjamas, socializing at Buxton's was a much more formal, black-tie affair, in the style of an English country mansion. Although he later married, at the time of Alice's arrival in Africa Geoffrey was still a bachelor, albeit rather a serious one.

Other immediate neighbours included the Honourable David Leslie-Melville, the second son of the Earl of Leven and Melville, and his wife, Mary, the granddaughter of Lord Portman. The Leslie-Melvilles were married in 1919 and arrived in Kenya soon afterwards, farming 5,000 acres. Their house was a broad and rambling affair, decorated in the English fashion with antiques, silver, family portraits and even a grand piano. Then there was Bill Delap and his wife, Bubbles, who owned Rayetta, a small pyrethrum farm. Pyrethrum was a valuable new crop and a natural pesticide grown by many of the farmers in the area, Idina included. Bill was a jealous and difficult man whose first wife – according to rumour – 'messed around with the troops'. After he married Bubbles he built a drawbridge around his house and threatened to shoot unannounced visitors. The Delaps kept themselves to themselves, and the Happy Valley set were evidently perfectly in step with this arrangement.

Thanks to Alice's friendship with Lord Delamere the de Janzés were also getting to know the crowd that gathered at the exclusive Muthaiga Club in Nairobi. The club had been founded by a group of settlers who had wanted somewhere to socialize away from the existing Nairobi Club, a place where they were likely to run into government officials with whom they were often at war. The new club opened on New Year's Eve 1913, with D as its first president, and soon gained a loyal and elite membership. Well-bred settlers were drawn like moths to the magnificent Muthaiga, its cellar filled with fine French wines, its well-appointed rooms offering comfort and elegance, along with the opportunity to socialize with friends over an infinite number of cocktails. Race weeks took place twice a year, at Christmas and in midsummer, during which times the Muthaiga overflowed with revellers – balls were held every evening, with members dressed to the nines, and the dancing lasted until dawn. Alice and Frédéric had been made temporary members of Muthaiga soon after their arrival, ensuring that they found themselves at the very centre of colonial social life. Full membership would follow by virtue of D's backing.

For the last two months of the de Janzés' stay in Kenya, Frédéric hired a Ford car so that they would be able to drive to the Muthaiga and explore the surrounding area without relying on Idina or Joss to chauffeur them around. It was on one of their regular visits to Nairobi that they were introduced to Roy and Margaret Spicer, a couple recently arrived from Ceylon. English-born Roy was serving as the Commissioner of Police for Kenya. His new wife was American and had a 9-year-old daughter from a previous marriage. Frédéric was delighted to strike up a friendship with the Kenyan Head of Police, but the strongest bond was between Alice and Margaret. Alice found she had much in common with this well-dressed 32-year-old mother: like Alice, Margaret was from the United States but had spent time in Europe and spoke fluent French, having been educated in Montreux. Margaret was often invited to stay at Slains, where she kept Alice, Frédéric, Joss and Idina in fits of laughter with her imitations. Margaret had a talent for mimicry: she would impersonate the people she'd encountered on the boat trip out and the pompous manners of the Nairobi government officials.

It was during visits to Slains that Alice taught Margaret how to play the ukulele. The two women would often entertain Joss, Idina and their guests after dinner with popular and traditional American songs. Alice and Margaret had complementary voices: Alice had a rather deep and husky contralto voice and Margaret, who had trained as a soprano in Florence, possessed a higher and sweeter one. The two women would sit together on the descending lawn in front of the house as if on a stage. Guests would drive their cars into a half-circle facing them, switching on headlights to illuminate the scene. One of Alice and Margaret's duets was the following folk song from the Deep South:

There is an old log cabin and it's a beautiful place
In that old log cabin, there is my baby waiting for me.
And it won't be long, until I hear that song
Ringing in the fields of cotton and I'll rejoice
When I hear that voice saying Bab-y
Oh yeah, there is an old log cabin . . .

They also performed George Gershwin hits such as 'Swanee' and 'Oh, Lady Be Good!' as well as duets in French. Such performances became much talked about amongst the settler society of the times, and Alice would be asked to play and sing wherever she went.

It was through Roy and Margaret that the de Janzés first came into contact with the Governor of Kenya, Sir Edward Grigg, and his wife, Joan. Roy Spicer had already won the respect of the handsome and commanding governor: Edward Grigg approved of Roy's impressive service record during the First World War (he had been awarded the Military Cross in France) and of his highly effective reorganization of the Kenya Police force, especially its African section. Roy's morale-boosting innovations were much admired and included attention to officers' dress and the newly coined Kenya Police motto 'Salus Populi' (the Latin motto means 'Service to the People' and it is still used today, although translated into Swahili). Roy also created cricket and football teams for the officers and developed Kenya's first mounted police force, all of which helped to give the right impression to the enthusiastic governor. Although the governor's wife, Joan, had become friends with Margaret, she did not share Margaret's enthusiasm for

Alice. Word had reached Lady Grigg that Alice had a decadent side and the very prim and proper Joan was insistent that wives had to conduct themselves in a ladylike fashion if they were to be admitted into her circle at Government House. Margaret, however, managed to endear herself to Joan, despite being a divorcee, and was never excluded from official gatherings.

While Alice spent a good deal of time with Margaret, her closest ally in Kenya was Idina. The two had much in common. Although Idina was six years older and lacked Alice's unimpeachable good looks – the former being known for her trademark weak chin – both women shared a fashionable elegance, an active disrespect for convention, and a passion for the Wanjohi Valley. It soon became clear that they had something else in common, namely their attraction to Joss. After Alice's arrival in Africa, she found herself increasingly attracted to Idina's handsome husband. For his part, Joss returned the compliment, flirting publicly with Alice at every opportunity. Idina was unperturbed by her husband's latest infatuation. In fact, she may have even encouraged Joss to set his sights in Alice's direction. The Hays had always maintained an open relationship, and the heavily pregnant Idina may have felt that at this time Joss should be permitted his affairs. The advantage of Alice was that she would respect Idina's precedence and would never attempt to rub her nose in it. Alice was someone who got along just as well with women as men, often making friends with the wives of her male friends. In many ways, Alice and Idina's mutual attraction to Joss became a bond between the two women.

We do not know exactly when Joss and Alice first consummated their relationship, but it seems that this happened at some point during Alice's first visit to Kenya. Although their affair wasn't openly acknowledged at this point – and neither Joss nor Alice sought to leave their spouses as a result – their on-again-off-again relationship would continue for the next two decades. In hindsight, their liaison has an air of inevitability about it. Alice was unfulfilled in her marriage, looking for excitement and escape: her relationship with Frédéric was stable, but far from passionate. For his part, Joss had always been magnetically attracted to wealthy and beautiful married women. Clandestine encounters between Alice and Joss would have taken place whenever Idina and Frédéric happened to be out at the same time, and the rarity of such opportunities would have only added to the excitement. By all accounts, Joss was an accomplished lover, known for his ability to bring a woman to climax easily: it is entirely possible that Alice experienced a kind of sexual awakening with him. For his part, Frédéric put a brave face on Alice's flirtation and subsequent affair with Joss. He was even heard to refer to Joss on more than one occasion as 'the boyfriend'. Frédéric had lived with Alice's moods for such a long time, it seems he was inclined to go along with anything that might make his unpredictable wife a little happier.

It was true that since their arrival in Kenya, Alice's health had improved enormously. For the first time in years, she was happy – her heavy moods had almost completely lifted. As the African trip began to draw to a close,

Alice realized she was dreading her return to Paris and her life there. It was at this juncture she made up her mind to buy a permanent home in the highlands. Frédéric's need to appease Alice was such that he agreed to help her purchase land in the Wanjohi Valley. The de Janzés arranged for a meeting with the Leslie-Melvilles and Geoffrey Buxton to talk about purchasing Wanjohi Farm, adjacent to Geoffrey's property. The acreage was small, only 600 acres, but could be easily managed and was ideal for growing pyrethrum. Frédéric and Alice would be able to employ the local Kikuyu farmers, who had smallholdings dotted about the area, to plant and harvest the crops. The de Janzés learned that the land was owned by Sir John Frecheville Ramsden, known as 'Chops', a local builder of settler houses. Before long, Frédéric was putting wheels in motion to buy Wanjohi Farm from Chops, driving to Nairobi to see Mr Barrat at the firm of Shapley, Schwartze and Barrat (the Hays' legal advisers). By the end of 1925, a deal had been struck and Alice began making plans to build a new house on the site. The de Janzés' future home would be situated about seventy-five yards from the Wanjohi River, facing a bend where a deep pool formed. There was a small manager's house on the land (still there to this day) that would provide the de Janzés with temporary accommodation while they supervised construction. Although Alice was anxious to start the building work, she would have to wait until the title for the land had been transferred and legal arrangements processed by the lawyers. This would not be completed until June of the following year.

The de Janzés stayed on with the Hays through Christmas and New Year, experiencing the customary revelry of Nairobi's race week. By January 1926, Idina had given birth to a daughter, Dinan, in Nairobi. It was at this point that Alice and Frédéric decided to go back to France, at least temporarily, to see their children. Alice refused to be parted from her pet monkey, Roderigo, and so she took him with her on the liner to France, successfully disembarking with him at Marseilles. On their arrival in Paris, the de Janzés were reunited with their children who must have been delighted at the sight of their mother with an African monkey perched on her shoulder. Nolwen and Paola, now ages three and a half and twenty months respectively, were staying with Aunt Tattie at her rather grand apartment on the rue de la Pompe. Their parents had been away for five months, an interminably long time for young children. Although Nolwen would have recognized her parents immediately, little Paola would have already grown completely accustomed to life with Aunt Tattie.

Meanwhile, Aunt Tattie was not at all happy about the arrival of Roderigo in her elegant home. Terrified that the monkey would ruin her furniture, she suggested that they all go and stay at the de Janzés' rue Spontini apartment. That January, Alice, Frédéric, their children, a French nanny, the monkey and a grand piano took up residence in the rue Spontini. Not surprisingly, Roderigo wreaked havoc. The children loved him, but the nanny was up in arms – every day the monkey would knock over another vase or ornament as he leapt from sofa to sofa. (We can only imagine what an African monkey made of being transplanted to the confines of a sophisticated Paris apartment.) For Alice, Roderigo was a living connection to Africa, to the Wanjohi Valley, and to her friends there, Joss in particular. Throughout her life, Alice would continue to show a greater attachment to her pets than she did to her two daughters. Although she was doubtless pleased to see Nolwen and Paola, she was also determined to leave them again as soon as possible to return to Africa.

After only a few weeks in Paris, the de Janzés received a cable from their lawyer, Barrat, to say that completion of the Wanjohi Farm acquisition could take place in Nairobi as soon as they returned to Kenya. By mid-February, after only a few weeks in France, they were ready to leave again. Both Alice and Frédéric feared that Alice's moods would return if she stayed in Paris a moment longer. Frédéric had kitted himself out with powerful rifles and a shotgun in preparation for going on safari – he was looking forward to hunting game on his return. Alice, meanwhile, packed up crates of linen, silver, books and other household essentials for their new African home. Based on her experience of living with the Hays, she knew exactly what was needed to make the place comfortable and personal. Her linen was exceptionally beautiful, with the de Janzé coat of arms embroidered on every sheet, pillowcase, hand-towel and table napkin. Pictures, lamps and carpets were also included in the de Janzés' luggage as well as a few pieces of antique French furniture to lend refinement to their drawing room. With four vast crates in the hold and some new Paris clothes in a cabin trunk, they said goodbye to their daughters once more.

For half the year, Nolwen and Paola would be installed in Château Parfondeval in Normandy, with Moya, their devoted grandmother. For the rest of the year they would be in Paris with Alice's Aunt Tattie. This second trip to Africa marked the beginning of what was to become for Alice a total separation from her children. Perhaps it was Alice's instinct – and in this respect she may have judged correctly – that Moya and Aunt Tattie would simply be better mothers to the girls. Evidently, Alice lacked the maternal instincts that her aunt and Moya so naturally felt for Nolwen and Paola. Alice had been severely shaken by both her daughters' births, enduring post-natal depressions that had only recently been relieved by her escape to Africa. Like many women of her generation and class, Alice would have found it not at all unusual to be living at a distance from them. Wealthy families of the period were often divided in this way – with parents overseas while their offspring stayed at home to be looked after by relatives or sent to boarding school. (Idina and Joss would also arrange for their daughter, Dinan, to be brought up by a relative, in this case Idina's sister in England, while they remained in Africa.) Later in life, both Nolwen and Paola always maintained that they adored their mother and did not resent her desertion. Perhaps they understood why Alice had to live away from them, and were pleased to see her happy. Nonetheless, they must have missed her deeply at times, anticipating and longing for her letters and return.

After the long journey from Europe, Alice and Frédéric arrived in Nairobi again. The de Janzés signed the documents for Wanjohi Farm in March 1926. The certificate of title reads as follows:

> Title I. R. 1494
> Frédéric le Comte de Janzé and Alice la Comtesse de Janzé, both of Gilgil in the colony of Kenya, pursuant to the transfer dated the 9th day of March 1926 registered at the Registry of Titles at Nairobi as I.R. 1052, are now the proprietors as owners of the fees subject to such encumbrances as are notified by memorandum written hereon to the conditions contained in the said transfer etc. – etc.

Alice lost no time persuading Chops to build her a house, on the site she had marked out. She also needed him to fix up the small manager's house at the rear of the property so that she and Frédéric could move in there immediately. With the help of Idina, Alice drew plans for Chops to follow. The lines of the house would be similar to those of so many of the settlers' houses in the area. It was to be built on a single level in the shape of a fat 'H' with stone foundations that were visible to a height of three feet. There would be cedar half-logs cladding the sides, a cedar roof and a square verandah. The house would overlook the Wanjohi River at its rear and the long silvery waterfalls of the Satima Peak in the Aberdare Mountains at the front. Inside, walls would be plastered and some basic wiring would be installed with a generator housed in the servants' quarters. Two wings would be devoted to bedrooms, with Alice's bedroom on the left as you faced the verandah and more bedrooms and bathrooms on the right. In the centre of the house, there was going to be a long drawing room with a central stone fireplace. A central chimney would also serve the dining room with its large pantry off to one side. As was traditional, the kitchen would be separate from the house – food would be cooked there and, when it was ready to serve, brought to the pantry in the main house. After the title for the land was transferred to the de Janzés on 2 June 1926, building work finally began.

On her return to Africa, Alice went about adding to her menagerie. To protect her dogs from night-time marauders she had an open wire kennel constructed near to her temporary living quarters. Here she also kept her baboon, Valentino. Joss lent the de Janzés two Somali ponies that were housed at Geoffrey Buxton's stables across the river. Every morning, Alice continued to ride out before breakfast through the morning mists with Frédéric, her new greyhound Fairyfeet running alongside. Frédéric recorded stories from these morning rides in his book of pen portraits about Africa, *Tarred with the Same Brush* (1929). The book – which is dedicated to one of its characters, 'Delecia', a pseudonym for Alice – describes one ride in particular which helps to paint a picture of Alice's close relationships with her animals. One morning, Delecia/Alice goes out riding alone with her greyhound for company. Her pony bolts, leaving Delecia/Alice winded but uninjured beneath a cluster of trees. The greyhound panics and tears off in the opposite direction. A few minutes later, the dog returns to his mistress, deeply scarred and bleeding after catching a paw blow to her side and front legs from a lion. The dog has saved her life. Greatly shaken, she walks home leading her pony and hound. Back at the farm, she bathes the poor dog and bandages his wounds, nursing him all day and into the night.

Looking at the photographs of Alice during this time, it is possible to see the degree to which she was evidently invigorated by her surroundings. In her Paris photos, Alice often looks pale and has a haunted expression. In the Kenyan photos, she radiates ease. The eyes look out to the horizon, her face tanned across her broad cheekbones. Alice told friends that she had never felt happier in her life. Her dreaded depressions had lifted: she felt cured, as though she had taken a miracle draught of smelling salts. In fact, there is a scientific explanation for this new stabilization of her moods. Kenya is on the equator, blessed with intensely bright light year round. Studies have shown that sufferers of cyclothymia often demonstrate a marked improvement in mood after being exposed to bright light therapy: it is thought that sunshine stimulates the pituitary and pineal glands, effecting the release of mood-altering hormones. Doctors all the way back to Hippocrates have recommended natural light as a cure for unhappiness – for her part, Florence Nightingale found patients recovered more rapidly when kept in sunny wards. Adding to the beneficial effect of so much sunshine, the Wanjohi Valley is 6,000 feet above sea level, and at such a height, alterations in psychology, behaviour and cognitive functioning are common. Then there was the sheer uplifting beauty of the place. Evelyn Waugh, who visited Kenya in 1931, described well the effect that the highlands have on those who visit. 'There is a quality about it which I have found nowhere else but in Ireland, of warm loveliness and breadth and generosity,' he wrote. 'It was not a matter of mere liking, as one likes any place where people are amusing and friendly and the climate is agreeable, but a feeling of personal tenderness. I think almost everyone in the highlands of Kenya has very much this feeling, more or less articulately.' He went on to evoke the particular quality of the light: 'Brilliant sunshine quite unobscured, uninterrupted in its incidence; sunlight clearer than daylight; there is something of the moon about it, the coolness seems so unsuitable. Amber sunlight in Europe; diamond sunlight in Africa. The air fresh as an advertisement for toothpaste.' In Kenya, those combined effects of sunshine, altitude and landscape continued to positively affect Alice's mental chemistry.

In other words, it was easy to be happy in Happy Valley. The de Janzés would drive over to Slains every day in their new 1925 Straight Six Buick with a drop head and spare wheels. They variously entertained their neighbours, the Leslie-Melvilles and Geoffrey Buxton. Alice had her new house to plan and her animals. There was the thrill of her occasional liaisons with Joss to add to her pleasures. Her life in Paris was fading to a distant memory. She no longer felt trapped by her role as countess and by her marriage. Certainly, she missed her daughters, but they were to be visited on a regular basis and Alice decided that as soon as her house was built and furnished she would return to see them. She wrote long descriptive letters for Aunt Tattie to read out loud to her girls, always starting 'My Darlings', giving news of her house, and her new servants, and including little stories about Roderigo and the other animals.

Perhaps for the first time since her early childhood, Alice was actually at peace. Then, as so often happens when a person finally achieves a degree of contentment in life, Alice was about to fall in love.

4

Raymund and the Coup de Foudre

A month after the de Janzés' return to Kenya, a new face appeared on the Happy Valley scene. It was that of Raymund de Trafford, a 26-year-old English aristocrat. Darkly handsome, slender and the youngest son of Sir Humphrey de Trafford, third baronet, Raymund could trace his ancestors back to the eleventh century and the time of King Canute. By all accounts, Raymund could also be described as something of a cad, a man who had already left a trail of broken hearts stretching from Mayfair to Buenos Aires and back again. Some years later, Evelyn Waugh, who visited Raymund at his farm in Kenya, described him as a 'bachelor farmer', adding 'though perhaps he is more typically bachelor than farmer'.

Raymund had been brought up in the rather starchy

environment of a Catholic English country home at the turn of the century before being sent away to boarding school, as was customary. He was educated at St Anthony's, a Catholic school in Eastbourne, and at the Oratory at Edgbaston (often described as the 'Catholic Eton'). At the age of eighteen, he entered the Royal Military College of Sandhurst and was gazetted as an ensign in the Coldstream Guards (1st Battalion) on 20 December 1918, thereby narrowly avoiding probable slaughter in the trenches of France. He left the army on 27 February 1924, after serving in the British Army of occupation in Constantinople. In his final year of army service he developed asthma and was told by his doctors to go abroad for his health. He embarked on a tour of South America beginning in 1925, spending time in both Uruguay and Argentina, where the dry climate proved conducive to his weak lungs. In South America, he learned to cut cattle on ranches, went boar shooting in Uruguay with one Aaron Ancharenas la Barras and was entertained by a family of wealthy polo-playing ranchers named Basualdos in Argentina. On his return to London early in 1926, Raymund decided to travel on to Kenya, with another dry climate and a popular destination for so many Englishmen of his age and class. As the youngest de Trafford son, he was a victim of primogeniture, meaning that his eldest brother would inherit the family estate. Although Raymund received regular payments from the family coffers, it was expected that he would begin to make his own money at some point, especially now that his health had improved.

He decided to try his hand at farming and business in East Africa. The prospect of big-game hunting was also a considerable lure, but other factors helped his decision. He had heard much about the Kenya highlands from fellow members at the London club White's, to which he was elected in 1922. Apparently, there were groups of English aristocrats living in decadent fashion in a place called the Wanjohi Valley. Raymund would have heard tales of drunken parties, wife-swapping and general debauchery. The joke would have gone around at White's, 'Are you married, or do you live in Kenya?' Given Raymund's appetite for alcohol and women, Wanjohi would have sounded like absolute heaven. Soon after his return to London from South America, he started to make preparations for his departure. Raymund could have begun his journey to Kenya from Southampton, but this would have taken him through the Bay of Biscay to Gibraltar, a route that could be rough, sick-making and even dangerous. Instead, like many English passengers bound for Africa, he chose to leave from Marseilles, after which the route to Mombasa was comparatively smooth sailing. Raymund took the train to Marseilles in early April of 1926, boarding the SS *General Duchayne* bound for Kenya on the 15th. He arrived in Nairobi via the Lunatic Line about four weeks later, and was seen soon after his arrival on the verandah of the Mombasa Club with a pretty fellow passenger, who probably succumbed to his charms on board the ship.

Next, Raymund set about finding himself a home in the highlands. Although he was not an Etonian – like so many of the upper-class settlers in Kenya of the time – he brought with him an impressive list of introductions from his father and friends in England. First he called on Lord Delamere and Sir Francis Scott, the two most prominent expatriate farmers in the region. He also went to see Geoffrey Buxton, a former Coldstream Guards officer. Soon after his arrival, Raymund settled on buying a maize farm near Njoro called Kishobo. Here he employed a manager to run the farm, purchased a lorry and rented a Buick car. There was already a house on Raymund's newly purchased land, albeit a fairly basic one, but he improved it, furnishing it for the most part with his extensive collection of books which he had brought out in crates. Photos of Raymund from this period show an immaculately dressed young man, slim-framed and athletic, with dark hair and a winning smile, his hat often set at a rakish angle. Needless to say, he soon established a reputation as something of a lothario amongst the small community of settlers – doubtless relishing his own notoriety. Raymund's primary interest, however, was hunting of another variety. Big-game safaris in Africa had been fashionable amongst aristocratic Europeans since the turn of the century, and by the time Raymund arrived in Kenya, Denys Finch Hatton, the most famous of the white hunters in Kenya, had just begun his new business venture escorting wealthy clients into the wilderness on safari. Raymund was keen to join in.

By June of 1926, Raymund had heard of Joss and Idina and their friends the de Janzés, but he had yet to meet them. When he called on Geoffrey Buxton early in June, he asked Geoffrey to engineer a meeting with Frédéric in particular. Raymund was anxious to undertake his first safari and had heard that Frédéric was also keen. What's more, Raymund was intrigued to meet the count for another reason. Although mostly self-educated, Raymund considered himself well read, and he had heard that Frédéric was a writer. Geoffrey arranged for Raymund to meet the de Janzés along with Joss and Idina at Satima Farm that June. Some years later, Raymund related to Margaret Spicer the details of his first meetings with Alice. He remembered Alice standing by the fireplace in Geoffrey's drawing room looking up over a glass of champagne, her grey eyes vivid and lit by the fire. He also recalled the next time he saw her, which was the following day. After staying the night with Geoffrey, Raymund decided to drive over to Slains to discuss a hunting safari with Frédéric. At Idina's insistence, Raymund stayed for lunch, which gave him the opportunity to study Alice in daylight. Raymund recalled in particular Alice's hair, which was beautifully arranged around her face, and her tight sweater, emphasizing her breasts. She had made up her eyes to kill. He also noticed that she drank spirits easily and was unaffected by them.

In later years, Alice would tell friends that she met Raymund 'on a lion hunt'. With her well-developed sense of drama, she had evidently decided that 'lion hunt' had a better ring to it than 'introduced by mutual friends'. In any case, Alice was immediately drawn to this good-looking unmarried arrival, with his polished conversation and tales of South American adventures. It was, for both parties, a mutual attraction of powerful proportions. Raymund resolved to find some way to see Alice alone. It transpired that he did not have to wait long for the opportunity. Frédéric was leaving on a safari the following week and there was no room for Raymund on this occasion. Instead, the count suggested another date in August and gave Raymund instructions as to how to obtain an elephant licence. While Frédéric was away, Raymund set to work arranging a secret rendezvous with Alice in Nairobi. She agreed to meet him there so they could then travel together down the coast near Mombasa.

For Alice, this entailed a double deception. Not only did she need to keep the trip secret from Frédéric, she also had to make sure that Joss would not find out. Since her return to Africa, Alice had resumed her affair with Joss and she sensed that he would not be keen on this new dalliance with Raymund. Idina was no fool, however, and when Raymund and Alice returned from their trip, Idina confronted her friend. Although Idina is often seen as Happy Valley's high priestess of free love, in fact, she was happiest when relationships were within her control – she may even have taken Alice's new affair as a kind of infidelity to Joss. Suffice to say, she sensed that the happy foursome of the de Janzés and the Hays had just been disturbed. Idina duly informed Alice that she was not pleased about Raymund and did not like him.

Undeterred, Alice returned to Wanjohi Farm to oversee the work on her new house and to welcome her husband back from his safari. Despite the reappearance of Frédéric, Raymund set about redoubling his attentions to

Alice, becoming a frequent visitor to Wanjohi Farm. As the de Janzés did not have a telephone, he would drive down unannounced in his box-bodied Ford. An accomplished amateur photographer, Raymund took many pictures of Alice during this period. In one portrait, Alice is standing chest-deep in the waves during a clandestine trip to the coast, her eyes obscured by a wide-brimmed sun hat, her swimming costume pulled down around her shoulders, revealing bare shoulders and torso. She exudes happiness, health and sex appeal. During the initial stage of this new romance, Alice continued her meetings with Joss, although her primary interest was now Raymund. Alice's new interest was unattached and could potentially help her escape from her situation with Frédéric, whereas Joss had never offered her any long-term commitment or a route out of her failing marriage.

Besides, Joss's eye was already wandering elsewhere. The object of his attention was Mary Ramsay-Hill, sometimes known as 'Molly' – a pale-skinned 33-year-old beauty with a red-lipsticked mouth and matching lacquered nails. At the time of her first meetings with Joss, Mary was already married and living with her husband, Cyril, in the ostentatious Spanish palace that he had built for her on the nearby shores of Lake Naivasha. This impressive structure and its mistress enthralled Joss, even if Mary's origins were dubious. Born in London in 1893, she was often referred to as 'Miss Boots' because it was rumoured that her fortune was from the chemist chain. In fact, her father was a bankrupted London clerk, who had lost all his money by the time Mary was fifteen (the exact source of Mary's wealth is not known). Cyril was her second husband: she had married her first at sixteen. Now she set her sights on Joss, or at least he set his sights on her. The attraction was mutual – he was lured by her money, lavish home and sexual experience. She was drawn by his title, good looks and considerable reputation as a lover. For both parties, the liaison may well have also helped to provide a route out of marriages that were turning bad.

With Joss directing his attentions elsewhere and Alice engrossed with Raymund, Frédéric was faced with a new dynamic. While the affair between Joss and Alice had never threatened the status quo, Alice's attraction to Raymund was altogether more destructive. If Frédéric guessed what was going on, he said nothing. Alice's moods were powerful and potentially destructive and Frédéric may have preferred to remain silent in order to preserve the relative peace. What's more, the de Janzés could still find plenty of common ground when it came to their animals. At this point their menagerie included Alice's baboon Valentino, a marmoset monkey, Fairyfeet the greyhound and a mongrel dog called Monster. Alice's prize pet, however, was her lion cub. Frédéric had discovered the cub one morning while out riding alone on his pony. In his description of the incident from his book *Tarred with the Same Brush*, about his adventures in Africa, he wrote: 'I had only a fleeting impression of a yellow streak darting out at us from behind a rock.' Frédéric and his pony eventually came to a halt, the poor horse trembling with fear. Frédéric guessed that he had just been saved from a lion's charge, so he decided to tie up the pony in order to see if he could locate the den. He approached the area from the opposite side and managed to get a glimpse of a lioness and her cubs. The next day he took Alice with him and they watched through binoculars from a safe distance. In the coming days, the couple frequently returned to the area, approaching to within fifty yards of the den. They could see four cubs inside. The lioness greeted these visits with low growls, but she did not attack.

Two weeks later, Alice and Frédéric received an unexpected visit from an Indian maharaja, his two young princes and an older man, an aide-de-camp or vizier. They explained that they were on safari and were hoping for lunch. Frédéric and Alice were happy to provide. After the meal, the maharaja invited the de Janzés to view his trophies – gazelles, kongonis (large antelope), and a great kudu (another species of antelope) as well as two lion skins pegged out in the sun. Frédéric enquired as to where the lions had been killed. 'Oh, quite near,' he was told. 'Among some kopjes (small hills) a few miles from here.' Frédéric asked, 'But didn't you see the cubs?' 'Oh no, they were all alone; the lioness charged from some rock piles after letting us get within fifty yards.' Frédéric was furious and immediately went to saddle up his pony. He found the poor lion cubs in a small cave. They had been starved for three days. One was dead. Frédéric brought the three remaining cubs back to the farm, but one more died in the night. He wrote: '. . . it is an unpardonable crime to shoot females of any species'. The maharaja's party was invited to stay the night, but the atmosphere between the de Janzés and their guests was strained and the visitors left the following morning.

Alice and Frédéric doted on the cubs, feeding them on tinned milk and raw meat. These new visitors were ravenous, sleeping together in a basket; two round, fat balls of fluff. Christened Samson and Judah, they were soon introduced to the other members of Alice's menagerie. They got along well with the dogs, and even the monkeys, particularly Valentino the baboon, who elected himself the cubs' keeper, and cuffed both of them if they got out of line. One night, when the cubs were older, Judah escaped and was never seen again. Samson, however, became a household pet. He was playful and often naughty, and possessed great character. In the evenings, he would often wander into the house and lay his head on the laps of his master and mistress. There is an iconic photograph of Samson and Alice taken by Raymund, in which Alice is sitting on the verandah with Samson draped across her knees – a Madonna and child with the cub playing the part of the infant. The cub's tail is hanging down to Alice's toes and his paws are bigger than her hands. He must have weighed at least fifty pounds, and was easily old enough to do some harm, but Alice appears completely unperturbed. She is wearing a loose shirt and baggy trousers, a large felt hat on her head, gazing into the middle distance with the look of a woman who has come into her own. The photo was sent to her children – whom Samson had literally replaced – and Frédéric's mother, Moya, as well as to Alice's father, William.

Although Alice and Frédéric adored their pets, their own relationship was becoming increasingly untenable. In his series of quasi-autobiographical stories about Kenya, *Vertical Land* (1928), Frédéric presented an accurate, if poignant, assessment of their marriage via the fictionalized relationship of 'Delecia' and 'Ned' (Alice and Frédéric). The names of the de Janzés' pets were not changed. The narrator is a new arrival in Kenya and is called 'Bob':

> After a long trek down, and the motor ride from Meru, I reach Nairobi fagged out. Washed and bathed, I'm carried off to Muthaiga for a drink.
>
> As we drive up we are passed by a low-bodied Buick, piled with luggage and boys. 'Ah – they are the Happy Valley crowd,' says the Colonel at my side. We stop and park the car behind theirs. 'Salaam! Mon colonel!' the boy cries, all dusty faced, orange shirt turned to brown. 'Hello, Delecia!' the Colonel calls, as the girl gets out, dark haired under a broad terai, in grey slacks and green jumper, small and dainty with firm, pointed chin and wide spaced grey eyes, much personality. We all meet and sit on the verandah for a drink. – 'You don't know Samson! – Oh, Ned, please get Samson.' He drags his long supple form from the deepest chair with a sigh of ennui, goes to the car, bringing back a four months' old lion cub.
>
> 'I never travel without him, but I've also got Roderigo and Bill Sikes, also Samson's pal, Gillie, the Airedale.'

They are all brought for inspection, the two monkeys tiny, and clinging like moths. Roderigo is sweet, but Delecia warns he is not very gentlemanly in his habits.

She talks and tells the Colonel all the gossip. Ned stalks off to the bar. He seems so nervous and jumpy, cannot stay still, wanders from group to group. Delecia tells of his accident with the elephant: 'His nerves are terrible and he will go hunting in the forest with only one good arm.' She smiles, 'He's difficult at times.'

'And, Delecia, do play to us to-night.'

'Well, maybe, but not at the club, and we must have dinner, a wash and thousands of drinks. I'm feeling completely passed out now. I'm going to my room, do send Ned along soon, he'll only get cross if he stays too long in the bar.'

'A great pity,' murmurs the Colonel as she goes. 'A great girl, Delecia, but she cares too much for her pets and he cares too much for her.'

Despite his growing sense that he was losing the woman he loved, Frédéric must have accepted his new rival's appearance with a degree of equanimity, because that August, the two men agreed to go on a four-week safari together. Frédéric invited Alice to join them and all three began making the necessary arrangements. On 20 August 1926, Raymund purchased a licence to shoot two elephants at a cost of £45. They engaged a white hunter to guide them and began to gather the necessary equipment for the trip.

A safari was perhaps not the best idea in the circumstances. Alice, Frédéric and Raymund would be spending both days and nights for a whole month in extremely close proximity to one another and without respite. Raymund would doubtless make frequent attempts to spend time alone with Alice and to persuade her to leave Frédéric. Meanwhile, Frédéric could be in no doubt of Alice's feelings for Raymund, and would have to stifle his husband's sense of hurt pride continually. Any underlying tensions were bound to erupt in the isolated environment of the wilderness.

Even in the weeks leading up to the safari, frictions between Raymund and Frédéric began to surface. There were frequent disputes, usually about literature, fuelled by drink and altitude. Too gentlemanly to argue outright over Alice, they elected to fight about books instead. Both of them moved in literary circles and considered themselves intellectual. Raymund had attended military school rather than university, but could nonetheless be dogmatic when it came to literary matters, readily defending his wide knowledge of the classics and his favourite nineteenth-century authors. He was indifferent to Shelley, loathed Byron, but loved William Thackeray, George Eliot and Charles Dickens. Frédéric, on the other hand, was a legitimate intellectual, a graduate of Cambridge University with a degree in English, and a friend and contemporary of Proust. He venerated in particular Honoré de Balzac, Gustave Flaubert and Charles Baudelaire. Exactly what took place during the trip itself is unknown but it is hard to imagine that the dynamic between the three participants was anything but fraught. It is perhaps not surprising that Alice decided to depart a week early and return to Wanjohi Farm without her husband or lover, anxious to leave the men to their own devices. Frédéric wanted to push on north to Uganda. Raymund was torn between going back with Alice – thereby ensuring he could have time alone with her – or going on with this next leg of the adventure. It is characteristic of Raymund that he put hunting first. He had been told that there were gorillas in the Ugandan forests near Lake Victoria and the Congo and had already decided that he would supplement his farming and family allowance by capturing live animals and selling them to European zoos. At the time, live gorillas fetched extremely high prices in Europe. Raymund elected to plough on.

Alice made her way home with a driver and a servant. It was mid-September, and building work on her house was almost finished. The Indian builders had moved quickly, working from dawn until dusk. In her three weeks away, the house had been transformed. Alice was able to unpack the rest of her crates and move furniture and beds into position. Idina was there to advise. Idina's French maid Marie made curtains. Soon, Wanjohi Farm House began to look like home. But it was no longer a home Alice wished to share with Frédéric. Alone, she had time to think. She confided in Idina, telling her friend that she was contemplating divorce. Although Idina disliked Raymund, she did not find this news in the least bit shocking. After all, she was a veteran divorcee. 'If Raymund makes you happy darling, then that's what you must do,' she advised. 'But for heaven's sake, don't leave us; do come and live here near us in your angelic little valley.' Next Alice drove to Nairobi in order to discuss matters with Margaret Spicer. Margaret warned Alice to be careful. The Spicers liked and admired Frédéric; they had met Raymund, knew of his reputation and were wary. Alice returned to Wanjohi, but not before ordering some extra furniture from a Scottish joiner called Mr Macrae who made excellent Georgian-style furniture for colonial homes. In more ways than one, Alice was attempting to set her house in order.

Even though Alice had sought Margaret's advice, it was becoming increasingly clear to her that she was not going to follow it. Frédéric and Raymund were due back very soon and Alice began to steel herself for their arrival. To her surprise, Frédéric returned alone. Raymund had remained in Uganda, trying to negotiate a game-capturing safari for which he needed special assistance and crates. It should have been Alice's first inkling that she was unlikely to be Raymund's first priority; instead, she reassured herself that it would not be long before he pitched up again. Meanwhile, there was obviously something terribly wrong with Frédéric. He was gaunt and complaining of fever. Alice sent him straight to bed, then drove to Nakuru to contact a doctor. The doctor offered the diagnosis of a severe and dangerous type of malaria, dosed Frédéric with quinine and ordered Alice to apply cold, damp towels to her husband's legs to draw the heat down from his head and reduce his temperature. Not wanting to take the local doctor's word for it, Alice asked Idina about good doctors in Nairobi. Idina told her to drive directly to Nairobi to pick up Dr R.W. Burkitt, the famed Irish surgeon, who was known for his rough but effective treatment of malarial patients.

Burkitt's diagnosis was gloomy. Frédéric was suffering from the early signs of blackwater fever, a condition brought on by malaria and the dosing of quinine he had just received. Frédéric had contracted blackwater fever previously while serving as aide-de-camp in Morocco during the First World War, and had been invalided out of the French Air Force as a result. Once contracted, the disease can easily return if stimulated by a new bout of malaria and quinine. Frédéric's urine was beginning to turn black, a sure symptom of the disease. It was decided that the count should return to Paris for treatment. The doctor also recommended that Frédéric stay away from places where he might contract malaria in the future. Remaining in Kenya on any permanent basis was out of the question. Alice was faced with the following dilemma: should she return to Paris with Frédéric or stay in Kenya with Raymund? She was in love with Raymund, but Frédéric was her husband and he was dangerously ill.

Alice was honest with Frédéric. She informed him that she was not prepared to leave Kenya for good. The couple considered their options. Frédéric could return to France alone, leaving Alice to look after the menagerie. Or Alice could return to Paris with him for a temporary period, but then what would they do with the animals? They contemplated turning Samson loose, but he was only four or five months old, still an uneducated cub, and unable to fend for himself. Neither of them could bear the idea of losing Samson. The lion cub was so concerned about his master he was visibly moping, laying his great head on Frédéric's sick bed and insisting on sleeping there. Frédéric agreed to travel to France alone unless Alice could find someone to look after the pets. Valentino the baboon had recently escaped, taking his collar, chain and ground anchor with him one night when everyone was down in Nairobi on a Muthaiga Race Week binge. So that was one problem less. But Alice and Frédéric still needed someone to buy or shoot meat for the other animals. Geoffrey Buxton's manager, who lived next door, agreed to supervise. Before they left for France, the de Janzés threw a house-warming and farewell party. That evening, Wanjohi Farm swarmed with cars, servants and guests. Everyone brought a contribution in the form of drink: vodka, gin, wine, whisky and brandy. Dinner was laid out for twenty on the extended table in the dining room, and Samson wandered in and out. At one point in the evening, the lion cub snatched the tablecloth in his jaws and began nodding vigorously, eventually pulling the cloth off the table altogether and thereby sending glasses, knives, forks and plates crashing to the floor.

In the days that followed, Alice and Frédéric said a last goodbye to their friends and their animals, and went by car to Nairobi and then by train to Mombasa. Of his departure Frédéric wrote in *Tarred with the Same Brush*:

> Ordered home – failing in health – miserable in mind. Much as I would greet a home leave of even a long period, just as much do I resent this ordering

> out of the colony. My heart is out here – with my house – my boys [servants] – my zoo . . . I would much rather die out here as they say I will, unless I return to temperate climes . . . I will rest in the shade of the [Mombasa] Club veranda, sipping pink gin – thinking, remembering, mostly Samson, his baby roundness; his affection which helped us through some hectic months of puppy hood, until he grew up to be a real man, fearless, quiet, understanding, a better friend than any of you could find in most men's lives.

Raymund, busy with his new business ventures, seemed hardly affected by Alice's departure. Even so, Alice was determined to shake herself free of Frédéric so that she could be with Raymund. She now had the travel time back to Paris in which to end her marriage. She needed to make clear to her devoted husband that after seeing him safely home, she intended to return to Kenya immediately. By the time the de Janzés reached Paris, Frédéric had agreed to Alice's conditions. They would remain good friends, but the marriage was over. Alice would ask her lawyer to file for divorce. Nolwen and Paola would remain in Frédéric's custody. On this matter Alice was adamant and Frédéric did not argue. Both girls had always been closer to their father than their mother. There was no question of Alice taking her daughters back with her to Africa. Yes, she loved her children, but if she did not feel well then how could she be a good parent to them? She could always return to Paris for visits. There is no doubt that Frédéric was heartbroken by Alice's decision to divorce. He loved her and was deeply attached to Kenya and to their animals. Now he was being banished, not only from Africa, but also from his wife's affections.

In Paris, the little girls were reunited with their parents, only to find their father sick and their mother on the verge of departure again. After only a month in Paris, Alice re-embarked at Marseilles for Kenya, leaving Frédéric in the care of his mother and placing Nolwen and Paola with Aunt Tattie. It was October of 1926. As a bizarre consolation prize, Alice promised Frédéric that she would bring Samson back to him in Paris before the end of the year. The count told her this would be impossible, but Alice was undeterred. Once again, she boarded the train to Nairobi at Mombasa. Alice was familiar with the route by now and she would have greeted the train's arrival at Voi with delight: dinner at the wayside station meant you had truly returned to Kenya. The menu was the same as it had been a year ago and Alice and the other old hands en route to Nairobi greeted each dish with acclamation: brown Windsor soup, tinned salmon, meatballs and fruit and custard. Alice was returning to Kenya alone and free of all obligations to her family, her husband, her children or her rank. Instead, she had a new husband in her sights; a new house; dozens of friends waiting for her in Wanjohi Valley; her animals, Samson, Fairyfeet, Monster, Roderigo, two more monkeys, and her dik-dik.

On her return to Kenya, Alice and Raymund officially became a couple, dining out together and sharing a bedroom. For the last three months of 1926, Alice spent most of her time with Raymund at Wanjohi Farm, channelling her energies into making improvements to her new home. She often visited Joss and Idina, whose notorious marriage had dwindled into a rather strained friendship by now. Raymund slithered over from his base in Njoro on a regular basis: it was not a long journey and there was a good road to Nakuru, and then on to Gilgil, before turning off to Wanjohi Valley. There is no doubt that with their dark good looks they made a striking pair, but while Alice's attraction to Raymund was developing into devotion, Raymund, although very keen on Alice, was instinctively more restrained. He was someone who would never be able to care about anyone quite as much as he did about himself. Nonetheless, Alice was determined to secure her divorce from Frédéric so that she could be free to remarry.

Alice was still resolved to return with Samson to France in December as promised and she enlisted Raymund's newfound expertise in capturing and transporting animals to help her accomplish this feat. There is a note in Margaret Spicer's diary that Raymund de Trafford dined and danced with Margaret at the Muthaiga Club on New Year's Day 1927. Alice is not mentioned. In fact, she had sailed in mid-December with Samson the lion cub and Roderigo the monkey, now on his second trip to France. Once back in Paris, Alice delivered the animals to the apartment at rue Spontini, where her daughters Nolwen and Paola were living with Frédéric and their nanny. When Aunt Tattie arrived for her regular visits, she would be greeted by a monkey climbing on the furniture, a lion in the living room and a baby Nile crocodile in the bathtub. It is not known whether Alice smuggled in this crocodile from Africa, or whether she had bought it in Paris. Certainly, Samson had the run of the rue Spontini apartment, because Paola, then two and a half, distinctly remembers riding on the cub's back while hanging on to his considerable ruff of a mane.

Alice remained in Paris for more than a month this time. One of the reasons for her delayed return to Africa was that Raymund was in England after having received word that his father had suffered a stroke. In February 1927, Alice told Moya and Aunt Tattie that she was moving out of the rue Spontini apartment to take a small pied-à-terre in rue Chalgrin: evidently she wanted to be free to receive Raymund without the encumbrances of her children, her husband and her animals. Alice's friends and family in Paris remained understandably concerned about this new relationship. Raymund was an unknown quantity, whereas Frédéric had proved himself to be loyal, devoted and tirelessly kind. But Alice was in love, she was a woman of means and she was determined. In Raymund's letters to Alice during this time, he cautioned her not to move so fast. Instead, Alice simply urged her lawyers to hurry through the divorce proceedings even faster, fearing that Raymund's interest was dwindling. She began to make plans for her wedding.

To his credit, Raymund had informed his family that he wanted to marry Alice. However, the de Trafford family, especially Raymund's brother, Humphrey, had grave reservations about this new relationship. As son and heir to the baronetcy, Humphrey was a much more conservative member of the de Trafford family than his wilder younger brother. The aristocratic de Traffords considered the countess far below their social status, despite her enormous personal fortune. Alice was American, still married and she had two children into the bargain. Above all, Raymund's family were strait-laced Catholics and did not approve of divorce. As far as Humphrey was concerned, Raymund had been instrumental in breaking up a Catholic marriage: scandalous behaviour in other words. Divorce was a mere technicality, meaning nothing in the eyes of God. Only the Pope could rule on an annulment, as he had done in the case of the de Traffords' sister, Violet, who had divorced her first husband, receiving an annulment in 1921. The mechanics of annulment were complicated. One argument was that annulment could be granted if the marriage had not been consummated. This obviously could not apply in the case of Alice and Frédéric who had two children. (Nolwen once asked her sister, Paola, in later years, 'How can mummy's marriage be annulled when we are her two children?') Another submission could be that the children had been unwillingly conceived. A large payment to the Pope (Pius XI) was also deemed to be a help. Alice's French lawyers provided a very competent submission, combining the argument of reluctant conception with a considerable offer of money.

The lawyers did not move fast enough, however. On Friday 25 March 1927, less than a year after their first meeting, Raymund visited Alice at her apartment in Paris in order to inform her that the relationship was over and that he was leaving the next day by the four o'clock boat train. His parents were threatening to cut him out of his inheritance and would stop his allowance altogether unless he ended the relationship immediately. The threat of disinheritance terrified Raymund: he relied on regular injections of the family's cash to fund his love of gambling, travel and luxury. Alice told him there was no need to worry about money. She had quite enough for both of them. Raymund explained that he could not turn his back on his family, his religion and his country. It was too much of a sacrifice. Alice reminded him that she had given up her husband and her children for him. Raymund could not be persuaded. He argued that if he continued his relationship with Alice, he would further jeopardize his father's health. He even went as far as to suggest that Alice would probably be better off going back to Frédéric.

After Raymund's departure, Alice was left in an unenviable position: she had abandoned her husband and children for a man who was now about to abandon her. Alice was a naturally unstable person, displaying a dangerous combination of vulnerability and determination. Faced with the sudden ending of the relationship with Raymund, she quickly began to unravel. That Friday evening, she visited Frédéric and her daughters at the rue Spontini apartment. Frédéric could see that Alice was distraught and he asked her what had happened. Alice told him about Raymund's announcement. Although Frédéric was already aware of Raymund's reputation and can hardly have been surprised, the count comforted Alice as best he could. Then, in an act that demonstrates Frédéric's impressive decency, he decided to defend the very woman who had rejected him. He went to see Raymund at his hotel, accusing his wife's lover of dishonourable cowardice and instructing him to marry Alice as promised. Frédéric's words, although well intentioned, had little or no effect. Later that same evening, Raymund arrived at Alice's apartment on the rue Chalgrin to inform her, yet again, that he was leaving. This offered Alice one more opportunity to change his mind. She begged him, shouted at him, tried to reason with him, offered him money, and even tried to seduce him. But to no avail. Raymund was determined to leave for London the next day. He told her that he had no source of income without his family's support and no intention of being kept by anyone else. He agreed to one more lunch to say goodbye the following day before he caught his train but nothing more.

That night, Alice decided there was no future she could imagine for herself without him. The best and only possible way out of this situation was also the most extreme. She barely slept. By Saturday morning, she was resolved. If she couldn't persuade Raymund to stay, she was going to have to take the most drastic action imaginable.

5

The Shooting at the Gare du Nord

On the morning of Saturday 26 March 1927, Alice awoke from a fitful sleep in the bedroom of her apartment at 20 rue Chalgrin. She got out of bed and began to prepare for lunch with Raymund. She dressed with great attention to detail; if this was to be their last meeting then she wanted to look her best. She had arranged to meet him at the Maison Lapérouse, a restaurant and *salon de thé* on the quai des Grands-Augustins, overlooking the Seine. That week, Alice was looking after a friend's Alsatian dog and she decided to take the animal with her, glad of the company. After a short cab ride along the banks of the Seine, she arrived at the Lapérouse. Alice and the dog made straight for a private dining room reserved especially for the meeting with Raymund. Lunch consisted of champagne, foie gras and salmon. Raymund must have been nervous but Alice was determined to lighten the mood and consequently the meal went smoothly as they ate and drank, laughing, and even joking together. So amusing was their meeting that Alice had to remind herself of the gravity of the situation: Raymund was planning to leave.

When lunch was over, Alice suggested they do some shopping before going to the station in time for Raymund's four o'clock train. She informed him that she had to run an errand for Frédéric at a nearby gun shop and suggested she could also buy a parting gift for Raymund there. The gun shop was on l'avenue l'Opéra, a short walk across the Pont Neuf and through the courtyards of the Louvre. The owner of the shop, a Monsieur Guinon, recognized Alice. She had visited with Frédéric to buy hunting equipment for their trip to Kenya in early 1925. For that reason, no special permits or licences were required for Alice's purchase. Raymund chose some knives and a twelve-bore shotgun. Alice elected to buy herself a small revolver – a 3.8 calibre Colt with pearl inlay handle and a box of nickel-plated bullets. The countess paid for the weapons and asked for them to be wrapped separately. She watched attentively as her gun was carefully enclosed in brown paper, with the box of bullets placed in the same bag.

The Gare du Nord was a cab ride away. When they arrived at the station, it was bustling with Saturday-afternoon shoppers on their way home to the suburbs. The boat train to Boulogne was waiting at Platform 1 at the far end of the station. Alice and Raymund made their way through the crowds, picking up some snacks from a *boulangerie* along the way. As Alice looked up at the station's enormous overhead clock, she would have realized that she had only a little time left. She told Raymund she would meet him on the train to say their farewells. Next she went to the Ladies to unwrap her gun from its parcel, load it with bullets and place it in her handbag. As she walked towards the boat train, Alice maintained her resolve. She had decided to die in Raymund's arms. Suicide was both a solution to her impossible predicament and a twisted restitution of justice. In other words, she would rather kill herself than allow herself to be abandoned by another man.

Alice boarded the train and found Raymund in his first-class compartment, stowing his luggage above his seat, ready to settle down with his newspaper for the journey ahead. He got up and moved towards Alice who was standing in the entrance to the first-class carriage.

'Do you really want to leave?' she asked him.

'Yes,' he replied.

The whistle blew and the train gave a jolt, signifying its imminent departure. Alice went for her gun, but at this moment, as she later described, she had a sudden change of heart. Why should Raymund continue to live without her? Why should he be allowed to go on with his life when hers was about to end? Alice leaned forward to kiss him, throwing one arm around his neck while removing the gun from her bag. Then she pressed the muzzle against Raymund's chest and pulled the trigger. He collapsed. Next Alice turned the gun on herself. Another crack. Witnesses reported that as she fell to the floor, she smiled.

Neither Alice nor Raymund remembered the furore that followed. The guards were summoned, someone was sent to call for an ambulance and within a matter of minutes train officials had boarded the train. The guards found the couple motionless and bleeding, their bodies half in and half out of the first-class compartment. Alice's Alsatian was growling so ferociously that it initially proved impossible to rescue the dying couple. Finally, someone threw a rock at the head of the dog so that the police were able to approach and remove the bodies from the train. Raymund was able to utter, 'It was she who fired,' while Alice's chief concern was with the Alsatian now lying unconscious on the platform. 'Take care of my dog!' she managed to gasp to an onlooker.

Alice and Raymund were taken to Lariboisière Hospital, directly adjacent to the Gare du Nord, where operations were performed to remove the bullets. The condition of both parties was desperate and there was a possibility that neither would live through the night. Raymund's family was notified and members of the de Trafford clan left the deathbed of their father to sit in the hospital's anteroom while the youngest son of the family slipped into a coma. An examination of Raymund's wound and clothing showed that the muzzle of the pistol had been pressed directly against his chest as he had leaned forward to kiss her goodbye. By a miracle, the bullet had missed his heart by a few millimetres and it is a tribute to the skill of the Parisian surgeons that he was revived at all. Meanwhile, Alice was faring slightly better. Her bullet had passed through her stomach before penetrating her lower abdomen.

The events at the Gare du Nord made headlines in the United States, France and Great Britain. The Fort Covington *Sun* in New York State printed the following account on 14 April 1927:

> America, France and England were all threatened in the tragedy in the Gare du Nord, Paris, when Countess de Janzé, estranged wife of Frenchman, shot Raymond [*sic*] V. de Trafford, scion of a prominent British family, and then put a bullet through her own body. The countess was Alice Silverthorne of Chicago, cousin of J. Ogden Armour and well-known in American social circles. Her relations with De Trafford recently led her husband to file suit for divorce. For several days after the shooting it was believed both the countess and De Trafford would die, but latest reports are that they are out of danger.

Certainly, the novelist F. Scott Fitzgerald must have seen the newspaper reports. At the time, he was hard at work on his novel *Tender is the Night*, which would finally be published after many redraftings in 1934. In the novel, an American acquaintance of Dick and Nicole Diver, a woman called Maria Wallis, is depicted shooting an Englishman on a railway platform in Paris. She 'plunged a frantic hand into her purse: then the sound of two revolver shots cracked the narrow air of the platform'. The train stops and the man is carried away on a stretcher while the police take the woman away. Dick is at the station seeing a friend to the train and races to find out what has happened. He reports back to his group that Maria Wallis just shot an Englishman. Although Fitzgerald changed the setting of the shooting from the Gare du Nord to the Gare Saint-Lazare, Maria Wallis is unmistakably Alice: 'The young woman with the helmet-like hair'. The murder weapon, like Alice's, is '*très petit, vraie perle – un jouet!*'

The French police soon pressed charges against the countess, with the District Police Commissioner preparing a tentative indictment accusing her of attempted homicide. The task of bringing these charges against her was assigned to the prosecution. All charges were deferred, however, until the two principals of the shooting either succumbed to their wounds or recovered. Alice spent nearly six weeks at Lariboisière Hospital recovering enough to be transferred to the hospital ward of the all-women's prison, Saint-Lazare. The French authorities had already tried to interview her on several occasions. The first time her sole response was, 'I decline to give the reason for my act. It is my secret.' However, as the police started to interrogate her more thoroughly, she was forced to seek legal advice. In April she made the following statement: 'I was determined to die in his arms, and when the whistle blew, I suddenly changed my mind and resolved to take him with me into the Great Beyond. Slowly, very slowly, I loosened my grasp around his neck, placed the revolver between our two bodies and, as the train started, fired twice – into his chest and into my own body.'

Alice's use of the phrase 'Great Beyond' is significant. Death was the ultimate gesture for Alice, the one aspect of her existence over which she could have complete control. She had been brought up in the Presbyterian faith and so she would have been taught that when a person dies, his soul goes to be with God, where it waits for the final judgement. After the final judgement, souls are restored to bodies, eternal rewards and punishments are handed out and everything and everyone is 'refreshed and restored'. In other words, in heaven, Alice would finally be reunited with Raymund and with her long-departed mother. The existence of an afterlife was a credo to which Alice passionately subscribed. Ever since her adolescent suicide attempt she continued to wish to 'escape this world'. According to her friends and acquaintances, she frequently made use of expressions such as the 'other side' or 'the Great Beyond'.

For now, Alice found herself far from heaven. After her arrest, she was imprisoned in a cell in Saint-Lazare Prison on charges of attempted murder. The cell had hosted several notorious female criminals in the past, including Marguerite Steinheil, the former mistress of French President Felix Fauré. In 1908, Steinheil had been held at Saint-Lazare Prison for a year while she awaited trial for the double murder of her husband and stepmother. She tried to pin the blame on a gang of intruders and members of her household staff – stories that the judge called a 'tissue of lies'. Eventually she was acquitted. Another notorious former inhabitant of the same cell was Henriette Caillaux, the second wife of the Finance Minister of France,

Joseph Caillaux. She was imprisoned for shooting the editor of the French newspaper *Le Figaro* after he published a letter about her husband that portrayed the minister in an unflattering light. Although Henriette admitted her crime, her lawyers pleaded that she was the victim of 'uncontrollable feminine emotions' and that the shooting was in fact a 'crime passionnel'. The jury also acquitted her. Alice's other famous predecessor at Saint-Lazare was Mata Hari (born Gertrud Margarete Zelle), the Dutch-born exotic dancer who was arrested as a double agent by the French in 1917 and convicted of treason, possibly on trumped-up charges. She had agreed to spy for France but her employees had lost faith in her and accused her of working for the Germans. Unlike Steinheil and Caillaux, she was eventually sentenced to death by firing squad. Alice's fate remained in the balance. As the weeks slipped away, her attorneys worked furiously to secure her release. On 19 May 1927, after nearly six weeks in the prison ward, Alice was temporarily released on the proviso that she would remain in secluded convalescence until she was sufficiently healthy to appear in court. It was true that Alice had been badly wounded and her lacerated stomach needed constant care. Despite everything that had come to pass, the obvious place for her convalescence remained her husband's country residence, Château de Parfondeval. In official terms, Alice was still married. What's more, she had been the love of Frédéric's life for six years and she was still in close contact with his family. Château Parfondeval offered countryside peace, the attentions of the kindly Moya, and those of her favourite manservant, Edward, both of whom had a soothing effect on Alice's health and nerves. Although Alice claimed she did not fear death, there is no doubt she was terrified of imprisonment should she be convicted of attempted murder (or murder, should Raymund die).

During the nine months of convalescence before her court hearing, Alice rested at Parfondeval and wrote a number of letters to her friends and relatives. Despite the de Janzé family's generosity in looking after Alice during this time, they felt the 'scandale' deeply, and at Parfondeval, she was made only too aware of her estrangement. During this dismal period of her life, she also visited her apartment in Paris to collect clothes and books. Meanwhile, the gossip about Alice continued to circulate in Chicago, New York and London and she soon found out that her imprisonment had isolated her almost completely. Although she received correspondence from her father, Louise her stepmother, and close friends such as Paula de Casa Maury, other members of her acquaintance were evidently keen to put distance between themselves and the notorious countess. Joss visited London for his grandfather's funeral in July, but there is no evidence that he made contact with Alice at that time, and besides, by the end of 1927, he was already hatching plans to marry Mary Ramsay-Hill. Alice heard from Margaret Spicer that Margaret was planning a visit to London via Paris in December 1927 and wondered if they could meet? They never did.

Alice did, however, exchange multiple letters with

Raymund. Although his wounds were still causing him considerable pain, he had emerged from his coma and was well enough now to order his nurses about, barking at them to appear at his bedside 'at the double'. Contrary to popular expectation, he was not about to cut Alice out of his life. In fact, her dramatic act seems to have piqued his vanity. On 19 May 1927 he even went so far as to tell the *New York Times* that a reconciliation with Alice was on the cards, although that may have had something to do with wishing to appear noble in the eyes of the public.

And what of Frédéric? It seems he remained generous and loyal throughout the 'scandale' – although many would have recommended he keep his distance from Alice. He did the reverse, agreeing that his family home was the best place for her recovery. By now, he had begun work on *Vertical Land*, his book of pen-portraits of Africa – which would be published the following year – in which the female characters were directly inspired by his relationship with Alice. Like many who have been spurned, Frédéric continued to remain attached to his lost love, at least on the pages of his notebook. Alice makes her first appearance in the book as Anna-Christine Mason, a cousin of the narrator, Bob, who has just arrived in Kenya by boat. Like Alice, Anna has wide-set grey eyes, wavy hair and a distinctive voice. Frédéric wrote:

> . . . her arms are marvellous, from the orange tinted nails to the shoulders, not a trace of colour, not

marble, not white ivory; perhaps of some old ivory held for generations in long Chinese fingers. On one finger an opium smoker's ring of green jade, no other ornament. As the ordered cocktail comes, she takes off her hat, revealing deep grey eyes set wide apart, long black lashes and eyebrows so minute and regular they might have been painted on.

'Pale moon face' of the old Chinese ballads. The dark red lips nearly maroon, the wavy shingled hair – a marvellous work of nature, a more marvellous work of art; and that on board a ship after three weeks at sea!

I am stunned and during luncheon can only mumble and be very British while she talks vividly now in English, now in French.

Later in the evening I take her off, the whole ship's company seems to man decks to see her go; I'm getting back my footing and we talk in the Customs house, and we talk in the taxi, and we talk in the hotel, she sitting on the edge of a bed, while my boy unpacks her things.

I go away to change, my mind whirling with the charm of this child of eighteen. It does not seem possible. She knows everyone – about everything, she seems to have been everywhere, and her voice, that flat voice, without tone or pitch, like voices heard in Islam's bazaars, reciting verses of the Koran. It worms into your mind, fascinates your senses, envelops, numbs one! What is natural? What is art? What is training?

As we start out for Tudor House, across the island, for dinner, she insists, and we take bathing suits just in case.

The hibiscus, the jasmine, the Bougainville [*sic*] trail overhead. Light fishes served on brown and grey dishes. Pawpaws and mangoes on the table.

Her stories of India bazaars and Hill stations way up in the Himalayas, and . . . dinner is over.

Her amber fragrance goes to my head, all my British training and self repose has fled. I am throbbing in heart and mind.

Down to the beach and into the rippleless creek, the moon throwing flashes of blue fire into our wakes as we swim.

Suddenly I miss her, no longer at my side; and turning, startled, see her emerge, naked, silver on the shining beach. Madness! I rush in to be told in that cold flat voice that the night is for night hawks, and, as there is no one there to see, I should not have to worry.

She lies on the sand beautiful as some goddess, silver statue of some Athenian athlete, all length and suppleness, and yet as cold as white marble, frozen in some Nordic garden.

At last we go home; she tells me with a wandering smile to sleep well and have no dreams.

Frédéric's subsequent description of Anna-Christine's wilfulness is particularly revealing of Alice's petulant temperament:

Today there was a clash of wills, and I lost as I am now doomed to lose for ever; I was reserving seats on the train and she wouldn't 'be put in with some maybe bathed but certainly not washed female'. She insisted in travelling in a big compartment with me. I battled my best, but was undone.

After the conflict, in soothing tones, one hand on my feverish hand: 'Bob, it's no use; I always get my own way. I always take what I want and throw it away when I like; don't forget this ever, I hate repetition.'

We are now in the train. Dinner at the wayside station amused her; the lights are out, and through the panes of glass shadow landscapes dwindle by.

There is a certain humour in it all; what a defeat Aunt Anna-Belle is in for. At that moment soft lips touch mine, but cold! Arms stretch above my head round my shoulders.

Those pure arms I saw in that first meeting, that silver body of the beach.

'I take what I want and throw it away'. When shall I be thrown? Thrown by a child!

Frédéric was writing from harsh personal experience: 'I always get my own way'; 'I take what I want and throw it away' – such exclamations could have been taken directly from Alice's lips. Whatever his opinion of Alice, Frédéric evidently remained fascinated by his exotic and dangerous former wife.

Nolwen and Paola were now in the legal custody of their father, who continued to do his best to protect them from their mother's growing notoriety. The girls were living in the apartment in rue Spontini with their Portuguese nanny, the crocodile, the monkey and the oversized lion cub, but because of the animals, the nanny was threatening to leave. Her name was Denise de Milo-Viana and years later Paola would remember her as 'horrible'. Denise told Fréderic that if he wanted her to stay, the animals had to go. Fréderic duly removed the crocodile and transported the monkey to Parfondeval where he was placed in the care of Alice's butler. The lion was donated to the Jardin d'Acclimatation, the children's park in the Bois de Boulogne. While Alice convalesced at Parfondeval, Aunt Tattie took Nolwen and Paola to the Riviera where Alice briefly visited them in Nice. She spent only a short time there before returning to Normandy. Alice's lawyers had warned Moya that Alice must convalesce and be seen to do so, as this was the special condition of the court.

Now that it was certain that both parties in the shooting had recovered, the date was set for Alice's official charging. Nine months after the events at the Gare du Nord, on 23 December 1927, in the 12th chamber of the Police Correctionnelle, Alice was charged with 'wounding and causing bodily harm' to Raymund de Trafford. According to the newspaper *Le Figaro*, she came to the courtroom that day 'a thin little woman in a grey suit. Big, shiny, feverish eyes; high cheekbones; great charm and style' and with 'the guilty look of a naughty girl'. In a photograph of Alice taken that day, she is certainly as beautiful as ever, if extraordinarily pale, looking up at her lawyer – the well-known advocate Maître René Mettetal – with an expression that lies somewhere between fear and defiance. She is wearing a dark cloche hat that masks almost completely her bobbed hair. There are pearls around her neck and in her white-gloved hands she holds a black fur stole. Her dress is to the knee, revealing her legs in their elegant white stockings. In the courtroom, she had attracted a crowd. *Paris-Soir* reported that: 'There were many women in the 12th Chamber where M. Fredin (the most Parisian of Judges) is presiding. All that is fair enough; is this not a beautiful love story? – one of those stories which novelists put together in moving phrases.'

The following description of the court proceedings is a composite taken from the newspaper pages of *Paris-Soir*, as well as *Le Petit Parisien*, *Le Journal* and *L'Echo de Paris*, for 24 December 1927. Alice answered the examiner with 'yes' or 'no' mostly, speaking French with an American accent. The judges had heard about the circumstances leading up to the shooting, but were eager to learn more.

'You have abandoned your husband and children for M. Raymund de Trafford?'

'Yes.'

'Your children?'

'It's so hard to explain; but I only thought of myself.'

'You don't seem to realize the serious situation in which you find yourself.'

'Oh yes.'

The examiner, M. Fredin, wondered about the two of them buying the gun together.

'It was I who asked M. de Trafford to accompany

me to the gunsmith shop. I told him I had to run an errand for my husband.'

The judge could not stop himself from asking: 'And M. de Trafford believed you? In his place, in the situation in which you both found yourselves, I would not have been very comfortable at all.'

Alice smiled sadly and added: 'He had no reason to doubt me. He knew I did not want him to go. I was suffering, but I was sure that he was leaving me – in spite of what he wanted, because he couldn't do otherwise.'

The next question: 'If you didn't want him to leave, why did you buy a revolver?'

She replied: 'But it was to kill me, not him.'

'But you shot M. de Trafford while you were kissing him.'

'Not quite. I was holding my gun when he kissed me. I don't know what went on in my head. I saw, like a drowning woman, all the memories of my life. I wanted to kill myself, but at the last moment in a sort of trance, I fired on him!' Alice was speaking in French: '*Alors, vraiment. Je ne sais pas ce qui c'est passé dans ma tête. J'ai vu comme une femme se noie, dénier tous les souvenirs de ma vie.*'

M. Fredin looked exasperated. 'Then, I don't understand,' he said.

'I was unhappy. I wanted to kill myself,' Alice emphasized.

Here in the French courts in front of the jury and a packed courtroom, Alice admitted that she had often wanted to kill herself.

> 'Yes,' replied the judge. 'There are some extenuating circumstances in your favour. M. de Trafford had promised to marry you. He did not keep his word. I would also present you, elsewhere, as a gentle person, an excellent mother . . .'

Meanwhile, Raymund, who was not called as a witness in the trial but had insisted on appearing, was permitted to speak. He was described in the *Tribunal Gazette* as 'tall, strong and speaking bad French'. He delivered his testimony rather coldly and flatly: 'I am responsible,' he insisted. He hardly glanced at Alice, who in turn stared unblinkingly at the man she had come so close to killing.

Raymund went on to explain to the court: 'I had asked Mme. de Janzé to become my wife; she wanted to. But my family didn't want to.'

Raymund then recalled what had taken place at the gun shop.

'And what did you think?' he was asked about Alice's purchase of the revolver.

'Nothing. I was in another part of the shop.'

His memory of the crime itself was confused.

'Mme. de Janzé approached me and asked me if I really wanted to leave. I replied yes. Then I saw the revolver in her hand. I seized it at the handle. She had already fired.'

The salesman who sold the gun to Alice gave brief evidence and so did Dr Paul, the surgeon who had operated on both Alice and Raymund, saving their lives.

Alice's attorneys delivered their pleas of mitigation. M. Gandel was said to have pleaded 'indulgently', saying: 'The accused is a sick woman for whom doctors have found extenuating circumstances. She has been an excellent wife and admirable mother, until she met the person responsible for the crime . . . But one must not forget the other dignified man, who has forgotten and forgiven everything. I hope that they get back together again.' (He was referring of course to the Count de Janzé.)

Finally, M. Mettetal entered his plea on Alice's behalf, his voice full of compassion and feeling, hinting to the tribunal that this had been a 'crime passionnel'. It was a crime that the French understood very well: a crime committed for love. In the end, the tribunal was lenient and the judge ruled in Alice's favour. She was ordered to serve six months but was '*condamner avec sursis*', given a suspended sentence, allowing her to leave the court on temporary probation. She was also ordered to pay a fine of 100 francs (around £1), a pittance for a wealthy heiress like Alice and a fraction of what she would have paid under French law for shooting a deer out of season.

Alice was free to go. No sooner had she walked out of Paris's Police Correctionnelle Court on the 23rd of December than she began making plans to travel back to Kenya. In April 1929, President Gaston Doumergue fully pardoned her, but he was later criticized for having done so.

6

Freedom and Exile

After her release, Alice informed Frédéric that she was leaving immediately for Africa. Again, there was no question of her daughters going: they would remain in Paris, in their father's custody, as agreed in the terms of the divorce. The lion and the monkey, however, would be returning with her. Although Frédéric knew Alice could easily arrange for Roderigo's return from Parfondeval, he forbade her from removing Samson from the zoo. By now, the lion was nearly fully grown and, besides, it was unlikely that the zookeepers would give him up. The count appeased Alice by promising to visit Samson regularly to make sure that he was well cared for. Alice left Paris for Marseilles and sailed for Kenya with her monkey in the hold.

She arrived in Mombasa in January of 1928 and immediately caught the train to Nairobi before motoring up to her house in Wanjohi. After surveying her empty animal cage and living quarters, she went to stay with Joss and Idina, perhaps reluctant to spend time in isolation after the ordeal of the trial. Joss was about to announce that he was marrying Mary Ramsay-Hill. Idina, meanwhile, had begun a new affair, this time with 'Boy' Long, a good-looking rancher who had been invited to Kenya by Lord Delamere to manage his cattle at a place called Elmenteita in the Rift Valley. In other words, the happy dynamic formerly enjoyed by Joss, Idina and Alice had shifted considerably. Each day, Alice went up to her house to visit her farm. Her servants had remained on during her year-long absence, paid for by Geoffrey Buxton's manager, and her old car was driven out of its garage and revitalized. There was much to do.

Alice's return had coincided with the arrival of a giant plague of locusts in the region. No one had anticipated the invasion: Alice's smallholdings of maize were devastated, along with most of the arable farmland in the area. David and Mary Leslie-Melville and Geoffrey Buxton, whose farms were both nearby, had been similarly affected. To each of these neighbours and her wider circle she related the dramatic story of her absence and explained how sorry she was to have caused everyone so much embarrassment. In her time away from Kenya, Alice's legend had grown. At the Muthaiga Club, the regulars had begun referring to her as 'the Fastest gun in the Gare du Nord', a title that stuck. After her arrival, Alice's movements were eagerly documented by the Parisian fashion and gossip magazine *Boulevardier* which often included a newsletter from East Africa. The settlers were evidently a little proud of the notoriety that the glamorous countess had brought to the heady world of the 'white highlands'. In general, Alice's Kenyan friends were inclined to forgive her. They had always been suspicious of Raymund, never really accepting him into their circle, and may have privately suspected he had got what he deserved. Only two of Alice's old allies were not so readily available. Lord Delamere, Alice's loyal supporter after her arrival in Africa, was now preoccupied courting Lady Gwladys Markham, daughter of the Honourable Rupert Beckett. He would marry her in May 1928. And Margaret Spicer, one of Alice's closest friends in Africa, had returned to London to have a baby.

Alice was relieved to find herself for the most part welcomed back into the highlands circle. Her return was to be short-lived, however. In February of 1928, less than a month after her arrival, Alice was contacted by an immigration officer, and given notice that she must leave the country. Her passport was removed and 'prohibited immigrant' written across it. She was given twenty-eight days to make arrangements for her departure. Alice was a divorcee, living alone without a new husband. As a general rule, single women were not admitted into Kenya at all. If a woman was engaged to someone living in the region, she arrived and went straight to Mombasa Cathedral to be married before even embarking on the train to Nairobi (Margaret Spicer went through this exact rigmarole in order to qualify for entry on her arrival in 1925). It transpired that Alice had made a powerful enemy in Kenya during her last visit: the governor's wife, Lady Joan Grigg. Lady Grigg, the colony's self-appointed moral guardian, had never liked Alice and now saw her opportunity to get rid of her altogether. After the incident at the Gare du Nord it would have been easy for Lady Grigg to argue that Alice was a single, dangerous and unstable character and should not be allowed to disturb the sanctity of other married families living in the area. Lady Grigg had her husband's ear on this matter and Alice had no other recourse but to obey orders. Lord Delamere was otherwise engaged and she had no influential connections amongst the authorities to argue her case.

With enormous reluctance, she began to arrange for her passage and to pack her possessions. She saw her lawyers and authorized them to rent her house, in the hope that the tenants would keep the place in good order and employ her loyal servants. In the period prior to her departure she was with Joss often, and there is plenty of evidence that she slept with him at this time, despite his new attachment to Mary. This pattern of frequent separations and intermittent sexual reunions between Joss and Alice would continue for years to come. Certainly, the couple were seen together on the afternoon of 28 February 1928. On that day, Karen Blixen, the future author of *Out of Africa* – who had been living and farming in Kenya with her husband Baron von Blixen-Finecke since 1914 – related in a letter to her mother that she had been visited by Joss and Alice. Karen had been running errands in Nairobi when she met Joss, the newly entitled Lord Erroll – he had succeeded to the earldom on the death of his father that very month – and invited him home for tea. Joss asked if he might bring Alice along.

That same afternoon, Karen Blixen received some unexpected guests: Lady Lucie McMillan, the widow of American millionaire Sir William Northrup McMillan, and the McMillans' old friend Charles Bulpett, both long-time Kenya residents. With them were two American tourists who had just arrived by steamer in Nairobi. Karen gleefully describes the ladies in her letter to her mother as 'really huge and corpulent'. They had been driving around the countryside, hoping to see a lion, so they could regale their fellow passengers on the ship later on. The Americans were also eager to talk about 'all the dreadfully immoral people in Kenya, Americans too unfortunately'. The 'worst one of all' was Alice de Janzé, whose exploits at the Gare du Nord had made headlines in the United States. Aware that the main subject of discussion was due to arrive at any moment, Karen let her guests continue with their tirade. When the infamous Alice arrived, Karen took mischievous delight in making the requisite introductions, to the extreme embarrassment of the American visitors. Karen told her mother, 'I don't think that the Devil himself could have had a greater effect if he had walked in; it was undoubtedly better than the biggest lion, and has given them much more to talk to the fellow passengers about.'

Alice left Africa in April. Back in France, she took up residence in the apartment in rue Spontini. Hairdressers, manicurists and masseurs were summoned to revitalize her. She visited her children who were living with Frédéric. Along with the loss of Kenya, she had one more sadness with which to contend. Soon after she had left France, Frédéric had decided to visit the Jardin d'Acclimatation to see Samson. On his arrival, he was told that all the cats there had been transferred to a circus. Frédéric went to the circus immediately. There he found a magnificent black-maned Masai lion half-asleep in a cage at the back of a tent. In his account of the incident in his book *Tarred With the Same Brush* Frédéric wrote: 'At last he got up and my heart stood still with horror – down his right hand quarter ran a jagged scar, Z shaped. It couldn't be Samson, but no two lions could have that same scar!' Frédéric called out to him. The lion cocked an ear and stalked over suspiciously. Frédéric put his hand through the bars. The attendant called out, '*Vous êtes fou, monsieur, il est très dangereux!*' The lion suddenly rolled over on his side, his back against the bars. Frédéric scratched him on the forehead; the lion put out his immense red tongue and licked Frédéric's hand, purring gently, delighted to be petted in a way that was evidently so familiar to him. It was Samson. Frédéric went to see the lion every day for a week, determined to buy him back from the circus. On his last visit, Frédéric was happily scratching Samson's brow when a female trainer, later described by Frédéric as a 'fiend in pink tights', arrived unexpectedly. She cracked her whip at Samson, ordering him to perform a new trick. The poor lion was driven panting and crouching into the corner of his cage. When the trainer turned her head for a second, Samson sprang at her, landing his massive paw on the side of her skull. A revolver shot rang out, then another. Frédéric wrote:

> Somehow I found myself in the cage, my hand on Samson's shoulder. I felt him shudder and he collapsed on my feet, knocking me over. I got up from under him and took his great head on my lap; a trickle of blood flowed from the side of his jaw onto me, then down to the floor; he tried one or two manful licks and snuggled his great shaggy head into my lap; he died in my arms – content, I hope, on the heart of a friend.

If Frédéric had permitted Alice to take Samson back to Kenya, the lion would have survived. We do not know if Alice reproached her former husband for his decision, but it is clear that she would have been deeply affected by the death of her beloved pet, especially as it coincided with her painful exile from Kenya.

On a happier note, it was during this time that Alice resumed her friendship with Paula de Casa Maury (née Gellibrand). Paula was in the process of separating from her husband, the Marquis de Casa Maury, and by the end of 1928 they had parted ways (de Casa Maury went on to marry Freda Dudley Ward, formerly mistress of Edward the Prince of Wales). Alice and Paula, as two newly single women, now had even more in common than ever. They accompanied one another on various adventures during this time: the following year, they decided on the spur of the moment to go to South America on a cargo boat with only two private cabins. Alice maintained her title of countess and, like the Marquise Paula, enjoyed playing the part of the beautiful, scandalous, titled divorcee. There is no doubt that the two women attracted a great deal of male interest wherever they went. In addition they could share their passionate interest in fashion. Alice eagerly began wearing her skirts short above the knee, and décolletée evening gowns hung from thin straps on her shoulders. Paula had become a fashion icon in Paris and was beginning to create her own clothes. 'It was a desire to have an occupation in life, instead of wandering from one tea party to another,' Paula later said of her designs, adding, 'I am tired of the eternal complaint that English women do not know how to wear their clothes.'

Alice was evidently inspired by Paula's new enterprise because it was after her return to Paris that she decided to invest in the fashion business herself, buying a substantial shareholding in the designer Jean Patou's Paris salon. Patou had opened his salon in 1919 and was making a name for himself as a haute couture designer, creating not only gowns but also sportswear for women, bathing suits in particular. He had already expanded into the American market, having dressed film stars such as Mary Pickford and Louise Brooks. On a visit to New York in 1925, he was so impressed by the long-legged American girls he encountered there that he auditioned 500 young women, choosing six of them to accompany him back to Paris as models (a masterful publicity stunt). In 1919, however, he was still struggling and Alice, along with her friend Idina, decided to help bail him out. Under the two women's sponsorship, Patou could begin to develop his new perfumes and other sidelines to help subsidize his couture line, a business model that fashion designers continue to follow to this day. Alice, Idina and Paula would both wear Patou and direct their influential friends to the salon.

Despite this new business distraction, Alice was restless. Although her time in Paris enabled her to explore her interest in fashion and play a more active part in the lives of her children, her focus remained on Raymund. She was in frequent contact with him and began visiting him regularly in England. It was as if by threatening to leave her, Raymund had triggered a need in Alice to hold on to him at all costs. The shooting had been her first attempt to prevent him from leaving. Now she resolved to get him back for good. Her sense of their relationship as unfinished business continued to blind her to his considerable character flaws. It is tempting to draw comparisons between Raymund and her father. Both men were unreliable, irascible, profligate, and compulsive gamblers and womanizers – which may go some way to explaining Raymund's continuing appeal for Alice. It is possible that her inability to countenance rejection by Raymund had its roots in her adolescence: one thinks of how Alice was forcibly removed from her father's care as a teenager, and wonders if she was revisiting and trying to rectify this trauma in her relationship with Raymund.

In June of 1927, less than three months after the shooting at the Gare du Nord, Alice and Frédéric had been granted a divorce. The marriage was officially annulled by Pope Pius XI in August of 1928. At this point, there was no longer anything to prevent a legal Catholic union with Raymund. What's more, if she could persuade Raymund to become her husband, she would be permitted to return to Kenya without delay, a high priority for Alice. But first, she needed the de Trafford family's blessing. In London, Alice called on Raymund's brother Rudolph at his house in Westminster. Rudolph's son, Dermot de Trafford, the future sixth baronet, recalled a visit from Alice during this period. Dermot's room and nursery were at the top of the house: Alice climbed all the stairs and warmly greeted him, explaining to his French governess that she was a friend of the family. Dermot remembered Alice telling the governess about her life in Africa and her animals there. (Afterwards, the governess remarked unkindly to Dermot that Alice's French was not very good.) Alice visited Rudolph and Dermot on more than one occasion, even going to stay with the de Traffords at their country home, Clock House, Cowfold, Sussex, where she signed the visitors' book with a flourish. Meanwhile, Raymund went back to Kenya at the end of 1928 to receive his other brother Humphrey, who had decided to see Raymund's farm and to meet a few old friends. That a single man like Raymund could travel freely to Kenya in this way must have rankled Alice and left her feeling doubly bereft.

By the end of 1928 Alice had decided that she would have to obtain a more permanent base in London if she was going to be a frequent visitor there. To this point, she had been staying in London's Ritz Hotel when in town, but at the beginning of 1929 she moved into an apartment block on fashionable Berkeley Street in Mayfair. Her half-sister, Patricia Silverthorne, and her stepmother, Louise Silverthorne, had recently moved into the same building. Louise and Pat had left the United States in 1919 following a drama in which the local sheriff had arrived at the family home in Sharon, Connecticut, to confront William Silverthorne. Pat remembers her father sitting downstairs puce in the face. Pat was sent to bed. In the morning, bags were packed and mother and daughter departed. When asked about this incident many years later, Pat refused to give full details, only revealing that, 'The chauffeur was the informer.' At such a distance, it is difficult to speculate on the nature of William's crime, but suffice to say that his behaviour was inappropriate enough that his wife and daughter sailed for France only a few days later.

Pat completed her education in Florence before being brought to London by Louise, who was determined to introduce her into English society. This was a tricky prospect for an Italian-educated American girl with no fixed abode or society sponsorship. Early in 1929, Alice, Pat and Louise found themselves living as neighbours. Alice had never been particularly close to Pat, but she had always got on well with Louise; however, she was careful to keep a certain distance from both women in public. 'With my reputation and the scandal surrounding me, I would not wish to spoil Pat's chances of meeting the right people,' she explained. Whenever Alice came over from Paris, they would breakfast together and it was during this period that Pat and Louise were often privy to Alice's unpredictable tempers and moods. On one occasion of Pat's recollection, Alice had been eagerly awaiting the day's mail, perhaps hoping for a letter from Raymund who had returned again to Kenya. That day, a single letter came and Alice opened it, only to find a large dividend cheque. Alice threw it to the ground, eyes welling with disappointment and disgust: 'I don't want all this damn money,' she told Pat. 'It doesn't buy happiness.'

Often Alice would walk alone up Berkeley Street at lunchtime, meeting a friend at the Ritz bar, where she would drink vodka cocktails spiked with absinthe. She was on the verge of her thirties, and her beauty, rather than waning, was maturing as the next decade of her life approached. Although a whisper of scandal accompanied her wherever she went, the countess was much in demand. Most Thursday evenings she could be found sitting at a table near the entrance of the Embassy Club in Old Bond Street, the famously exclusive London dance club. Thursday evening was the most fashionable night of the week, when the Embassy's dance floor swam with royalty, socialites and celebrities. The walls were painted in a soft green, with pink sofas placed against them, and low-level lighting was provided by twin candelabras fitted low on the walls. At the Embassy, Alice socialized with a small circle of Kenya connections that included, when he was in London, Denys Finch Hatton. Alice was also seen regularly with the club's most illustrious members, Edward, Prince of Wales – who would later abdicate the throne in order to marry Wallis Simpson – and his decadent younger brother, Prince George, the future Duke of Kent. Prince George kept up a long line of affairs with both men and women throughout his short life (he was killed in an aeroplane crash in Scotland in 1942). Alice could often be seen at the 'Royal Box', a table on the right at the front of the club, usually the rowdiest table in the room. Another member of the Embassy set was banking heiress Poppy Baring, christened Helen, daughter of Sir Godfrey Baring of Baring banks, and one of Prince George's many consorts. Gloria Vanderbilt, the widow of railroad heir Reginald Vanderbilt and mother of the future jeans designer, was also a regular. Kiki Preston, the drug-addicted great-niece of Reginald's mother, Alice Vanderbilt, could also be found there. Known as 'the girl with the silver syringe', she was the woman Prince George had fallen in love with on a trip to Kenya in 1928.

The novelist Barbara Cartland's description of Thursdays at the Embassy evokes something of the glamour of the female members of the club:

> The faces of the women dancing and sitting round the room have an almost monotonous beauty. They all have large eyes with mascaraed eyelashes, full crimson mouths, narrow aristocratic noses and fine bones. Their hair, cut short and styled close to their well-shaped heads, is like exquisite satin, shiny and neat. Everything about them is neat and the expensive perfection of simplicity. Their skins are white – very white, the only exception being the warm golden loveliness of Lady Plunket as she floats by in the arms of Prince George. Dorothe is the first person to be sun-tanned, and she has whispered to me that in the winter she keeps the same colour by applying diluted iodine to her skin.

It was at the Embassy that Alice and Prince George discovered their mutual love of French bulldogs. Alice had come into possession of a bulldog called Jimmy; Prince George had a bitch of equal breeding. It was decided that the two dogs should be married. To demonstrate Jimmy's eligibility, Alice flew privately from Paris to London with him and her two children. Paola remembers being pulled across Regent's Park by Jimmy on his long leather lead. The prince must have approved of Alice's hound because, despite quarantine regulations, the royal bitch was boxed and flown over to Paris to mate with Jimmy the next time she was in season. Twenty guests toasted the canine consummation with champagne at Alice's rue Spontini apartment and the dogs were decorated with orange blossom. While guests got drunk, Jimmy and his consort were locked in a bedroom. At one point, Alice decided to see how they were getting along, whereupon she discovered that Jimmy was facing 'south' and the prince's dog was facing 'north'. Horrified, Alice rang her vet, informing him, 'My dog is killing the Prince's poor girl!' The vet advised her to remain calm, assuring her that in twenty minutes all would be well.

When not arranging wedding parties for pets, Alice continued her campaign to secure a marriage of her own. After Raymund returned from one of his Kenya trips, Alice whisked him away to the South of France where he could indulge his love of gambling. Raymund had always been a keen gambler. He belonged to six clubs in London, including Buck's and White's, where he regularly lost money. *Reynolds Illustrated News* reported that he had lost

£7,000 playing cards in London in the course of one year. Occasionally, he got lucky. Soon after leaving the army, he had visited Deauville in France and cleared £5,000 winnings in a week's play. While in Cannes with Alice, Raymund scored an even bigger win. As he later recounted to Margaret Spicer, he had been playing roulette and betting on 0 and 0, 1, 2 and 3. When 0 came up twice running, followed by 3, which was half covered by 0, he won many thousands of francs. Inspired, Raymund piled on the chips and won even more. Sensibly, Alice encouraged him to cash in his chips: the amount he received exceeded his total allowance for the year. Later, Pat Silverthorne – who met Raymund only once and took an immediate dislike to him – would describe this incident as the time he 'broke the bank at Monte Carlo' (in fact, the win took place at Cannes).

Alice was not the only member of the Happy Valley set in the process of remarrying. As soon as Joss's divorce from Idina was made absolute at the beginning of 1930, he married Mary Ramsay-Hill on the 8th of February of that year at St Martin's Register Office in London. Soon afterwards the couple returned to Kenya and set themselves up in the sumptuous former Ramsay-Hill residence, which Mary had secured in her divorce settlement from her former husband. Frédéric remarried that same year. The wedding took place on 9 January 1930 at the Church of Saint-Pierre-de-Chaillot in Paris. His bride was Genevieve Ryan (née Willinger), another American and the widow of Thomas Jefferson Ryan, a prominent New York lawyer and politician. Not to be outdone, Idina would also wed before the end of 1930. Her fourth husband, Donald Haldeman – born in England and educated at Eton – was the son of an American shirt maker. Their nuptials took place in Steyning, Sussex on 22 November 1930. After a honeymoon in the United States, the couple returned to Kenya, where Donald had already made a name for himself as a white hunter.

All these weddings galvanized Alice's resolve. Despite Raymund's evident flaws, she continued her campaign. After almost four years of Alice trying to persuade him to marry her, Raymund finally relented. In 1931, the couple announced their engagement.

7

The Bride in Black and White

By the end of 1931, Raymund had convinced his family that there was no longer anything to prevent him from marrying Alice. Her marriage to Frédéric had been annulled by the Pope, which meant that, as far as the Catholic Church was concerned, Alice had never been married at all. Humphrey and Rudolph gave their consent and secret plans were hatched for a discreet wedding to be held in Paris early in the new year. Raymund must have been anxious to avoid publicity. He was still conscious of his family's underlying disapproval of his relationship with Alice, and the ongoing scandal of the Gare du Nord shooting. Humphrey was warning him to keep the wedding a low-profile affair. Alice was more realistic. She felt that the presence of the press at the nuptials was inevitable and that only so much could be done to control the coverage of the event. In fact, she hoped that the ensuing publicity might actually mitigate the 'scandale' in the eyes of the public and silence the lingering recriminations surrounding her relationship with Raymund.

Alice and Raymund decided to get married in the wealthy Parisian suburb of Neuilly. Alice busied herself with the preparations. She needed to find a dress to wear for the ceremony that would be both chic and appropriate. Alice knew she would be photographed extensively and she enlisted Paula de Casa Maury's help in selecting a suitably striking outfit. Paula advised Alice to wear black. 'I am not in mourning!' was Alice's response. 'You can hardly wear white,' Paula replied. A compromise was reached: Alice would wear black *and* white. Her former employer, M. Arnot, created Alice's wedding outfit at his shop on rue Saint-Florentin. Arnot made a close-fitting black cloak with black and white feathers, worn over a tight broad black tail jacket with white gauntlets and an ermine collar. Under the cloak and jacket was a black frock with a white insert, and to top it off, a dramatic black hat. The colour scheme matched Alice's black and white bulldog Jimmy to perfection. Jimmy would accompany Alice to the ceremony. The dog was given a special shampoo in honour of the occasion.

The wedding took place on 22 February 1932 in a room adjoining the historic Salle des Fêtes (where the treaty of Neuilly between Bulgaria and the Allies had been signed in 1919) in Neuilly town hall. The deputy Mayor performed the short service in French. The bride was resplendent in black and white with her bulldog Jimmy at her side. Raymund wore a dark suit and a white shirt and tie and sported a bowler hat. The witnesses were Rudolph de Trafford and Paula de Casa Maury. As with her first marriage, Alice's father did not attend. Neither did her two children, who were with Frédéric in Paris. Alice was later described as 'charming and smiling', and apparently she signed the register with 'a firm hand'. (Even though the register was an official document, usually available to the public, in this instance, it was carefully removed and put away in anticipation of the pack of press waiting outside.) When the brief formalities were over, Raymund escorted the guests down a side staircase and Alice meanwhile slipped away down another. She then caught a waiting car and drove off separately to Paula's residence in Neuilly, where a small reception was held.

That night a religious ceremony was performed in the Church of Saint Pierre at Neuilly. This time Alice wore a white veil. The wedding was widely reported in the French, American and British press. On 23 February, the *New York Times* printed the following pithy headline: 'American Woman Weds Man She Shot'. On the wedding day itself, London's *Evening News* gave the event front-page coverage with the headlines 'Black and White Bride' and a subheading of 'Coat, Hat and Dog to Match'. The *Evening Standard* went with 'Romance of Happy Valley' in large type and a subtitle of 'Mr Raymund de Trafford Marries Former Countess'. The *Star* printed: 'Locked Room Wedding' and 'Mr Raymund de Trafford's Bride Takes Her Bulldog'. The *Daily Telegraph* was more discreet, covering the story on page nine with a photograph of the couple and a short caption. (At least three reporters spelled Raymund's first name incorrectly. It must have happened all his life. He was Raymund, not Raymond.)

It is true that the majority of Alice's friends and relatives found her fixation on Raymund impossible to understand: for six years now, she had refused to let go of the idea of marrying a patently unpleasant man who clearly had few redeeming characteristics. Even Raymund's closest friends were never particularly complimentary about him, referring to him as '*tête brûlée*' or hothead. After Evelyn Waugh returned from Kenya in 1931, he wrote a letter to Lady Dorothy Lygon in which he described Raymund as 'very nice but SO BAD. He fights and fucks and gambles and gets DD [disgustingly drunk] all the time.' Alice, meanwhile, had continued to overlook Raymund's bad behaviour, clinging to the hope that the relationship would improve if only she could marry him. Now that she was Raymund's wife, she had a new British passport to boot, presented to her by the British Embassy in Paris. It declared she was a 'British Subject by Marriage' which also meant that she could return with Raymund to Kenya.

But first there was the honeymoon, which Alice and Raymund spent in Monte Carlo and Cannes. The newlyweds settled down at the Hôtel de Paris in Monte Carlo where Alice installed them in a grand suite overlooking the harbour. No expense was spared, and each day passed in preparation for the night ahead. Raymund, of course, made straight for the casino and its Salon Privée where he proceeded to play roulette at the high table until the early hours. Unlike his luck in Cannes, his losses during the honeymoon were considerable and Alice funded him throughout. He was placing maximum bets on numbers 'en plein' which never came up. Alice was understandably distressed – after all, he was playing with her money – and they quarrelled. Although Alice must have been aware of Raymund's more unappealing qualities before the wedding, it was in Monaco that she began to have some idea of the full extent of his failings. Marriage, it seems, was having the effect of bringing out the worst extremes of Raymund's character. This was a man so completely unsuited to being a husband that it makes one wonder why he agreed to marry Alice. But Alice had been extraordinarily persistent, and there were the small matters of her beauty and wealth, both of which would have been powerful incentives for someone as vain and profligate as Raymund. He may have also had a lingering sense of 'honour' about the woman he had jilted in very public circumstances.

Before the honeymoon was over, Raymund decided his luck might take a turn for the better if they had a change of venue. They moved along the coast to the casino at Cannes, where he had been successful in the past, and where they stayed in the equally majestic accommodations of the Carlton Hotel, with its grand terrace facing the corniche. Raymund's luck did indeed change in Cannes and he won back at least half of his considerable losses in Monte Carlo. His mood improved and Alice diverted the discussion to Kenya, reminding Raymund that she hoped to return there as soon as possible. The couple flew to

London in late March 1932, staying initially at Rudolph de Trafford's home in Cowfold, Sussex. Here the rows continued. Alice was determined to return to Kenya. Raymund would not be told what to do. Although Alice had hoped that the presence of Raymund's family would tame her new husband's temper, this was not the case. Alice confided their problems to Rudolph, but it did nothing to alleviate the rancour.

The more Alice tried to talk about returning to Kenya, the more Raymund retreated from the marriage in general. By April of that year, Alice decided it would be best to go away for a while without him. The couple had been married barely two months when she made plans to take the waters at the Thermia Palace spa in Piestany, Slovakia, with her new sister-in-law, Mrs Keith Menzies. Raymund's sister – christened Violet Mary – was a little older than Alice, having been born in 1893. Like Alice, she had been divorced from her first husband, receiving an annulment from the Pope in 1921. She married Colonel Keith Menzies in 1922. The new sisters-in-law agreed that a trip abroad would allow Raymund a cooling-off period. Built in 1912, the Thermia Palace was famous for its curative thermal spring waters, healing mud pool and luxurious art nouveau accommodations. It was a place frequented by Hollywood film stars, European royalty and Indian maharajas alike. Alice and Violet booked in for a complete course.

While in Slovakia, Alice wrote a letter dated 8 May 1932 to her Uncle Sim (Simeon Chapin) who was still the trustee of her fortune and her financial adviser. Alice wanted to thank him for his wedding present and for his letter of good wishes. She also wrote that she was 'suffering considerably from my "tummy"'. Alice's self-inflicted bullet wound to her abdomen continued to trouble her and the injury seems to have been exacerbated by stress and overexertion. Years later, her eldest daughter, Nolwen, remembered that her mother underwent multiple operations over the years and was rarely free of abdominal pain. In Alice's letter to Uncle Sim, she put a brave face on her ailment as well as her new marriage, even managing to explain away the fact that she was travelling without Raymund only two months after the wedding. After five years of being independent, she wrote, she couldn't imagine being married 'to anyone who had no respect for one's privacy . . .' Obviously, Alice did not wish to confide her marital problems to Uncle Sim because she went on to say that her new marriage was harmonious precisely because Raymund never interfered with her plans and she never interfered with his. After Slovakia, she would join Raymund in Paris. Despite Alice's valiant effort to give Uncle Sim the impression that all was well with the marriage, matters with Raymund had grown untenable. When Alice returned from Slovakia, she met him for lunch at a pavement cafe in Paris. Onlookers reported to the American gossip columns that Alice and Raymund were in the middle of a very vocal fight when Raymund picked up his champagne-brandy cocktail decorated with a glacé cherry – and threw it in Alice's face. Alice, her face dripping with drink and a cherry sticking to the little black veil on her hat, was seen to reach for her handbag to retrieve a compact. Raymund apparently misinterpreted Alice's movement, assuming that she was going for her gun again. Terrified, he made off down the street. Alice wasted no time, contacting her lawyers and advising them that she wanted an immediate legal separation. She agreed to buy Raymund a first-class passage to Australia, and to fund him sufficiently to stay there for a considerable length of time.

Raymund took the money and left for Australia as instructed. Mere months after the wedding, Alice was alone again. Determined to return to Kenya, even without Raymund, she travelled to London to pack up her flat in Berkeley Street and went once more to see Rudolph de Trafford. Rudolph seems to have taken pity on his sister-in-law as she stayed with him throughout August of 1932 (according to his visitor's book). Alice also managed to make contact with a visiting white hunter from Kenya who was arranging a safari for members of the Vanderbilt family. The planned hunting trip would take the party into the Congo from the west coast of Africa and towards the Ugandan border. Alice offered to pay her way if she could tag along, with the idea that she would cross over to Uganda and then get a train down from Kisumu on Lake Victoria to Nairobi. The Vanderbilts were delighted to have this interesting American girl as part of their entourage and so Alice packed her bags.

She said goodbye to Nolwen and Paola, who were now aged ten and eight years old respectively, promising them she would return for regular visits. Although Alice had been living in Europe for almost six years, her daughters were so accustomed to their mother's regular disappearances that this one would not have seemed very different from all the others. Alice de Trafford, as she was now known, entered Kenya via the Congo and Uganda with her new British passport and went straight to the newly appointed governor, Sir Joseph Byrne, who had assumed office the previous year. Lady Joan Grigg was no longer in a position to block her return, and so Alice presented her letters of support (one from Frédéric de Janzé himself). Sir Joseph granted her the right to stay. It was 1933, and Alice had been away since 1928. With her ferocious determination and an unrelenting desire to get what she wanted, Alice had managed to find her way back to Kenya again.

Part Two

8

Return to Happy Valley

Whenever Alice arrived in Nairobi from Europe it was her habit to go immediately to stay with Joss and Idina at Slains. But this was 1933 and Happy Valley was much changed. Joss and Idina had separated in 1928 and Slains had been sold while the divorce was still in progress. And so instead of making her way to Slains on her arrival, Alice went immediately to Idina's new home, Clouds, about six miles up the road from Wanjohi Farm on Mount Kipipiri (a Masai word meaning rain). Here she took up temporary residence in one of Idina's three guestrooms while Mr Barrat, the lawyer, gave notice to the family renting Alice's farm. Clouds was another settler house laid out in the typical manner, with a large central drawing room opening up on to a sixty-degree verandah where Idina often dined with her many guests. Along with her new residence, Idina had a new husband: in 1930 she had married an American, Donald Haldeman, but the union was an unhappy one, with Idina intent on carrying on her usual affairs. Donald's money came from a clothing manufacturing business and after one of the couple's blazing rows Idina was heard on the verandah of Clouds wailing: 'You makers of shirts, how can you understand us who have been wanton through the ages!' Another legend has it that Donald shot at the tyres of a car owned by one of Idina's boyfriends in protest.

Joss, meanwhile, could be found living in great style at Oserian, built on the beautiful shores of Lake Naivasha, where hippos roamed freely at night. The house had been awarded to his new wife, Mary, as part of her divorce settlement and was a much crenellated and domed North African-style castle, complete with minarets. Here Joss had installed squash courts and a swimming pool, and he bred polo ponies and hosted matches every week. Locals called Oserian the 'Djinn Palace' and although it did indeed look like an oversized Aladdin's lamp, the pun on 'gin' was intentional. Through the years, plenty of alcohol was consumed at Oserian, most of it by Mary who was developing a serious dependency. The poor woman desperately wanted to conceive a child, and when this did not happen, she fell back on her favourite black velvet cocktails. It didn't help that Joss and Mary's closest neighbours were Kiki and Gerry Preston: Kiki was the 'girl with the silver syringe', the American socialite whose conquests included Prince George, the Duke of Kent. Addicted to heroin, Kiki is said to have introduced Mary to the habit.

What did Joss see in Mary? The general consensus was that he had married her for her money.

At the time of Alice's return to Kenya, Joss had begun another new chapter in his life. Kenya's governor, Sir Joseph Byrne, had recently nominated Joss for the position of Councillor on the Naivasha District Council. Meetings, speech-giving and the responsibilities of public office now became part of Joss's regular routine. Of course, Joss was happy to see Alice – she continued to exert a powerful attraction for him and he had a talent for keeping on good terms with former mistresses – but he was busy. Not surprisingly, Mary wasn't inclined to tolerate Joss's extra-marital activities with the same laissez-faire as Idina. As a result, Alice's time with Joss would have been limited. The other lynchpin in Alice's Kenyan social life, Lord Delamere, had died in November 1931. Overall, the mood amongst Alice's friends was considerably less frivolous than it had been in the 1920s. Along with the rest of the world, the colony was entering a recession. Everyone, Alice included, was a little older, and without Joss and Idina to anchor her friendships or D as her champion, she would have felt adrift. What's more, she no longer had Frédéric or Raymund to partner her in social situations: as an unaccompanied woman, even in the relatively free-wheeling atmosphere of the highlands, there was only so much she could do alone.

Determined to make the best of things, Alice set about making a new life for herself. In her absence, her house in Wanjohi had been let to an English family called Case. The Cases had land in the area and were building their house slightly north of Alice's Wanjohi property. They were serious farmers and pioneers, not in the least socially ambitious, and as such they had little interest in their wilder, grander neighbours. Their daughter, Noel, was in her twenties, and determined to run a good establishment. While Alice had been away, she had created a proper garden on the property (something Alice had overlooked), laying out lawns and a rose garden. She had installed new curtains and comfortable sofas in the house and generally trained the servants who, under Alice's tenure, had grown used to operating without instruction. Under Noel – the household staff were smartly decked out in long white kanzus and red hats and the cook could make European dishes – Wanjohi Farm had been quite transformed. Now that Alice was back, Noel Case asked if she could remain at Wanjohi as an employed housekeeper, and Alice happily agreed – Noel possessed the necessary household and managerial skills that Alice so sorely lacked. When it came to settling bills and paying staff, Alice's lack of acumen was appalling: this was never due to meanness or lack of funds, it was simply that she had no desire to deal with such mundane matters. The title deed of Wanjohi shows that on several occasions, close friends such as Geoffrey Buxton and Idina were paying for Alice's outstanding bills and taking a charge on Wanjohi Farm until Alice handed over the amounts in question. Once the furniture had been reinstated from the manager's house, Noel moved in and ran the main house and kitchen. Alice bought herself a new Plymouth car and hired a driver who was to remain with her for the rest of her years: his name was Ruta (he was of the Kalengin tribe, and therefore known as 'Arap Ruta'). Alice brought her maid over from France, rounding out the new order at Wanjohi.

As always, Alice began acquiring pets. On her return, she adopted a little dachshund, called Minnie, who became her particular favourite. She acquired a Rhodesian ridgeback hunting dog, often called the African lion dog for its ability to keep lions at bay by barking. Also included in her menagerie was a magnificent pet eland or East African antelope that roamed her grounds freely. Alice's days at Wanjohi were spent playing backgammon, riding, walking her dogs, reading and drinking. She socialized with her neighbours, striking up a friendship with Fabian Wallace, an old friend of Joss's from Eton. Openly homosexual and strikingly handsome, Fabian lived on a small but well-appointed farm at the entrance to the Wanjohi junction near Gilgil where he grew pyrethrum. As well as being a remittance man, Fabian was also something of an epicure: he loved fine food and had his own cigarettes specially made for him in St James's Street, London, which were sent out to Kenya in boxes of a hundred. Another new friend was Pat Fisher, who had a cottage not far from Kipipiri, which she occupied while helping her husband, Derek, manage Sir John 'Chops' Ramsden's cattle on an estate near Clouds. Pat later remembered Alice's potent home-made cocktails, which included a whisky sour that was doused with grenadine and fresh lime and took immediate effect. Together with Idina, these new friends provided Alice with a much-needed social outlet on her return to Wanjohi Farm.

Just as Alice was establishing herself in Kenya, however, the recent past came back to haunt her. Towards the end of 1933, Raymund emerged on the scene. The couple were still legally married, but even so, Alice had not expected to hear from Raymund so soon. She had put up the money for him to travel to Australia, on the proviso that he did not return for some time. Instead, it seems he had so alarmed his Australian host and hostess in Melbourne with his general debauchery that he had thought it best to leave, deciding to return to Kenya in a bid to revive his relationship with Alice. She fended him off to the best of her ability, but she often had to run to Idina for protection. One evening, Raymund arrived at Alice's farm having driven over from his farm at Njoro. He was already drunk and threatening, demanding dinner and accommodation. Alice allowed him to take a bath before giving him something to eat, but when Raymund failed to appear at the dinner table, the French maid put her head around the bathroom door, only to find him drunk and asleep in the bath. 'Madame, one small push of the head under the water,' noted the maid to Alice, 'and all your troubles will be over.'

Then, in the new year, Alice received very sad news. Frédéric had died suddenly in Baltimore, Maryland, on 24 December 1933. He was in the United States on assignment, writing a series of syndicated articles for the French papers on economic conditions, but had fallen ill soon after his arrival. Two weeks later, he died of a septic infection complicated by meningitis. By his side was his new American wife, Genevieve, who had been married to

Frédéric for nearly four years. Frédéric was only thirty-seven. Nolwen and Paola were eleven and nine, respectively, at the time of their father's tragic death. Although they had been in Frédéric's custody after the divorce, it was decided that they should remain in the able care of Alice's Aunt Tattie now that their father was gone. Alice's reaction to this loss is not recorded, but there is no doubt that she would have felt it deeply: Frédéric had been a loyal husband and good friend, not to mention a devoted father to her two children. Even so, her reaction must have been tempered by her desire to keep in abeyance difficult memories of her own early loss of a parent: although she made sure to write to Nolwen and Paola, she did not return to France to attend the funeral nor to comfort her two children in this immediate period after Frédéric's death. Many years later, Alice's housekeeper, Noel, would remember that Alice almost never spoke of her past or her children during this time, nor did she keep any photographs of the family at Wanjohi, not even of her two daughters. On one occasion, Alice mentioned to Noel that her father was in a home in the United States and that it was costing her a lot of money but, otherwise, she continued to promote the illusion that she was a woman without ties or a past.

What is clear is that she did not neglect Nolwen and Paola entirely. In this period after their father's death she sent letters and later made visits to France to see her daughters. In 1931, the Imperial Airways flying service had begun a regular schedule from Southampton to Kisumu on Lake Victoria, which meant that Alice could travel back and forth to Europe without enduring a month-long sea voyage. Flights were swift, if expensive, usually only stopping at Alexandria for refuelling. Paola later remembered being taken out to restaurants in Paris by her mother who would regale her children with stories of animals and Africa. Paola remembers that on one occasion, Alice was convinced that an African waiter serving them hot chocolate was from Kenya, and so she tried to give her order in Swahili. In fact, the waiter was from Algeria and spoke fluent French. According to Nolwen, Alice had a delightful sense of humour, willingly laughed at herself and was a good leg-puller. She was, Nolwen said, '*très pince-sans-rire* [very deadpan] despite that dreamy gaze of hers which was due to her extreme near-sightedness'.

Despite her regular visits to Europe, Alice had already given up her apartment in London and was beginning to expand her residences in Africa. She acquired a new cottage, called Portaluca, conveniently located in the Muthaiga area, close to the centre of Nairobi, which made it ideal for socializing with her city friends and for those times when she felt unduly isolated at Wanjohi. Alice's new pied-à-terre was approached by a secluded drive, surrounded by a garden terrace. The main living room formed a central tower in the house, with two bedrooms on one side and a maid's bedroom on the other. During her stays at Portaluca, her driver, Ruta, and her French maid would accompany Alice. The house was conveniently located close to the Muthaiga Club, which she could only visit on Raymund's membership. Entry was a tricky proposition for a single woman: the bar was for men only, as was membership in general. Alice found herself having to sign her name 'de Trafford' despite the fact that she was doing everything in her powers to put a distance between herself and her estranged husband.

During this period of her life, she also began to look for a house on the coast. Most people from the Wanjohi area – upcountry people as they are known – regularly spend a few weeks at the coast every year as a respite from the high blood pressure induced by living at 6,000 feet above sea level. Alice set about exploring the Diani area, south of Mombasa, where she discovered an old coastal house at a place called Tiwi. The house, also called Tiwi, was small and in disrepair, but it was close to a quiet beach lined with palm trees and facing the Indian Ocean. Sunshine was tempered by ocean breezes and the nights were magical, lit by moon and stars and lulled with the gentle lapping of waves. Alice quickly negotiated a rent for the house, hired two local servants and proceeded to do it up, surrounding it with bougainvillea. Water was drawn from an old Arab well and the outside 'long drop' was the only available latrine: it consisted of a grass-roofed hut with an eight-foot pit, fitted with a wooden box to overhang the pit. While Tiwi wasn't particularly smart or comfortable, it was idyllic, and Alice loved staying there and hosting friends. There was plenty of fresh fish and seafood to eat, along with tropical fruits such as paw paw, mango, pineapple and watermelon. The house had four bedrooms, but Alice, who was never good with numbers, often invited too many guests for the existing space. On one occasion, she was forced to add more bedrooms at short notice;

such was the haste with which the rooms were assembled that none of them were symmetrical, nor were they interconnected with the original house. At all three of her houses, Alice kept an especially big and luxurious bed for herself. The guest beds, however, were notoriously hard and uncomfortable. And so Alice began a new chapter in her life, moving between her three residences frequently. Back at Wanjohi Farm, Noel Case would often be driven to distraction by her mistress's impulsive behaviour. Alice never thought to give notice of when she would be leaving or returning, often disappearing for days on end. Part of this secrecy was probably based on general carelessness and a need to avoid Raymund, but it also had to do with the general air of privacy that Alice cultivated during this time.

As for her relations with Joss, these were complicated by the fact that Alice did not approve of his recent political attachments. In April 1934, Joss had flown back to London with Mary, spending the summer there. It was during this trip that he became a card-carrying member of the British Union of Fascists. Sir Oswald Mosley – known as Tom – had founded the Union in 1932 and had been an acquaintance of Joss's since the early 1920s when the two men had first met. Now, with a worldwide depression entrenching, support for Mosley's brand of staunch protectionism was growing, especially amongst members of the English upper classes. The cause was a controversial one from the start. In June of 1934, only a month after Joss's initiation into the Union, Mosley's blackshirted stewards clashed violently with police and hecklers in

London, causing an outcry and damaging the party's already dubious image. The Union never recovered and was unable to gather sufficient support to play a part in the general election the following year. But Joss was convinced of the rightness of Mosley's solutions, especially in terms of their application to the economic difficulties being experienced in the colonies. If the threat of foreign markets could be removed and trade within the British Empire developed into an economic stronghold, Joss reasoned, then the possibilities for Kenya would be enormous. In Mosley's thrall, he spent the following months attending rallies, meetings and parties, appearing at the annual Blackshirt Cabaret Ball of 1934 with the Union's badge in silver on his sporran. By the time he returned to East Africa in August, he had been made Mosley's delegate in Kenya.

The timing of Joss's political conversion couldn't have been worse when it came to garnering support for the fascist cause in the settler community of Kenya. By the middle of 1934, Kenya itself was feeling the direct threat of fascist forces. The Italian fascist leader Benito Mussolini had stationed his armies on the Abyssinian border with Italian Somaliland. It was believed that British Kenya, which bordered Abyssinia, could well be the next line of attack. Up to this point, Abyssinia had managed to fend off her aggressors, remaining one of the few independent states in European-ruled Africa, but everyone was beginning to feel nervous about Mussolini's intentions in East Africa. In October of 1935, a border incident between the Abyssinians and the Italians gave Mussolini the opportunity he had been waiting for: with the League of Nations failing to intervene, Mussolini and his troops pushed back the Abyssinian army, taking Addis Ababa on 5 May 1936. Abyssinia's young leader, Haile Selassie, was forced to flee to Jerusalem via the Suez Canal and Haifa with the help of the British, taking with him 150 cases of silver coins so heavy that the sailors could carry only one case at a time. As head of the Coptic Church he was given a sensational reception in the Holy City. Mussolini's troops were now even closer to Kenya's northern border.

None of these events would have gone unnoticed by Alice, but unlike Joss, her politics inclined her strongly to the left. During one of her mother's trips to Paris in 1936, Nolwen, then aged fourteen, was sternly cautioned by Alice for expressing a preference for the fascist leader Francisco Franco over the Republicans in Spain. 'My mother rebuked me with restraint but real indignation in being wrong thinking about the Civil War in Spain. She was fervently republican. I, on the other hand, had been told how the Communists pumped up the bellies of innocent nuns with bicycle pumps . . .' This was evidently not the only political situation about which Alice had a definite point of view. Alice's eldest daughter also admitted to being 'alarmed by my mother' on several other occasions – 'not for fear of being shot by her, or because of some latent undercurrent of violence which I might perceive in her, but because I was inclined to much forthrightness in expressing opinions . . . Poor mama! Luckily there was Paola who cared nothing for religion or politics and preferred animals above all.'

It was during the same trip to Europe that Alice extended her visit to include a rare trip to see her father in Myrtle Beach, South Carolina. William Silverthorne was in ill health. In 1925, he had married again, a woman called Myrtle Plunkett, 'in order to have a nurse to look after him', according to his daughter Pat Silverthorne. William was nearing seventy and had only a few years to live – perhaps Alice sensed that this would be one of her last opportunities to see him. Father and daughter had remained in contact via their correspondence and – as Alice had suggested to Noel Case – she was helping to foot his medical bills. But even so, the visit does not seem to have constituted much in the way of a reconciliation between father and daughter. It was too late for that. Again, Alice left for Africa, putting a distance of many thousands of miles between herself and her troubled past. She was thirty-seven and living an independent life, one she had chosen for herself, removed from America and Europe, without a husband, shored up in her beautiful African houses with her books and her cocktails, a woman apart.

9

The Gathering Storm

In 1936, Joss and Mary moved into a bungalow in Nairobi, close to Alice's own pied-à-terre in the Muthaiga area. Alice and her old boyfriend became neighbours again, as they had been during the days of Slains. Despite Joss's political leanings, it was true that he remained one of the few constants in Alice's life. Their intermittent love affair had weathered their respective marriages to Idina and Frédéric, and the divorces thereafter, Alice's runaway romance with Raymund, her trial and imprisonment, her exile from Kenya, and her subsequent marriage and separation from Raymund, not to mention Joss's numerous other affairs and his marriage to Mary. In 1936, however, Mary's health was worsening and she needed to be near a hospital and her doctors. What's more, Joss was planning to stand for election to the Legislative Council, and so he needed to have a more permanent base in the capital than his usual rooms at the Muthaiga Club. With Joss living in such close proximity to Alice, it would have been impossible for him to resist the occasional secret meeting with his old flame, a habit that had been established for so many years. Alice had always made herself available to Joss and she continued to do so.

In that same year, in his role as Lord High Constable of Scotland, Joss was expected to take his place in the coronation procession of the new king, Edward VIII. Then came the abdication crisis, during which Edward declared he would rather marry a divorcee – Mrs Wallis Simpson – than ascend the throne. The coronation of Edward's brother, George Albert, was delayed until May of the following year. Alice would have followed these events keenly: Edward was one of her old friends from her Embassy Club days in London. When Joss did finally return from the coronation, in 1937, it was announced that he would stand for the Kiambu constituency in the forthcoming elections. Kiambu was at the very heart of the Kikuyu tribe, about eight miles from Nairobi, and had its own club, mainly supported by local coffee planters. Joss Erroll was duly elected and sworn in on 8 April 1938. By now, he had put his affiliations with Oswald Mosley behind him, celebrating along with the rest of his expatriate friends when the Munich crisis was averted in September of 1938. When Chamberlain arrived in London waving a non-aggression pact signed by Hitler, there was a new optimism that 'peace for our time' was not only possible, but a certainty.

Towards the end of 1938, Alice had good news of a more personal nature: she received word that her old friend Paula Gellibrand would be arriving in Kenya before the end of the year. After divorcing the 'Cuban Heel', the Marquis de Casa Maury, Paula had married William Allen in Paris but the marriage lasted only a year. (Bill Allen worked for British Intelligence – and would in time visit Kenya in the run-up to the outbreak of war in 1939.) For her part, Alice had finally become officially divorced from Raymund in October of 1937. The two women were single again and Paula, who wanted to try living in Kenya, decided to stay with Alice for a time. The friends proceeded to make the most of one another's company, living at Wanjohi and riding out each morning with Alice's dogs. The warmth of the relationship between these two attractive women is obvious from photographs they took of one another at Wanjohi Farm. Taking turns holding the camera, wearing identical short-sleeved gingham shirts and cord trousers – a boyish look that Alice cultivated and that the stylish Paula had evidently adopted since arriving in Kenya – they posed with Alice's dogs. There were frequent trips to the beach house at Tiwi in Alice's new 1938 DeSoto car, her old Plymouth having proven too uncomfortable for the frequent eight-hour trips along the hot and dusty murram road south from Nairobi to Mombasa. By contrast, the DeSoto had a straight-six-cylinder engine with enormous wheels and excellent suspension: it effectively steam-rolled rough roads, making driving in Kenya an altogether smoother experience. The front windscreens were split and could be opened by two handles on either side, keeping passengers both cool and comfortable. The two friends and Alice's little dog Minnie would have made an elegant sight as they motored from the city to the highlands and to the beach.

This happy time together was to be short-lived, however. One evening, Idina invited Alice and Paula over to Clouds for dinner and to stay the night. Idina had recently separated from her husband, Donald, and had taken up with Flight Lieutenant Vincent Soltau of the Royal Air Force, who would soon become her fifth husband. That evening, Boy Long – the handsome rancher and one of Idina's former conquests – was amongst the guests. He was recently divorced from his first wife, Genesta, and became immediately smitten with Paula. Paula returned the compliment and the couple wasted no time in marrying. The wedding took place towards the end of 1938. Boy's actual name was Edward Caswell Long, but he had been called Boy for as long as anyone could remember. Genesta once said of her former husband: 'Life with Boy was electric. I think he was the handsomest man I have ever seen, with infinite charm but "difficult".' Boy was certainly a flamboyant dresser, with a penchant for wearing stetson hats and colourful Somali shawls. Together with Paula, one of the most fashionable women in Europe, they made a striking pair. But although Alice was delighted that Paula had found her true love, Paula's marriage registered as a loss. Later, in 1941, she would write in a letter '. . . Paula is gone in a way. Our way of life lies apart and her big, bold paramour has changed her nature a little.'

With Paula otherwise engaged, Alice began seeking out the company of new female friends. In 1938, she met Patsy Bowles at the Muthaiga Club. Barely out of her teens, Patsy had married one of Alice's doctors, Roger Bowles, a man sixteen years her senior. Patsy was happy to let Alice take her under her wing and in the coming years the pair would often join one another for drinks or dinner around town, often accompanied by two other girlfriends, Rose Delap and Noreen Pearson. Patsy later confirmed that Alice retained all of her beauty during this later period of her life and that her distinctive wide-set grey eyes continued to captivate. Although it was clear that Alice had depressive tendencies and was dramatic into the bargain, she was nonetheless excellent company, someone who thrived in social situations, who was quick to laugh and adored a good party. Certainly Alice continued to rely on strong cocktails to mitigate her moods, but Patsy was certain that her friend was too intelligent to use drugs. She also confirmed that Alice never spoke of her family or of Paris during their friendship. By now, Alice's American accent was barely discernible – after all her years away from her native country, she spoke in the almost neutral tones of one who has left her home nation long ago.

Patsy also remembered Alice's rather odd taste in reading material. Over the years, in part thanks to two literary husbands, Alice had collected a large library. Towards the end of the 1930s, however, she began collecting volumes on medical problems, psychology and the occult. Patsy recalled one of these books in particular, *A Journey Round My Skull* (1938) by the Hungarian author Frigyes Korinthy (which has since been declared a masterpiece of medical autobiography). Korinthy's memoir tells the fascinating if grisly story of his brain tumour and the operation he had on it with only a local anaesthetic. Noel Case also recalled Alice's 'morbid mind' and 'books on horrible diseases' and how Alice would repeatedly ask Noel to mark out one place after another for her future grave site. According to Noel, Alice would sit on her verandah at Wanjohi Farm gazing at the river bend opposite her house, and pointing to the bank beside the deep pool as one possible burial place. Then she would change her mind and point to a completely different location: the iris beds on the edge of the 'cut' which she had made to take the stream water right round the edge of her house and garden. Perhaps the traumas that Alice had never managed to acknowledge fully – her mother's death, her father's abandonment – were beginning to manifest themselves in these morbid obsessions. Or perhaps as she grew older, Alice merely sensed that her years were numbered.

The new year would not be a particularly happy one for many of the inhabitants of Happy Valley. Locusts would devastate crop production, droughts were imminent and the news from Europe continued to go from bad to worse. Despite Chamberlain's pact with Hitler, war now seemed unavoidable and the colonists began making nervous preparations. In February Joss took on his new role as deputy director of the Central Manpower Committee, his patriotism trumping any lingering fascist allegiances (unlike many of his right-wing contemporaries, he was now fervently opposed to Chamberlain's appeasement of Hitler).

Joss's new job involved, for the most part, planning for the necessary distribution of military and civilian manpower and, as such, kept him well occupied. He was often away for weeks at a time, travelling throughout the Kenyan countryside mobilizing somewhere in the region of 2,000 European settlers. Despite his marital problems and considerable professional commitments, he still found time to see Alice – his offices, by coincidence, were located right next door to her Muthaiga cottage.

Always eager for a new conquest, however, Joss was also turning his attentions elsewhere. Phyllis Filmer was the wife of Percy Filmer, the managing director of the Shell company in East Africa who had arrived in Nairobi in 1935. No one in Joss's circle quite understood his fascination with Phyllis; she was considered rather dumpy and ordinary, at least by the standard of his more glamorous previous wives and mistresses. Even so, Joss continued to seek her out. Rumour has it that he was once discovered making love to her before dinner on the billiard table at the Norfolk Hotel. Alice would doubtless have not felt threatened by someone as unexciting as Phyllis – a small, rather conventional-looking blonde with none of Alice's flair – but it is safe to assume that the affair would have rankled nonetheless.

To make matters worse, Alice's health was in decline. In March of 1939, she visited her favourite doctor, William Boyle, complaining of stomach pains. The injury she had sustained during the shooting at the Gare du Nord often bothered her, but it is also possible that she was developing the first symptoms of ovarian cancer. Dr Boyle arranged to have her hospitalized and a drain was inserted. As soon as she was well enough, Alice flew up to Nakuru in an ambulance plane with a nurse, and went home to Wanjohi Farm. By now, Alice's devoted housekeeper, Noel, had left Wanjohi and Alice began to rely increasingly on Flo Crofton for help running her household. Flo was the daughter of a former Kenyan Governor, General Edward Northey, and was married to Dick Crofton, a white hunter living near Gilgil. After Alice's return from the hospital, Flo agreed to look after the house so that Alice could leave Kenya to visit her children in France. Despite her recent operation, Alice was determined to make the trip, aware that if war was declared, it might be one of her last opportunities to see Nolwen and Paola for some time. On 16 March 1939, she wrote to Aunt Tattie in France that the large rubber drain had been removed from her stomach, replaced by a gauze one which the nurse would remove in small pieces each day. It was still hard for Alice to sit up, and so her doctor had attempted to convince her that she should stay for another week to build up her strength for the journey home, advice that Alice had decided to ignore. She admitted to feeling greatly unsettled by the German army's recent march into Prague, but despite her anxiety about events in Europe, she went on to say that she was making all the necessary travel arrangements. It is revealing that Alice's greatest concern in the letter was not for her children, but her fear that passage on British ships might be restricted if war broke out and that she might somehow be prevented from returning to Africa. If all went well, she hoped to visit friends in Athens on her way home in June, travelling on a Belgian line. 'I do hope and pray there will be no war,' she wrote. 'Heaven knows what happens to our homes in such a case.'

Alice arrived in Paris in late March, as planned, remaining there for two months in order to spend time with Nolwen and Paola. Soon after her arrival, however, she decided to change her travel plans. She began to make arrangements to return to Kenya via Belgian West Africa, rather than by way of Athens. The Congo interior was a place that her friend Idina had visited two years previously, venturing deep into the rainforests to see the indigenous pygmy tribes. In the 1930s, there were still many thousands of pygmies living in the region – Idina must have returned to Wanjohi and regaled Alice with stories of her trip because now Alice became determined to see the pygmies for herself. Although Alice had also visited the Congo during her 1932 safari with the Vanderbilts, she had not been able to visit the tribes as her American host was interested only in hunting. And so on 29 March 1939, just after her arrival in France, Alice wrote to her Uncle Sim in New York to ask for funds from her 'Fifth Avenue Account' to be processed, so that a letter of credit of $2,400 and a further $400 in travellers' cheques could be provided for her Congo trip. She wrote that she intended to leave on the 4th of June, travelling across Central Africa all the way to Kenya. The trip would last in the region of four months. For two months she would be in places so remote that she would be unable to send or receive mail or cables. She asked that her cheques should be cashable in the Congo towns of Matadi, Kinshasha and Stanleyville, as those were the places where she 'will be quite alone, and between the first and last place mentioned, out of all communication'.

The decision to travel to the Congo was extraordinarily bold and, some would say, even dangerous. She would be venturing far into Central Africa, a single woman, alone, unwell, with Europe on the verge of war and – as she underlined in her letter to Uncle Sim – travelling to a remote area where she would be unable to make contact with the outside world. The tribal region she was to visit was 300 miles south-east of Stanleyville, now Kisangani, the provincial capital of the Tshopo Province and itself the furthest navigable point upstream from the capital Kinshasa. Certainly her doctor strongly advised against her going. But Alice was determined and, after leaving Paris, she sailed for West Africa. In some senses, the adventure was an act of defiance – Alice had always been headstrong and prone to making impulsive decisions – but perhaps it also represented her continuing need to live on her own terms during this period of her return to Happy Valley as a single woman, without Frédéric, Raymund, Joss, or her American or French families. In any event, Alice survived her extraordinary expedition, and returned to Wanjohi towards the end of the summer of 1939.

On her return, there was news of her ex-husband. Raymund had left Kenya in disgrace after getting very drunk one night at his farm in Njoro and striking one of his employees, whom he injured very badly. The matter was taken up by the police and the local district officer. To avoid any further scandal, Raymund was asked to depart for England immediately. Back in England, something altogether more serious had happened: he had been driving from a race meeting in Cheltenham and accidentally killed a woman cyclist. There had been a witness in the car – someone he had offered a lift to on his way back to London – and this person testified that Raymund was under the influence of drink when the accident occurred. On 7 June 1939, just after Alice left France for the Congo, Raymund was given three years' penal servitude for manslaughter. In sentencing him at the Gloucester Assizes, Justice Charles said, 'You have been found guilty – and very properly found guilty – of as bad a case of manslaughter by driving a car in a criminally negligent manner as I can well imagine. You drove like a lunatic. The sentence I pass upon you must necessarily, not only from a punishment point of view, but as a deterrent to others, be severe.'

Raymund was sent to Parkhurst Prison on the Isle of Wight, one of the toughest and most secure prisons in Great Britain. Escape was known to be impossible – water between the island and the mainland was unswimmable, multi-currented and with four strong tides every twenty-four hours. Alice must have taken pity on Raymund because she wrote to him often during this time and he replied. Evidently she remembered her own time in prison and how Raymund had been one of the only people to write to her while she was there. Despite everything that had taken place, she felt sorry for him. At the time of Raymund's incarceration, Parkhurst housed some of

Britain's most hardened criminals, including at least four leading IRA militants and several forgers. With his charm and ability to turn matters to account, Raymund had already discovered how to do his time in reasonable comfort. He made arrangements via the warders for extra provisions, including his favourite foie gras; he learned how to place bets on the horses, and to get the results. He also learned to communicate with his fellow Catholic convicts, who were IRA members, talking to them during exercise without moving his lips. His cell was scrubbed and washed out by other inmates who were keen to earn a few extra pounds, an arrangement which Raymund was able to honour. As usual, he read voraciously and had an ample supply of books, not only from the prison library, but also from friends who brought them in to him on a regular basis.

Then, in September of 1939, a month after Alice returned to Kenya, war was declared in Europe. Alice's two children were taken to the United States where they remained at Aunt Tattie's house in Chicago for the duration of the conflict. Although Alice was removed from hostilities on Wanjohi Farm, the war had one immediate consequence for her: she was no longer able to travel freely to see her children. In November, she wrote to her daughters via Aunt Tattie, unsure if any of her letters would ever arrive. At this time, airmail letters sent from Kenya could be delivered only to the countries of the British Empire. Alice worried that it might be years before her letters reached their destination, 'if they're not sunk on route'.

Enclosed with this particular letter was an article about Wanjohi Valley written by George Kinnear, editor of the *East African Standard* newspaper and a friend of Alice's. Alice asserted that George was a good writer and that his description of the valley and the mountains was apt. Of the stunning Wanjohi Valley, Kinnear wrote poignantly, 'The trees and the streams and the great mountains, the cattle and the sheep and the horses, the plump, chattering Kikuyu women picking daisies in the fields are still at peace.' While Alice always included descriptions of Africa such as these for her children to read, Nolwen and Paola were never invited to join her in Kenya. Now, with the advent of war, this would have been impossible, even if Alice had wished it.

In her letter to Aunt Tattie just before the war, Alice suggested that she had signed up as a Red Cross volunteer, but there is no evidence that she ever served in this capacity. For his part, Joss, like many of the colonists, was deeply engrossed in the war effort. He had been given a temporary commission in the Kenya Regiment as a second lieutenant, quickly rising to Assistant Military Secretary. There were fears that after the plagues of locusts and the recent drought, Kenya would simply be unable to produce enough food to feed its populace, especially with so many young and able male farmers being called up for the army. Events in Abyssinia continued to make the conflict feel very close to home: everyone knew that Mussolini would probably ally himself with Hitler and the invasion of British Kenya would be the logical next step. Colonial troops had already been assembled on the northern borders and there were plans to have parts of the highlands evacuated in the event of an invasion. Joss was very much involved in these arrangements.

A month after the outbreak of war, Joss's wife, Mary, who had been virtually housebound since the summer, finally succumbed to her illnesses. The cause of death given was kidney failure. She was buried that October at St Paul's Church in Kiambu, eight miles outside Nairobi and the main town in her husband's constituency. Alice did not attend. The money Mary had left she willed to Joss, but after the extravagances of their marriage, the amount was far from substantial. After Mary's death, Alice confided to her neighbour, Pat Fisher, that she would like to get back together with Joss. Evidently, this did not happen. Although short of cash and thrown off kilter by Mary's death, Joss was disappearing into his work and social activities, while also continuing his affair with Phyllis Filmer. He was ever more engrossed in his wartime duties. The following year, in June 1940, Mussolini declared war on Great Britain and the threat of Kenya's invasion by the Italians redoubled. Bombings were expected and Nairobi was blacked out in anticipation of air attacks; sandbags surrounded official buildings, and hundreds of new military personnel flooded the city.

Meanwhile, Alice's ever-delicate grasp on her moods was worsening. Like many people suffering from cyclothymia, the symptoms of her illness were becoming more severe as she grew older, her mood swings more pronounced and her unhappy periods lasting for a longer time. The effect of the light and altitude of the highlands was failing to work its magic as it had done in the past. It has been shown that various psychosocial factors – for example stressful circumstances, complicated living conditions and personal difficulties – can play a large part in exacerbating symptoms of the disease. Alice, who had been dogged by depression since adolescence, now had to deal with the considerable stresses of wartime, solitude, illness and middle age (she had just turned forty). Over the years, she had learned to ameliorate her condition with alcohol and used barbiturates to help her sleep. Now she seldom woke up before noon. Alice was entering an altogether disquieting time, with the outbreak of war foreshadowing the beginning of her sad decline.

10

The New Elements

In 1940, Alice was given her own chance to play a role in the war effort. In his capacity as Assistant Military Secretary Joss had decided that his old friend Lizzie Lezard (real name Julian Joseph Lezard) of the King's African Rifles should be stationed at Wanjohi Farm in order to undertake intelligence work in the area. Alice knew the Wanjohi Valley and its residents well and could help Lizzie report back on any local events that smacked of subversion. Alice was excited at the prospect of serving as an intelligence gatherer. For his part, Joss was evidently making a protective gesture towards his old girlfriend. Alice was alone and isolated at Wanjohi. Lizzie, meanwhile, had a reputation as a joker, someone who was excellent company. Joss was correct in his assumption that the pair would get along: Lizzie and Alice became good friends and, for a time, lovers.

Lizzie was Jewish, a striking-looking man of thirty-eight at the time of his arrival in Kenya, with hooded blue eyes and a mass of curly black hair. Born in Kimberley, South Africa, in 1902, he attended Cambridge University where he studied law between 1918 and 1922. He was a talented tennis player who captained the University Lawn Tennis Team and later represented South Africa with distinction in Davis Cup matches. When Alice first met him, he had recently separated from his wife, Hilda Wardell. She had filed for divorce after tiring of funding Lizzie's gambling, which resulted in considerable losses. With war imminent, he joined the military, where his quick-wittedness and poise attracted the attentions of the Field Intelligence Services. He was immediately commissioned as a lieutenant and posted to the Sudan before being reassigned to Kenya. Lizzie was known for his talent with women: he was a good listener and perceptive, usually in a humorous way, but always with enough flattery thrown in that his girlfriends would instinctively feel 'Here at last is someone who really understands me – the real me.' He also had a habit of speaking his mind. Throughout the first drive to Wanjohi, he complained bitterly to Alice about the abysmal road conditions. It was pouring with rain that day and the DeSoto was slithering from side to side as Alice battled to negotiate cavernous water-filled potholes. 'Stop the car!' Lizzie is said to have cried out. 'I can't take any more of this. I don't want to be a pioneer in Kenya. I'd rather be a bloody shit in London!'

Despite this unpromising start, Lizzie went on to enjoy his stay at Wanjohi, conducting his field intelligence duties during the day and playing hours of backgammon each evening with his hostess. Most likely he lost often as Alice was an expert at the game. Lizzie's natural diagnostic ability would have drawn his new girlfriend into telling him about herself, especially as her trust in him increased. Alice may also have enjoyed their more intimate relations: during his time in London, Lizzie had earned a reputation as an accomplished lover and he was always the first to boast of his skills. 'You see, I was regarded as rather intellectual and interesting, and that gave me a special position,' he would explain. 'Yes! I used to be London's ethereal lover!' According to Pat Cavendish O'Neill, in her memoir *A Lion in the Bedroom* (2004), Lizzie was also in possession of an exceptionally long penis which he sometimes produced while playing bridge: he would announce 'Full house', and everything went on display. Whether this knowledge had reached the ears of Idina, we do not know, but it is possible that she had heard something because on a visit to Clouds, Lizzie was prevailed upon to play the 'sheet game'. This unusual after-dinner game involved stringing up a sheet with holes in it across the living room. Half a dozen men could stand on one side with their penises through the holes and an equal number of women would stand on the other side, selecting their favourite appendage by calling out a number. Lizzie often joked that he had been the 'Number 3 lover in London in 1934' and so there would have been plenty of cries of 'Three!' from the women in attendance that evening. After his stay with

Alice, Lizzie returned to Nairobi where he took up residence at Joss's two-bedroom cottage in Muthaiga, continuing to fulfil his field intelligence duties, while still finding time to show off his serves at the Muthaiga Tennis Club. The brief relationship with Alice petered out, naturally and without rancour.

Then, one night at the Muthaiga Club Alice met another military man stationed in Nairobi. He was Richard (Dickie) Pembroke, a charming and good-looking Coldstream Guards officer who had been transferred to Kenya in 1939. Alice immediately marked him out as a possible conquest now that her affair with Lizzie was over, but to her dismay Dickie turned his attentions elsewhere. His object of interest was a cool blonde with blue eyes called Lady Diana Delves Broughton, who arrived from London in November of 1940. At the time of Diana's appearance in Nairobi, she was newly married to Sir Henry Delves Broughton, the eleventh baronet of Doddington – known as Jock, an imposing man with slicked-back dark hair who walked with a limp due to an old war wound. At twenty-seven, she was thirty years younger than Jock, and had been his mistress for five years when she agreed to travel with him to Africa. Although the timing of this emigration might seem unusual, in fact, Jock was entitled to land under the 1919 Soldiers Settlement Scheme and saw his departure to Kenya as a way of being useful in some way to the war effort. By the time the Delves Broughtons reached Cape Town towards the end of October 1940, Jock's divorce from his first wife was official and the couple were married in Durban on the 5th of

November. Before the two married, they agreed on the following unusual terms: if Diana wished to separate, Jock would let her go.

Although Diana evidently adored her new title of Lady Delves Broughton, she was not so enamoured with Jock. The issue of marriage had been forced because it would have been extremely difficult for Diana to gain entry into Kenya as an unmarried woman. After disembarking from the train at Nairobi, the newlyweds took up temporary residence at the Muthaiga Club where Diana made it clear to the members of this male-dominated establishment that she was very much available. For his part, Dickie was smitten with the glamorous Diana, but Diana was less enthused. Although Dickie was wealthy – having inherited his money from his grandfather, Edward Pembroke, Chairman of the Baltic Exchange – he, unlike Jock, lacked a title. Although the affair was over before it had begun, Dickie's attentions to Diana proved to be of immense annoyance to Alice, who found herself rebuffed in favour of Diana. Alice had never had any problem attracting men before. When she had first arrived in Kenya in 1925, it had been Alice who was the new girl in town, gaining the attention of all the prominent men of the settler community, Joss included. But this was 1940. Alice had turned forty the previous September and although her beauty was still very much in evidence, her looks could not last for ever. To make matters worse, she was in ill health and becoming increasingly reliant on alcohol and sleeping pills. She could only watch as this younger interloper drew the gazes of the most attractive and available men in Nairobi.

Everything about Diana conspired to irritate Alice. Not only was Diana younger, she was Alice's exact opposite in terms of looks and temperament, blonde and extrovert whereas Alice was dark and complex. While Diana was obviously voluptuous, Alice was delicately slender (her Kikuyu servants nicknamed their mistress 'Wacheke', meaning 'the thin one'). Simply put, Diana had the kind of blatant sex appeal that often inspires an instinctive dislike in other women. Alice was also alert to Diana's social ambitions. Diana had been born into a solidly middle-class English family – in her younger years, she had been a working girl, serving for a time as a hostess in a somewhat seedy cocktail bar called the Blue Goose in London. Although Diana had hoped to meet a wealthy and titled husband, instead she managed to marry a piano player called Vernon Motion: the marriage had lasted less than a year when husband and wife discovered that neither had any money. When Diana met Sir Jock Delves Broughton at the Blue Goose in 1935, she wasted no time in becoming his mistress. Now she seemed to be casting around for another titled lover amongst the pool of available Nairobi men. Alice detected Diana's underlying ambition and found it distasteful. After her time as a French countess, Alice knew exactly what it was like to be judged by one's pedigree (or lack thereof) and she had developed a considerable antipathy for those who valued titles over substance. Writing to Raymund in Parkhurst she described Diana as a 'new element' who had upset the delicate balance of a number of relationships within the close circle of Kenya society.

In the end, Alice did not have to wait long for her chance with Dickie. Diana quickly rejected Dickie on the grounds that he was 'dull', clearing the way for Alice to begin a relationship with the handsome guards officer. Dickie was thirty-six at the time of his affair with Alice. Unlike Raymund, another ex-officer in the Coldstream Guards, he took a certain pride in his status as gentleman soldier. His manners were polished and his courtesy to all, including Alice's staff, made him both popular and respected. In many ways, this new boyfriend constituted another Frédéric figure in Alice's life – someone who was dependable and loyal but lacking in the spark that ignited her relationships with Raymund or Joss. For Dickie's part, the affair with Alice offered him newfound happiness after a very difficult period in his own life. Born in Epsom on 18 December 1904, he attended Malvern School and entered the Military Academy at Sandhurst on 30 August 1924. On passing out he was offered a commission in the Coldstream Guards, which he accepted, beginning a career of steady promotion. But just prior to his arrival in Kenya, Dickie had begun an affair with a fellow officer's wife. As punishment, he was put on temporary leave, seconded to the Colonial Office and made a Brigade Major in the King's African Rifles. Such a turn of events constituted an enormous embarrassment for Dickie, who took his military career extremely seriously, and he was anxious to make amends. He retained his Coldstream cap star and always wore his Coldstream Guards uniform and buttons during his time in Kenya. After the disappointment of being seconded and then cast aside by Diana, Dickie quickly embraced the relationship with Alice, spending more and more time with her, not just at Wanjohi but also at her cottage in Nairobi and the beach house at Tiwi where they were photographed together. But even though Alice had succeeded with Dickie, a rivalry with Diana had been established.

Imagine Alice's growing dismay, then, when it became clear that Diana was beginning a very public affair with Joss. By Christmas of 1940, Joss and Diana were seen regularly dancing together at the Muthaiga Club, their bodies locked together in a way that many of the club members considered indecent. Diana evidently found Joss irresistible: his good looks, high ranking in settler society and title of Lord High Constable of Scotland made him extremely attractive to her. A mutual infatuation was underway. Alice sensed that the relationship with Diana was different. Joss was consumed with Diana in a way that Alice had never witnessed before. Still smarting from the Dickie–Diana affair, Alice felt herself dropped by her old friend Joss. Again, she wrote to Raymund about her fury regarding Diana's appearance on the scene.

Jock Delves Broughton, meanwhile, seemed to be accepting his new wife's infidelity with a degree of good humour. Joss and Jock were friends: they had attended the same school, Eton, and had been enjoying one another's company now that they were living in the same part of the world. That December, the Delves Broughtons had moved into a large house in Marula Lane, in Nairobi's Karen district, and Joss would often visit both of them there. The Delves Broughtons' close neighbour in Karen,

Derek Erskine, spent a good deal of time with the three of them during the last few months of 1940. Another old Etonian, albeit one with politically liberal leanings, Derek had arrived in Kenya in the early thirties to become the news announcer for the Kenya Broadcasting Service (but because he had a lisp and was unable to pronounce his r's, he mangled his introduction – 'This is the Naiwobi Bwoadcasting Sewvice' – and soon quit the job). After starting up a bakery with his wife, Elizabeth, he went on to form a successful grocery business. In later years, Derek always maintained that Jock was surprisingly tolerant of the liaison between Joss and Diana. Derek recollected that on one occasion Jock was looking out of his library window, which overlooked the swimming pool at Marula Lane. That day, Diana was swimming in the nude. Joss was standing beside the pool and holding up a towel, ready for her exit. Jock opened his library window and shouted jokingly, 'Joss! It's my turn to dry Diana today!' According to Derek, the relationship between the two men was always grown-up and good-spirited, regardless of Jock's hurt feelings. There was a sense of 'no grudges' between these two men who shared the same alma mater and had been brought up to believe that 'all's fair in love and war'.

As 1941 began, it was becoming increasingly clear to Jock that his wife was in love with Joss. Like Alice, Jock could only look on as yet again Joss and Diana danced publicly and amorously with one another at the Muthaiga Club. What's more, Jock was receiving anonymous letters. The first read 'You seemed like a cat on hot bricks at the club last night. What about the eternal triangle? What are you going to do about it?' The next one was even more unpleasant in its insinuation: 'There is no fool like an old fool. What are you going to do about it?' In mid-January, Jock decided that he would take it upon himself to confront his wife and her lover in order to discover their true intentions. As was later revealed in his trial, Jock went first to Diana, asserting his right to know the nature of her feelings for Joss. Diana did not lie: she told Jock that she was in love with Joss, saying, 'It's something I cannot help.' Jock then suggested that Diana come away with him for a few months, in order to allow for a cooling-off period. If she still felt the same way about Joss after time away, he would agree to a separation. 'I promise you, Diana, I will stand by it,' he said. 'But let us give our marriage a longer trial.' Diana would not consent.

Next Jock went to visit Joss at his Nairobi bungalow, demanding that he also reveal his intentions. 'I take no notice of gossip,' Jock declared, 'but it has been clear to me for some time that you are in love with Diana. I have spoken to her and she says she is in love with you too.' Joss was truthful: he told Jock that he was 'frightfully in love' with Diana although he hadn't realized she felt the same way until now. Jock reiterated that he wanted to take Diana away for a number of months. 'If she still believes she is in love with you and wants a divorce to marry you, Joss, I'll make no objection.' When Joss pointed out it was unlikely that Diana would agree to such a plan, Jock tried another tactic, begging Joss to allow him the chance to make something of the marriage: 'Won't you arrange to leave Nairobi? Perhaps if you apply to do service elsewhere, they will let you go.' Again, Joss declined, citing his attachment to Diana and pointing out that, apart from anything else, he could not go away, as there was a war on. Jock gave it one last try, demanding that Joss reveal how he intended to support Diana. 'You've got practically nothing apart from your pay and allowances,' he reminded Joss. 'I know Diana would not take a penny of the money I've settled on her if you two were to be married. She is the straightest person I know where money is concerned.' Joss's reply did not reveal his own concern about Diana's financial situation: 'Of course, I would not expect her to take it nor would I live on her money. But we'll manage somehow.'

Jock's attempt to save his marriage had resolutely failed. He told Diana he had no choice but to go ahead with a divorce. Later, at his trial, he would say, 'I made up my mind to bow to the inevitable. The only thing for me to do was to cut my losses and go, say, to Ceylon. Perhaps I would return to Kenya in a few months. She might then no longer be in love with Erroll.' Jock still held out a final glimmer of hope that Diana's infatuation would peter out, and that 'all might still come right in the end'. It was at this point Jock wrote to a friend, Jack Soames, to inform him that Joss and Diana were in love, and that he was going to 'cut his losses' and leave. 'There's nothing for me to live in Kenya for,' he wrote. According to Lizzie Lezard, who also gave evidence at the trial, Joss had informed him that 'Jock could not have been nicer. He had agreed to go away. As a matter of fact, he has been so nice that it smells bad.'

On the morning of Thursday the 23rd of January, Jock sent word to his lawyer that he wished to begin divorce proceedings. Over lunch, he informed Diana of his decision and told her that he would soon be leaving for Ceylon. That evening, the Delves Broughtons were expected at the Muthaiga Club where they were to meet Joss and another friend, June Carberry. When Jock arrived, Joss and Diana were already lounging on a sofa, limbs entwined. The evening constituted an odd celebration of sorts: champagne was ordered and Jock even went so far as to toast his wife and her lover. He held his glass aloft and in a loud voice declaimed: 'To Diana and Joss. I want to wish them every happiness in the future and may their union be blessed with an heir. To Diana and Joss.' Everyone in the room could hear his words. Jock was deliberately making a great show of giving up his wife. Later he would say, 'The dinner party was a most cheerful affair. Mine was an attitude of complete resignation in view of the circumstances I had encountered. There was nothing else to be done. I realized it.' After dinner, Joss and Diana decided to go off dancing at the nearby Claremont nightclub, with Jock stipulating that Diana should be returned home by 3 a.m. Dickie Pembroke was at the Muthaiga Club that night and when he returned to Alice's Portaluca bungalow, he informed her of the extraordinary celebration he had witnessed that evening.

The Delves Broughtons' friend June Carberry later testified that she had remained at the bar with Jock while he drank a quantity of brandy. 'We've only been married three months,' he told June, 'and look how it is for me now.' When he left with June at 1.30 a.m., Jock came close to passing out from too much drink and the sudden impact of fresh air. Jock and June left for Karen, arriving at the Delves Broughton residence at 2 a.m. June, who was staying at the house, went to her room. Shortly afterwards, Jock put his head round her door to say goodnight. He was wearing his dressing gown. Fifteen minutes later, Joss and Diana pulled up at the Karen house in the Buick that Joss had borrowed, as his own car was out of order. Diana's maid was there to greet them. Joss said goodbye. Diana cautioned him to 'drive carefully'. Everyone knew that Joss always drove too fast. June and Diana chatted for a while before Diana went to bed.

11

The Murder of Lord Erroll

After saying goodbye to Diana, Joss drove back in the direction of his Muthaiga bungalow. It was after two in the morning and the road ahead would have been hard to make out. In accordance with blackout regulations, Joss's headlights were half-shaded, and he would have been forced to lean forward in his seat to see his way. Despite the lack of visibility, there is no doubt that he was driving at his usual top speed. He would have been keen to get home. It was late, he was tired, and he needed to be at his desk first thing in the morning. Although Joss almost always lived up to his reputation as a philanderer, he rarely neglected his professional duties.

Joss soon approached the intersection of the Ngong–Nairobi road, where he was intending to turn right, which would have taken him back towards Nairobi and Muthaiga, where his cottage was located. Only so much is known for certain about what happened next. What we do know is that he was persuaded to stop his car well before the crossroads. Two shots were then fired at him at close range. One bullet missed but the other entered his neck under his left ear, passing through the base of his skull and killing him instantly. Next, Joss's body either fell or was pushed under the dashboard of the car. The Buick then rolled or was pushed off the road so that its front wheels were hanging precariously over a gravel pit by the side of the verge. The person who fired the shots fled the scene.

It did not take long for Joss's body to be discovered. At around 3 a.m., two African dairy workers (milk boys) driving along the Ngong–Nairobi road saw the Buick which appeared to have swerved off the road. As the milk boys came closer, they could see that the car's headlights were still on and that blood was spattered on the windscreen. There was a man in the car but it was difficult to see who this might be as he was crouched down on the floor beneath the dashboard. The milk boys drove immediately to the nearest police station at Karen to sound the alert. Two constables arrived at the scene. Again it was assumed that some kind of accident had taken place. Another set of tracks could be seen in the mud, heading off in the direction of Nairobi. Perhaps this was a case of hit and run. At 8.15 a.m. an ambulance arrived and the body was taken out of the car so that a government pathologist could examine it. The man was obviously dead: rigor mortis had begun to set in and there was blood clotted around his left ear. At this point, someone recognized the body as that of Joss Erroll.

Word spread quickly. Back at Joss's bungalow, Lizzie Lezard was awakened by a hysterical Diana. She had heard that Joss had died in a car accident and she was inconsolable. After gathering up what she wanted of Joss's possessions – his pyjamas included – Diana departed in floods of tears. Next to visit the bungalow was Idina, Joss's former wife, in search of the Erroll family pearls, which she hoped to pass on to her daughter Dinan. The pearls were nowhere to be found. Lizzie realized that it now fell to him to inform the other woman in Joss's life, Alice. He drove the short distance to the Portaluca cottage where he found Alice ensconced with Dickie. Here he repeated the news that Joss had died in a car accident. Alice's reaction was immediate. While Diana and Idina had chosen to race to Joss's home to retrieve his possessions, Alice had a very different idea. She asked to be taken to the mortuary. She wanted to see Joss. Lizzie agreed to this request and drove her there himself.

Together, Alice and Lizzie were permitted to view Joss's body, which was laid out on the mortuary slab. What could have been Alice's thoughts at the sight of him? Joss had been a key figure in her life for almost twenty years. Her on-again-off-again relationship with him had weathered their many marriages, divorces and affairs. Now he was gone, his body stretched out, his pale features drained of all animation and life. But if Alice had come to say a final 'goodbye', this was not the word she chose to use. Instead, she bent down, put her lips on Joss's, kissed him passionately and declared: 'Now you are mine for ever.'

The visit to the mortuary and her declaration while there were the first of many bizarre reactions from Alice in the aftermath to Joss's death.

Later in the day, Joss's body was taken to be examined by a pathologist, Dr Vint. When the clotted blood behind the left ear was cleaned away, Vint could see that Joss had been shot in the neck and at close range. The bullet had passed through the neck below his left ear and was lodged in the right side of his neck. Joss was right-handed, so it would have been impossible for the wound to have been self-inflicted. He had been murdered. There were black powder marks around the wound, which meant that the killer had most likely been sitting in the passenger seat or standing on the car's running board when he or she took aim. Later that afternoon, another .32 calibre bullet was found under the accelerator pedal of the Buick. Joss must have ducked the first bullet, but the second shot killed him on impact. Dr Vint estimated that the murder had taken place between 2.30 and 3 a.m. He also suggested that the body might have been pushed into its curious position beneath the steering wheel so that someone else – the killer or an accomplice – could then drive the car off the road. The car itself was virtually undamaged and the mechanic who examined it asserted that the car was being driven at no more than 8 miles an hour when it had stopped. The gear lever was almost, although not quite, in top position, an oddity. In the front of the car was further evidence: a bloodstained hairpin.

Despite Vint's revelation that Joss had most definitely been shot, the newspapers were duly informed that Lord Erroll had died in a car accident. Assistant Inspector Arthur James Poppy, formerly of the Metropolitan Police, London, and head of the Nairobi Criminal Investigation Department, had been immediately assigned to the case, but he deliberately chose to keep the truth under wraps for twenty-four hours until more details could be ascertained. It seems that the police were keen to stave off speculation until more was known: after all, Joss was a high-ranking official and a well-known British aristocrat into the bargain. This was an investigation that needed to be handled with diplomacy and care. Joss's funeral took place the following day on 25 January 1940 at St Paul's Church in Kiambu, Lord Erroll's constituency. Here he was buried next to his wife, Mary, his headstone inscribed with the following words:

In loving memory
of
Josslyn Victor Hay,
twenty second Earl of Erroll,
Hereditary High Constable of Scotland,
born 11th Day of May 1901,
met his death on 24th Day of January 1941.
Thy will be done.

The funeral was well attended. Most of Kenya's officialdom was present, including the governor, Sir Henry Moore, as well as an impressive line-up of military and governmental representatives. Alice had composed herself enough to make an appearance amongst the other mourners. Jock Delves Broughton arrived late. Diana was too upset to attend but she had given her husband a note to drop into the coffin. Almost everyone who was present was still under the impression that Joss had been killed tragically in a car accident. This made sense. Joss had always driven too fast and recklessly. Alice even went so far as to suggest to Jock that perhaps Joss had suffered from heart trouble and that this could have been the cause of his death.

It wasn't until the day of the inquest, in the afternoon of Monday the 27th, that the news broke that Joss had been 'probably murdered' and that an investigation was underway to find the killer. Assistant Inspector Poppy was known to be thorough and expert, but the odds were stacked against him from the start. Many aspects of the crime scene had already been carelessly bungled. Joss's body had been removed from the car before exact measurements of the position of the body could be ascertained. The car had been washed out before fingerprints could be taken. No one had thought to put a rope around the Buick and so a second set of tyre tracks going off in the direction of Nairobi had been trampled into the mud by the police before they could be correctly recorded. With hard evidence in short supply, Poppy was going to have to rely on psychological factors, and a great deal of supposition, to determine the identity of the murderer.

Of course, the most obvious suspect was Jock Delves Broughton. It was common knowledge that Joss had been having an affair with Diana and in the eyes of most Jock was immediately cast as the cuckolded husband, seeking revenge on the man who had stolen his wife. In the coming weeks, Assistant Inspector Poppy drew up a list of suspects with Jock high on the list. Poppy's suspicions were heightened further when he went to visit Jock at his house in Karen. Here he discovered a fire burning in a pit in the garden with remnants of a bloodstained golf stocking in the ashes. The blood type, although human, could not be established, and, strangely, Jock could neither explain the presence of the stocking nor why it had blood on it.

Other names on Poppy's list included that of Phyllis Filmer's husband, Percy. He too fitted the description of jealous husband but his secretary confirmed his whereabouts on the night of the murder, and besides, he just 'wasn't the type'. And what of Diana? She was the last person to have seen Joss alive and possibly had some hidden motive for wanting him dead. But Poppy could not conceive what such a motive might be and Diana's obvious distress at the death of her lover seemed to rule her out. Although many in the settler community later hissed 'murderess' behind Diana's back – and it was later rumoured that she had killed Joss in a fit of pique after he refused to marry her – it is hard to imagine her motive for doing away with the man she evidently hoped to wed. Also, in practical terms, it would have been very difficult for Diana to kill Joss. After saying goodbye to him, she had chatted with June Carberry for some time before going to bed. In order to shoot Joss, Diana would have had to make the drive to the crime scene in an impossibly short amount of time.

Then there was Alice. Of all Joss's many former mistresses, no one was more unsettled by his love affair with Diana than Alice. More importantly, she had known that Joss would be coming home from Marula Lane before 3 a.m. Alice's lover, Dickie Pembroke, had been at the Muthaiga Club the night of the murder and had overheard Jock say to Joss, 'Bring Diana back before 3 o'clock, there's a good fellow.' Dickie had duly related this to Alice on his return to her cottage that evening. In a further strike against her innocence, Alice had a history: she had already been convicted of attempted murder in Paris, after the shooting of Raymund at the Gare du Nord. When Poppy's men questioned the erstwhile countess, however, they discovered that she had an airtight alibi. Dickie Pembroke swore that Alice had been in bed with him at her Portaluca cottage for the duration of the night of the murder. Alice's name was removed from the list.

In the period after Joss's death, Alice's state of mind was precarious to say the least. Fate had decreed that the two most important men in her life would die within a week of one another, Joss on the 24th of January and William Silverthorne, her father, on the 30th of January. William, nearly seventy-four at the time of his death, was buried in Savannah, Georgia, where he had been living. Alice did not contemplate attending the funeral. Apart from the fact she was unable to travel because of the war, she was consumed with the events of Joss's murder investigation. We do not know her reaction to the news that William had passed away, but we can only assume that his death, coming so soon after Joss's murder, placed even more pressure on her already fragile equilibrium. Alice's relationship with her father had always been central to her unhappiness and now the lifelong rift between father and daughter had been made perpetual, dangerously mirroring her separation from her beloved Joss.

With Alice and Diana discounted as suspects, the police refocused their attentions on Jock. If they could find the murder weapon and link it to Jock – or at least identify that one of his guns had fired the bullets that had been recovered from Joss's body and car – then they would have sufficient evidence to charge him. The Karen house and its grounds were duly searched but nothing was found. After Jock was questioned further, it turned out that his two revolvers had been stolen the Tuesday before the murder. Poppy was immediately suspicious. The stolen pistols were a Colt .32 revolver and a Colt .42. Joss had been shot with a .32 calibre bullet. Had Jock deliberately arranged for the guns to go missing prior to the murder to divert attention from himself? It was also discovered that Jock had shot rounds from his revolvers at his friend Jack Soames's farm. Bullets taken from Soames's shooting range were examined and deemed to match those found in Joss's car and body.

Poppy felt certain he had found his man. Jock had the motive to kill and also seemed to have owned the gun that could well have been the murder weapon. Even so, the police still had to ascertain how Jock could possibly have left the house at Karen and then returned there without anyone hearing his movements. June Carberry was prepared to testify that she had seen Jock at 2 a.m. and again at 4 a.m. The shooting had taken place before 3 a.m., but the staircase at Karen creaked loudly and Diana, June and the maid had not heard anyone going downstairs, driving away or coming back between two and four that morning. Could Jock have climbed down the drainpipe at the side of the house or over the side of the balcony? Did he lie in wait for Joss, driving away with him until they were at a far enough distance to accomplish the shooting without anyone hearing the shots? Was Jock capable of the physical prowess required to climb out of the house and walk the two miles back home from the scene of the shooting? This was a man who walked with a limp and had a fractured wrist that would have severely impeded his climb and ability to walk long distances. Jock also suffered from night blindness and had been advised by his doctors not to drive after dark. As a further impediment, he had drunk excessively that night, as June would attest.

Despite shaky evidence Jock was arrested on 14 March 1941. Jock's words to Poppy at the time of his arrest were, 'I'm sorry. You've made a big mistake.' That evening, he was placed in a cell at the Nairobi police station and the following day, he was charged with Joss's murder at the residents' magistrate's court. Immediately afterwards, he was sent to Nairobi Kilimani Prison and given his own cell (where he was permitted to order the food of his choice from the nearby Torrs Hotel). By mid-April, the magistrate had ruled that the Crown had a prima facie case of murder.

Although Diana was grief-stricken over Joss's death, she proved herself to be a loyal wife, visiting Jock in prison on a regular basis. One of Jock's most frequent visitors, however, was Alice. She took him supplies – books in particular – counselled him and tried to cheer him up. She told him he could not possibly be found guilty. Indeed, what evidence was there? Alice was fixated on the idea that Jock might be found guilty, and repeatedly told Pat Fisher how worried she was that this might come to pass. Why would Alice have taken such keen interest in this man's imprisonment while remaining convinced of his innocence? She had never had any desire to befriend Jock before, and his marriage to Diana would only have marked him out as 'off limits'. It is possible that Alice merely sympathized with Jock: she had spent time in prison and knew how it felt to be socially ostracized as a result. Or was something else altogether preying on her mind?

If Jock was found to have committed the murder, it was likely that he would be hanged. As with her peculiar visit to the mortuary, Alice's attentiveness to Jock seems strange to say the least.

12

The Trial of Jock Delves Broughton

On the advice of Jock's solicitor, Lazarus Kaplan of the law firm Kaplan and Stratton, Diana flew to South Africa to see if she could hire Henry Harris 'Harry' Morris KC, who was the leading South African defender of the times. Not only was Morris a brilliant cross-examiner, he was also a noted ballistics expert. Diana must have been persuasive because Harry Morris accepted the job of defending Jock Delves Broughton, at the cost of £5,000, a very large sum for the day. While in South Africa, Diana took the opportunity to buy herself a large number of new outfits and her wardrobe soon became a matter of note in the Nairobi newspaper, the *East African Standard*. On day one of Jock's trial, she arrived dressed dramatically in widow's black and diamonds. The ensuing trial lasted for twenty-seven days, extending over a period of five weeks, the longest on record for Central Africa. But nonetheless – as the *Standard* gleefully reported – Diana never wore the same outfit twice.

The trial of Jock Delves Broughton began on 26 May 1941 in the Supreme Court of Kenya in Nairobi. Chief Justice of Kenya Sir Joseph Sheridan presided. Mr Walter Harrigan KC prosecuted for the Crown. Henry Harris Morris KC defended. A large crowd of Broughton supporters attended each day – all seats were taken. Diana was not the only female mourner for Joss in the packed courtroom. Idina came each day: she and Joss had remained friends until the end. Accompanying Idina was Joss's girlfriend Phyllis Filmer, who had returned from South Africa after hearing the terrible news. Since the murder, Idina and Phyllis had become fast friends, grieving for Joss together, to the point where Phyllis even moved in with Idina at Clouds. Then there was Alice. Although she was never called upon to give evidence, she attended the trial daily, always arriving early to secure a good seat, beautifully turned out, as if in competition with the other women in the courtroom. According to Harrigan's secretary, Peggy Pitt, Alice made copious notes throughout the trial.

Proceedings began with the prosecutor for the Crown, Walter Harrigan, making his powerful opening address. Harrigan reminded the men and women of the jury that 'motive' should guide their verdict: Sir Delves Broughton had killed the Earl of Erroll because the latter had stolen his wife. 'We shall try to establish that Erroll died from a bullet in the brain fired from a revolver which, at any rate, had been in Broughton's possession three days before,' Harrigan declared.

Next, Harry Morris set about laying the groundwork for Jock's defence. Morris wanted to show that it would have been impossible for Broughton to climb down the drain-pipe or over the balcony of the Karen house before climbing into the car with Joss that night. '. . . Sir Delves consumed a quantity of liquor at the Muthaiga Club on the night of January 23rd and was under its influence by the time he returned to Karen,' Morris advised. 'He was extremely tired as well and night blindness prevented his driving his car after dark, let alone in a wartime blackout. He also has a broken wrist, the result of a car accident some years ago.' Equally, the two-mile walk back to the house after the shooting would have been extremely challenging for Jock. Friends of Broughton's – including Jack Soames and June Carberry – gave evidence of Jock's good nature and general equanimity when it came to Joss and Diana's affair. Soames described his friend as neither 'quick tempered [n]or passionate'. June portrayed him as 'courteous, considerate and most cheerful, with a sense of humour, and not at all jealous.' Morris also cited the anonymous letters that had been sent to Broughton before Erroll's murder as proof that Joss had many enemies – former mistresses and cuckolded husbands included – who might have wanted to stir up bad feeling between Jock and Joss during this time. Morris even hinted that the murder might have been politically motivated: Joss had been a sometime member of the British Union of Fascists after all.

Lizzie Lezard was called in as a witness. Described in court as 'Lieutenant Julian Lezard', he related the conversation he had had with Joss the day before the murder during which Joss had told Lizzie how 'nice' Jock was being about the whole affair. Dickie Pembroke also gave evidence, having been brought in by the Crown in order to rule out Alice as a possible suspect. Dickie clearly loathed playing his part in such a public event, although he duly confirmed that Alice had been in bed with him on the night of the murder.

The Crown's case therefore rested on the following supposition: Jock Delves Broughton had killed Joss Erroll with a bullet fired from the Colt .32 revolver allegedly stolen a few days before the murder. In order to affirm Jock's innocence, Harry Morris knew that he had to prove that the bullets fired from Jock's revolver at Soames's shooting range were different from the ones used to commit the murder. For the prosecution, Harrigan brought in two ballistics specialists to show that the bullets fired at Joss and the bullets discovered on the shooting range had been fired from the same gun. According to both specialists, all the bullets in question had right-hand rifling grooves and therefore were from the same equipment. It was at this moment that Morris knew he could win his case.

It had already been ascertained that Joss had been shot with five-grooved bullets. Morris knew that Jock's Colt was a six-grooved revolver. He had cabled the Colt company in the United States to confirm this fact.

'It stands to reason,' Morris proposed, 'that you cannot get a five-grooved bullet out of a six-grooved gun. And the missing Colts were six-grooved, were they not?' The ballistics specialist on the stand was forced to agree. Morris had it on the record: the bullets and the supposed murder weapon did not match. The Crown was forced to drop its line of argument that Jock had arranged for the Colts to be stolen in order to cover up the murder.

Now it was Jock's turn to give evidence and be cross-examined. This process took place over a period of six days.

'Sir Delves,' Morris began. 'Did you have anything to do, directly or indirectly, with the death of the Earl of Erroll?'

'Certainly not,' came the reply. Jock went on to mention his limp, his fractured wrist and his night blindness. He described himself as devoted to his wife, Diana. He told the story of their recent marriage and the pact that they had made before the wedding, that if Diana wanted a separation, he would let her go.

Morris then asked Jock if he had been prepared to sacrifice his marriage in order to secure his wife's happiness.

'I realized that she had all her young life in front of her,' Jock replied. 'I have not. The only thing, therefore, was for me to cut my losses and go away to Ceylon.'

He went on to describe in some detail the events preceding the murder, his evening at the Muthaiga Club and how he returned home at 2 a.m. before going to bed.

'I do not mind how many men fall in love with my wife as long as she does not fall in love with them,' he explained. 'She never gave me the slightest cause for jealousy till she started going out with Erroll. This, I admit, came as a bit of a shock and I did my best to persuade her to come to Ceylon with me. But she did not want to.'

On the prosecution side, Harrigan needed to show that Jock's line of argument was implausible.

'Do you seriously mean that if you suspect a man of making love to your wife, you are incapable of making it clear to him you would like him to desist?' he asked.

'Before you know for certain,' Broughton replied, 'that your wife is in love with another man, or a man is in love with your wife, I think it would be an extremely foolish thing to do. Once you know, you have to do one of two things – either give up the contest and go away, or have a frightful row and tell the other man you won't have it. As we had a pact and my wife was thirty years younger, I felt bound to honour it. Otherwise what's the use in making it?'

To clinch his case, Morris brought in another small-arms expert who confirmed that the bullets used to shoot Joss could not have come from Jock's Colt revolver. More witnesses spoke about Jock's general good temper and his difficulties with walking long distances at any great speed.

Finally, Morris made his closing remarks. Referring back to Harrigan's original supposition that motive would guide the jury in their verdict, he spoke definitively: 'We live in an age of mathematics and machinery. The appeal is no longer to the hearts and to the passions of men. The appeal is to their reasoning power.' It was not the responsibility of the defence to come up with the true identity of the murderer, Morris asserted, it was up to the Crown to show, beyond reasonable doubt, that Jock Delves

Broughton had murdered Lord Erroll. Morris reminded the jury that the murder weapon had never been found and that the bullets from Jock's gun did not match that found in the Buick and the one in Joss's body. The Crown needed to prove that Jock had shot Joss with bullets from a five-grooved gun on the morning of the murder. The Crown could not prove this. Also, there was no evidence that Jock had left the Marula Lane house on the night of the murder. What remained of the case against Jock? The motive of jealousy? Morris reminded the jury of Jock's equanimity in the matter of his wife's affair.

'There is no proof he uttered a single threat against Erroll's life at any time. Habit, gentlemen, is a compelling thing. Breeding is powerful and tradition omnipotent . . . You are asked to believe, gentlemen, that Sir Delves Broughton suddenly became transformed into a cold-blooded, crafty individual who decided after his interview with Erroll, to slaughter him . . . I can only make this submission to you gentlemen: it is incredible.'

Morris concluded his summing up with the following words: 'The evidence does not support the conclusion that Sir Delves Broughton had a hand in the murder, directly or indirectly. You cannot find him guilty of this crime.'

Next it was Harrigan's turn to conclude. He informed the jury that the bullets needn't have come from a Colt revolver. It was possible that Broughton had used another gun. Besides, the Crown's ballistics experts had spent many months researching and verifying the bullets at the shooting range and the bullets found at the crime scene and had confirmed these were the same. It was clear to him,

Harrigan informed the jury, that Jock had decided to murder his rival. He had arranged to have the revolvers vanish, reporting the burglary to the police to distract attention.

'I have already suggested, and I repeat, this was a faked burglary,' insisted Harrigan.

Harrigan then moved on to the central question of motive. Jock had every motive to kill the man who had taken away his wife. During the period leading up to the murder Jock had acted the part of a husband happily conceding his wife to another man and done so 'magnificently'. As to Jock's disabilities, Harrigan reminded the jury that Jock had recently returned from hunting big game. 'He has stalked lion. He uses an elephant gun. There was nothing wrong with his walking or powers of endurance on the hunting expedition to the Masai Reserve.' As for his night blindness, Harrigan suggested that Jock had simply made up this particular impediment to suit his story.

'The Crown has put forward jealousy as the principal motive for this crime,' declared Harrigan. 'In your deliberations, gentlemen, you will consider human nature. None are exempt from passion or temptation . . .'

Harrigan finished his conclusion just before six on the evening of the 1st of July 1941. Three hours later, at nine o'clock, the jury filed back in. Jock stood to receive the verdict.

'Not guilty.'

Harry Morris's expertise in ballistics had indeed ensured Jock's acquittal. It had not been proven beyond reasonable doubt that Jock was the murderer. For his part, Jock thanked the Chief Justice and turned to face his jubilant supporters, Alice included. Diana had stayed away from the courtroom that day (at Jock's insistence in case of a guilty verdict). Morris, who had returned to South Africa, wrote the very next day to tell Jock he had been certain of his innocence from the beginning, and that Jock had been an exemplary witness. Copies of the letter were made and sent to Jock's many acquaintances, in case they should be in any doubt of his blamelessness. In his reply to Morris's letter, Jock wrote: 'I can never thank you enough for saving my life. Apart from what it means to me there is a deep debt of gratitude my family owe you for clearing my name.'

Alice had followed every moment of the courtroom proceedings with compulsive attention, making jottings in her notebook, investing so much in the outcome of the trial. Now a 'not guilty' verdict had been given, just as she'd prayed for and predicted.

13

The Case for Alice

If Jock was innocent, then who shot Lord Erroll?

No other suspect was ever tried for Joss's murder. It was wartime after all and, after the furore of the trial, Walter Harrigan in particular was keen to play down the scandal which many in Kenya's colonial community had found extremely embarrassing. The Kenya police duly dropped their investigations. At the time of writing, nearly seventy years have passed and yet the Erroll murder remains officially unsolved. The many 'unexplained details of the case' – as they are described in *White Mischief*, James Fox's classic work about the mystery – continue to tantalize the amateur sleuth. Who was the owner of the hairpin found in the car? What happened to the murder weapon? Why had the Buick rolled off the road with the lights left on and the ignition switched off? What was the exact position of Joss's body under the dashboard and why was he crouched there?

It is no surprise that a succession of respected authors have been drawn to the rich territory of such a notorious uncracked case. What *is* surprising is that two of the most distinguished of these writers, both Fox and Errol Trzebinski, Joss's biographer, agree that Jock Delves Broughton was indeed to blame. Fox believes Jock was motivated by jealousy and that Harry Morris simply confused the jury with his ballistics jargon. Trzebinski concluded that Jock was a pawn but that MI6 operatives were entrusted with Joss's assassination. Yet when one examines what is known about Jock's character, weighing this with Harry Morris's persuasive case for his acquittal, along with the technical evidence presented by the defence and the lack of a murder weapon, it becomes difficult to disagree with the jury's verdict of 'not guilty'. The Crown's case failed and with good reason. The mismatch of the bullets and the weapon clinched the case for Morris, but even so the idea that Jock had murdered Erroll never really felt right. This was a man in his late fifties who had difficulties with walking and who was visibly drunk on the night of the murder. Yet in order to shoot Joss he would have had to climb down a drainpipe or over a balcony before walking the two miles home. The police plodded to the conclusion of Jock's guilt on the grounds that he must have been 'jealous' but Jock was a man who had learned how to live with his losses. As he said at his trial, he was accustomed to losing. He had lost in life before – his wife had divorced him after going off with her lover – and as a gambler who regularly bet and lost huge sums on the horses, Jock knew how to be sporting about such things. He had written Diana off as a bad but unavoidable business.

The Kenya Police never even considered the possibility of a professional hit by an MI6 team, although Harry Morris did raise the idea at Jock's trial. In this respect, I am inclined to agree with the Attorney General, Walter Harrigan QC, who said of this particular supposition: 'If a jury could believe that, I have nothing more to say.' There were many prominent men in 1939 and 1940 who were pro-Oswald Mosley, and quite a few from Scotland, yet none of them became the victims of assassination plots. The Duke of Montrose was an avid Mosley supporter, as was the military scientist J.F.C. Fuller and the novelist Henry Williamson. Charles Stewart Henry Vane-Tempest-Stewart, seventh Marquis of Londonderry, visited Germany in 1936 and was entertained by Hermann Goering and Joachim von Ribbentrop; Adolf Hitler himself gave a dinner in the marquis's honour. Hitler, on the other hand, *was* a target for MI6 and had he been eliminated in 1939 the course of history might have been very different. But Lord Erroll? A man who had been a member of the British Union of Fascists for only a few months? Not worth bothering about. Joss had presented no danger to Britain or to its colonies and, if suspected, he could easily have been watched.

The lack of a clear suspect other than Jock was

evidently very much on the mind of Harry Morris during the course of the trial. Morris knew he would have to convince the jury that someone else was responsible for the crime. In summing up, he asked the jury to consider a number of alternatives. It was possible that Lord Erroll – once a card-carrying member of the British Union of Fascists – might well have been the victim of a political plot. Equally, a jealous husband could have been to blame. If not a husband, then it could well have been one of Joss's former girlfriends, seeking revenge. 'Hell hath no fury like a woman scorned,' Morris reminded the jury.

In fact, Morris had good reason for supposing that one of Joss's lovers might well be responsible for the murder. Shortly after Morris's arrival in Nairobi for the trial, he had received two anonymous letters. The first note read: 'Under separate cover I have written to the Chief Magistrate, Kenya, asking him why the murderer of Joss Erroll, a relative of mine by marriage, was not looked for in the proper quarter. Sir Delves Broughton is not the murderer . . . (the name of a leading socialite and Nairobi personality was given) murdered him in a fit of jealousy.'

The second read:

> Have you found out what lady (?) had the privilege of the late Lord Erroll's affections before he fell in love with Lady Broughton? I think if you put a good detective on the job to find out and follow this lead, you will be pleased . . .

> Lord Erroll would stop his car if such a woman (he knew) signalled that she wanted to speak to him. The rest would be easy . . . If she could not have Erroll herself, no one else would.
>
> Think it over – two birds with one stone. I'm sure Sir Delves didn't do it . . .

Morris took the notes to the police, but the identity of their mysterious author could not be ascertained. The notes were never seen again. Fortunately, Henry Morris kept records and these were reprinted in *Genius for the Defence*, Benjamin Bennett's biography of Morris, published in 1959.

So who was the mysterious leading socialite and Nairobi personality mentioned in the notes? Joss's other love interest was Phyllis Filmer but she was out of the country at the time of his murder, and, besides, she could hardly be described as a 'leading socialite and Nairobi personality'.

The description fits Alice perfectly. Alice was a central figure in the Nairobi social scene. She was ferociously jealous of Joss's relations with Diana. She had certainly enjoyed 'the privilege of the late Lord Erroll's affections before he fell in love with Lady Broughton'. Joss would certainly have stopped his car if he had seen her in the road. What's more, Alice *knew* that Joss would be driving back to his bungalow from Marula Lane on the night of the murder at around 3 a.m. because Dickie Pembroke had told her so. It was thanks to Dickie that Alice also learned that Jock had given his blessing to Diana and Joss's union that very evening. The idea that Diana might now be free to marry Joss can only have sent Alice into a 'fit of jealousy'. Nothing caused Alice more anguish than when the men in her life attempted to reject her. 'I always get my own way'; 'I take what I want and throw it away.' These were the ominous words that Frédéric had used to give voice to Alice's wilful destructiveness in his book, *Vertical Land*. 'If she could not have Erroll herself, no one else would,' wrote the author of the anonymous notes.

There is no doubt Alice had the motive and the knowledge. She also had the nerve. In 1927 she had turned her gun on Raymund when he tried to break off their engagement. She had been tried for his attempted murder and found guilty of a 'crime passionnel'. In other words, she was entirely capable of acting on her passionate impulses. She was a brave and competent shot, someone who seldom left home without a revolver. According to Margaret Spicer, Alice had first owned a gun in Chicago when she was eighteen years old, given to her by her mobster boyfriend 'for her own protection'. This Colt-type weapon was an American pocket revolver: hammerless with automatic extraction, nickel-plated and .38 calibre. Alice bought one very like it in Paris, with its pearl inlay handle, just prior to shooting Raymund. In Kenya, she kept such a revolver on her bedside table. But what of her alibi, Dickie? It is possible that Dickie slept through Alice's departure and her return on the night of the murder. Even if he had heard Alice leaving or coming back, he certainly loved her enough to want to protect her. When questioned by the police, he would have been anxious to minimize his association with the Erroll case so that he could be reinstated into the Coldstream Guards as soon as possible. Either he lied to the police for Alice's sake – and in order to preserve what remained of his already tarnished reputation – or he was telling the truth. Alice had simply managed to leave and then return without waking him.

That night, Alice could have easily taken her revolver from the bedside table and soundlessly climbed into her car, and then sped away. Her route would have been swift and without traffic. Turning left out of Portaluca, she would have driven downhill over the Nairobi River and then past the Catholic church until she reached Ainsworth Bridge and the Da Rajah House, where she and Frédéric had visited the Spicers many times during 1926. At Ainsworth Bridge, Alice would have turned left to pass the Norfolk Hotel before reaching the Ngong road, which led to the Karen road and its intersection with Marula Lane. She could have parked her car on the Karen road at this point and doused her lights to save the battery. She knew that a car being driven by Joss would be coming down this road sometime before or around 3 a.m. Checking her revolver, she would have made sure it was fully loaded. When a pair of half-shaded headlights appeared over the horizon ahead, Alice would have opened the door of her car and walked into the middle of the road, waving her arms as she did so. Joss would have immediately recognized Alice's slim figure illuminated by the Buick's headlights. He probably would have slowed to a full stop but with the engine still running, his foot on the clutch and the top gear still engaged. The Buick was right-hand drive so Joss would have needed to lean across the long front bench seat in order to open the passenger window to speak to Alice. With his foot still on the clutch, the length of his body would have been almost parallel with the seat.

At this point, Alice would have pulled out her pistol and fired. Undeterred by the first miss, she would have immediately pulled the trigger again, letting loose a second bullet. This one met its mark, entering Joss's neck just below his ear. On the bullet's impact, Joss would have slipped from his stretched-out position, falling in a crumpled heap under the dashboard, his left foot coming off the clutch. With the engine still ticking over, and with top gear engaged, the car would then have inched forward. The huge torque of the engine could have permitted the Buick to move without stalling, and Alice would have watched the car turning slightly right and going over the embankment into the ditch on the right-hand side of the road, where it came to rest, stopping with the headlights still ablaze and the key still in the ignition.

In this scenario, both Joss's position under the dashboard and the position of the car with its wheels over the verge are explained. The second pair of wide car tracks found at the scene of the crime, going off in the direction of Nairobi, is also explained: Alice's car was a DeSoto, which had enormously wide tyres. Could the hairpin found in the car have belonged to Alice? And what of the ignition and the headlights? The car was apparently discovered with its lights on but the ignition off. It is my guess that the first constables who arrived at the scene attempted to turn the lights off by switching the ignition key to the 'off' position. In fact, the lights were operated independently but the light switch was broken and could not be operated without pliers. Hence when the car was later examined, the lights were on and the ignition off. A larger question is why Alice didn't try to kill herself that night, just as she had attempted to do at the Gare du Nord after shooting Raymund. Did she go as far as to press the gun to her own head on the night of the murder? Did she lose courage, too horrified by what she had already accomplished? Did the thought of the loyal Dickie draw her back to the Portaluca Cottage? For whatever reason, after committing her horrible crime, Alice would have climbed into her car and raced back to bed where Dickie was waiting. She could not have been absent for more than one and a half hours. As for her revolver, she could have easily disposed of it during the following days. Alice's Muthaiga cottage, her beach house and Wanjohi Farm were never searched by the police.

If Alice *did* shoot Lord Erroll, this would certainly help explain her reactions in the aftermath of Joss's murder. It would explain her decision to see his dead body on the morning of his death: she would have needed to be sure that she had succeeded. This would also explain why she was so completely involved in the outcome of Jock Broughton's trial. If Jock had been found guilty, he would probably have been hanged and in all likelihood Alice would have felt bound to confess in order to save him. No wonder she visited Jock so frequently in his cell, reassuring him that she had perfect faith in his innocence. She knew that he was innocent because she herself was guilty. If Jock had been convicted, Alice would have had Jock's death – as well as Joss's – on her conscience.

14

A Green Bedroom Full of Flowers

Both during the trial and after the verdict, Alice spent as much time as possible with Dickie Pembroke, leaning on him with an increasing devotion. While she remained gripped by every detail of the Erroll case, Dickie could not share her interest. He had been highly uncomfortable about giving evidence in court: after the disgrace of being placed on leave from the Coldstream Guards, he was acutely sensitive when it came to matters of his reputation. It was agonizing for him to have his name associated with the general ignominy surrounding Joss's murder. Although Dickie loved Alice, his clear priority was to rejoin his regiment in North Africa where the 3rd Battalion Coldstream Guards was stationed at this time. Even before the start of the trial, he had made his application to HQ in

London to be reposted. While Dickie waited to hear whether he would be accepted back into his regiment, the possibility of his departure only served to increase Alice's attachment to him. As with all the men in her life – Raymund and Joss included – Alice would always experience her greatest passions for those who were attempting to leave her.

In June 1941, with Jock's trial still in progress, Dickie's application for transfer was granted and he was asked to travel to Cairo where he was to be made acting Regimental Lieutenant Colonel. He left on the 24th of July, only a few weeks after Jock's acquittal. Alice knew there was every possibility Dickie would see action and be killed and so she put off saying goodbye to him for as long as possible, travelling with him as far as Kampala, Uganda, before bidding him farewell. In Dickie's luggage was a letter Alice had written to him before his departure from Wanjohi: poignantly, she had wanted him to have something to open on his arrival in Cairo. Very few of Alice's letters have been preserved, but the ones she wrote to Dickie during the war were kept. They are immensely revealing of this woman during a period of her life when she was struggling with grief, separation, solitude, uncertainty, depression and physical illness, not to mention possible culpability in a murder. Despite Alice's predicament, the letters are marked by tenderness, and a self-knowing humour.

The first letter to Dickie is dated the night before his departure, 23 July 1941. Alice wrote in it that it seemed ridiculous to be writing a letter to someone who was still sitting in front of her. Even so, Alice said, she would rather give him something to read when he arrived in Cairo than for him to wait weeks for a letter to arrive in the mail. She told him that she'd had a lovely week with him, and that she hoped she could manage to say goodbye the next day in decent fashion. She went on in a less stoical vein: 'I can't imagine the immediate future at all . . . all of you are gone or going and my self-pity wells up when I realize that I can follow no one.' Alice's close circle was certainly diminished. Joss was dead. Idina had moved to her coastal house north of Mombasa. Lizzie Lezard had been posted to Cairo. Alice's closest friend in Kenya, Paula, was absorbed in her marriage to Boy Long. Even Alice's French maid had been dispatched back to France at the beginning of the war. Alice could count on her neighbour Pat Fisher, her friends Patsy Bowles and Noreen Pearson, and her housekeeper, Flo, for companionship. But she often found herself spending long days alone. Another letter to Dickie, this one undated – but which must have been written soon after his departure – offers more evidence as to her precarious state of mind during this time: '. . . the fact of you going away in these uncertain times, even for only a short time, as we hope, is pure and absolute pain . . .'

After Dickie's departure, Alice's health certainly took an immediate turn for the worse and in early September of 1941, she had a hysterectomy. Her regular doctor, William Boyle, performed the operation at a hospital in Nairobi. Since he first attended to her in 1932, Dr Boyle had taken a special interest in Alice and the two had long since established a flirtatious rapport. Years later, Boyle's daughter, also called Alice, would recall that her father was 'rather in love with Alice de Trafford'. While it would have comforted Alice to know that Dr Boyle would perform the operation, she remained terrified of the recovery period. In her next letter to Dickie – whom she knew was facing much graver dangers in North Africa – she managed to keep her tone light, at least initially. She spoke of the matron and the nurses, all of whom she knew from previous visits, greeting her warmly. Flo had travelled down to Nairobi with her, a trip that was marred by the fact that they had two punctures and only one spare tyre. Alice observed that now she had arrived at the hospital her operation was cheerfully referred to as 'the op' by the nurses, accompanied by much pillow-thumping and towel-shaking. But she also wrote of events that took place before she left for Nairobi. Immediately before her departure, Alice made the extraordinary decision to put down her beloved dachshund, Minnie. The reason Alice gave Dickie was that her poor dog had begun to panic every time she was put in the car and that recently the hysteria had worsened. Unable to bear Minnie's distress, Alice gave her pentobarbital, a short-acting barbiturate (often given the trade name Nembutal). Alice could have taken Minnie to a vet, and yet she chose to do this herself. For someone who loved her animals as much as Alice, it seems a desperate act, one that reveals her increasingly morbid state of mind during this time. Her choice of language in the letter was equally chilling. Alice said she 'killed' Minnie, and that she felt as if she had 'committed a murder'. She went on in an even more sinister vein. She remembered

Dickie once counselling her that 'life must go on'. Life need not go on, Alice observed: 'In Joss's case someone decided that, in Minnie's case I did, and the length of our own lives lies entirely within our own hands (unless someone else gets at us first!).'

Alice buried Minnie in the iris beds at Wanjohi Farm, at the edge of the 'cut' she had made to take the stream water right around the edge of her house and garden. After her operation, Alice returned to Wanjohi to recover. It has been suggested that Alice was suffering from ovarian cancer. However, Patsy Bowles (who was married to Alice's second doctor) recalls that although her womb was removed, no cancer was discovered. On 15 September 1941, Alice was well enough to attend an all-girls lunch with Patsy and Noreen Pearson, along with another friend, Rosie Delap.

Years later, Patsy would recall Alice's mysterious words that day: 'If you have an obsession or a very deep wish,' Alice informed her friends, 'or even two wishes which you dream about and want – they often happen. The first of my wishes has happened. I wonder if the second one will occur?'

If Alice did shoot Lord Erroll, then presumably her first wish had been to commit the murder. Her second wish would also soon come to pass.

After lunch, Alice asked her driver, Arap Ruta, to take her to the small church of St Paul's in Kiambu, where Joss was buried. At the far side of the graveyard, she found his headstone with that of his wife Mary close behind. This was not the first time that Alice had visited the gravesite:

since Joss's burial, she had made regular trips to Kiambu to put flowers on his resting place.

In her next letter to Dickie, written two days later on 17 September, she described her visit, and how pleased she had been to see new pots of flowers on his grave, which in recent times had been neglected. She also wrote about the difficulties of her recuperation. Although her surgical wound had healed, she remained extremely weak and ill. The matron had told her to expect to feel depressed, but not to let that get her down, advice that Alice wryly brushed aside. 'What these periods of depression will be like, plus the ones I get anyway, I can't imagine . . .' she wrote, adding that she felt 'desolate beyond words' now that Minnie was gone.

As September progressed, Alice's forty-second birthday was looming. In frail health and failing spirits, she must have dreaded its arrival. To make matters worse, her neighbour Pat Fisher was hosting a joint birthday party with Phyllis Filmer. Alice had never much cared for Joss's old flame and, not surprisingly, she decided to back out of the birthday party at the last moment. Flo Crofton was dispatched to Kipipiri with the excuse that Alice was unwell. After Flo's departure, Alice took to her bed and ingested a dose of Nembutal, the same barbiturate she had fed to Minnie.

A few days later, on 27 September 1941, Alice sent Flo off to Olkalau, a small town near to Wanjohi Farm, to do some shopping and collect mail. She told her African staff not to disturb her. This wasn't at all unusual as Alice usually breakfasted in bed and didn't get up until about

11 a.m. Then she went out into her garden and collected armloads of flowers. Back in her bedroom, she decorated her room, placing the flowers on her bed and furniture. Her large bedroom was painted with green oil and water paint mixed together, an effect that was both peaceful and striking, especially with the added decoration of the flowers. Alice then attached the names of close friends to her furniture, including the large Knole settee brought from France (one of her favourite possessions), and two large African drums, which served as side tables near her substantial bed.

She had already written five letters. Two of these were to her children, one was a suicide note and one was addressed to the police. The other was to Dickie and was sent to him in Cairo. She described the beauty of the African morning as she sat writing to him by a pool in her garden, surrounded by the sunshine, colourful flowers and a sense of peace. She told Dickie she loved him and predicted that he would find it very hard to understand her actions. Even so, she said, he should know that she believed she was doing the right thing. Then she revealed that the reason she had found it so hard to say goodbye in Uganda was that she knew it would be their last goodbye. Alice ended the letter with the following words to Dickie: 'I simply can't write again, and there is nothing more to say.'

Alice locked her bedroom door and wrapped a large bandage around her chest. By now, it had begun to rain. She put on her best nightdress and climbed into bed. Next she swallowed 10 grammes of Nembutal, a huge dose. She placed her revolver to her heart. Before she slipped out of consciousness completely, she pulled the trigger. Alerted by the sound of rasping breathing noises coming from Alice's bedroom, one of her African servants forced the door open only to discover a terrible scene. By the time Flo returned from Olkalau, Alice was near death.

Flo drove out to Kipipiri where there was a telephone and called Dr Boyle who was in his surgery in Nairobi. Boyle knew his own car was too small and slow to drive up to the heights of Wanjohi so he borrowed Dr Bowles's powerful Lincoln and raced up to Alice's house in the pouring rain. He arrived to find Alice was dead. At her bedside, Dr Boyle discovered the painting that she had labelled and left for him. She must have known he would come. The oil, possibly painted by the Russian-American surrealist Pavel Fedorovich Tchelitchew, shows three figures done in several shades of blue. On the back Alice had written teasingly to her favourite doctor: 'To the one who is too frolicsome . . .', a final joking gesture of sorts.

Dr Boyle knew he must now carry out his legal duties. A coroner's inquest would be required. He found Alice's five letters which he handed over to the police before lodging a death certificate at the coroner's office.

Alice was buried at the side of the river on Wanjohi Farm, near to the place where her dog Minnie had been laid to rest. Her staff, together with Pat Fisher and Flo Crofton, attended her funeral. In one of her suicide notes, Alice had asked that a cocktail party be held at her grave, but it was not to be. Most of her other friends stayed away, dispersed by war or ill health. In her final years, many friends had fallen away. Alice's grave was left unmarked, as was often the case in this part of the world – the local Kikuyu believed that the white settlers died with their wealth still upon them, and they often dug up graves in search of money and jewellery.

The coroner duly investigated the circumstances surrounding Alice's death and an inquest was held on Thursday 9 October 1941 at Gilgil. At the inquest, the doctor submitted the letters found at Alice's deathbed along with his report: by law, suicide notes have to be submitted to the authorities and the coroner. Dr Boyle gave his evidence, but the hearing was adjourned pending the result of the post-mortem. In December 1941, the hearing was again delayed 'owing to certain witnesses being in Mombasa', namely Alice's housekeepers, Flo Crofton and Noel Case. When the inquest was reconvened on 21 January 1942, the coroner, who had been unable to locate the missing witnesses, stated that he did not wish to prolong the inquiry, so he brought the hearing to a close. In his statement, he asserted, 'Alice de Trafford took her own life on 27th September 1941' and that 'the proximate cause of her death was shock and internal haemorrhage from a gunshot wound. It is clear that the deceased's taking of her own life was intentional, and there is no evidence of mental instability . . .'

There is no doubt that Alice's suicide was intentional. She had planned her death carefully. She had said goodbye to Dickie for the last time. She had tested the Nembutal on Minnie first, ensuring that her dog would not survive her. She had visited Joss's grave to pay her final respects.

She had written letters to her children and amended her will, assigning her furniture and other items to her friends. She had prepared her bedroom and the manner of her death. Above all, she made sure that she would not fail and that this suicide attempt would be final.

Alice's two daughters – now nineteen and seventeen respectively and living in Chicago with Aunt Tattie – learned of their mother's suicide from a newspaper headline announcing her death. They had not seen Alice in two years due to the war. Alice had always lived at such a great distance from them that it must have been easy for Nolwen and Paola simply to imagine their mother going on with her life in Wanjohi, with her animals and her stories. Although Alice's daughters had never visited their mother in Africa, the terms of her will contained a belated invitation. Nolwen and Paola were to inherit Wanjohi Farm and her house on condition that they come to live in Kenya and look after the place for five years, spending eight months each year there. As Nolwen later pointed out, these were impossible terms for two adolescent girls during wartime. In the event that her daughters were unable to live at Wanjohi, Alice's African estate was to go to a fatherless child of eight, the daughter of Noreen Pearson. Noreen's husband had died in the war, and Alice had evidently decided to take pity on this young child who had recently lost her father. Nolwen later recalled that, 'Alas, the child who inherited was taken away to Washington, her mother having remarried in Kenya an American Officer. So, the Wanjohi Farm was sold on the girl's 21st birthday. My mother's wishes all to the wind.'

In the coming years, Wanjohi Farm was given over to the authorities, becoming the Satima Primary School for Girls.

After their mother's death and the end of the Second World War, Nolwen and Paola left Chicago and returned to France. Nolwen had taken a course in Maryland with the Women's Army Corps and she joined the Free French Army in 1944 as a diplomatic liaison officer. On 23 September 1948 she married Lionel Armand-Delille and together they had two children, Frédéric and Angélique. In the 1950s, Nolwen embarked on a career in fashion, becoming the president of the Incorporated Society of London Fashion designers, which would have no doubt delighted her stylish mother. After divorcing Armand-Delille, Nolwen married twice – first to Edward Rice and then to the art historian Kenneth Clark. She died at the family château, Parfondeval, in 1989. Paola married twice, first to Walter Haydon and next to John Ciechanowski. She had two sons, Guillaume and Alexander. She died in 2007. Both Alice's daughters remained loyal to their mother's memory throughout their lives. Their apparent lack of resentment must be some indication of their good feeling towards her, despite their long separations from her, and of Aunt Tattie's excellent care of them in Alice's absence. Sadly, Nolwen and Paola never did visit Alice's beloved Wanjohi Valley. The only de Janzé member of the family to have seen Alice's farm to this day is Nolwen's daughter, Angélique Fiedler. On a visit there in 2004, Angélique was so taken by the breathtaking beauty of the place that she set about negotiating with the authorities to have the school renamed the 'De Janzé Primary School'. Angélique is now seeking to endow the school to enhance its prosperity and future, in memory of her grandmother.

Dickie Pembroke received word of Alice's death while posted in Egypt. He was devastated by the news. Undoubtedly he had had it in mind that if he survived the war he would return to Kenya and marry Alice, but this was not to be. Throughout the rest of the war, he carried Alice's letters in the left-hand breast pocket of his battle uniform, along with his AB64 (the document denoting his number and rank). In March 1943, Dickie's battalion entered Medenine in Tunisia where the British won a decisive victory against Field Marshal Rommel, one of the finest German generals of the Second World War. Towards the end of armed conflict, Dickie returned to England, later going on to the War Office where he was granted the status of full Colonel in 1951. His medals and awards included the 39/45 Star; the Africa Star; the Defence Medal and an OBE. After marrying a Mrs Dermot Pakenham in 1950, he left the army and embarked on a career in the bill-broking business. He died in Upham, Hampshire, in 1967 at the age of sixty-three. Brigadier H.R. Norman, formerly of the Coldstream Guards, wrote an obituary for Dickie Pembroke in which he described him as 'the most modest of men', someone who had the gift of creating friendships with all sorts of people, old and young.

Lizzie Lezard also outlived Alice. On arriving in Cairo in late 1941, he began boarding with several other bachelor officers, one of whom was the future diplomat and translator of Turgenev, Charles Johnston. Later, Johnston would immortalize Lizzie and their time in Cairo in his book, *Mo and Other Originals* (1971), where Lizzie appears as Monty Malan, a bon vivant who spends all day lounging in bed, being brought trays of chicken sandwiches, and whisky and sodas by his servant, Mo. In 1943, Lezard, who had recently completed his parachute training, was dropped near Monte Carlo, where he fell heavily and broke his back, henceforth becoming known as 'The man who broke his back at Monte Carlo.' Lizzie was rescued and hidden by the local Free French until the arrival of the Americans, at which point he returned to London on a steamer and was welcomed home a hero. He was next heard of living in a butler's room at the top of the Ritz Hotel, leading an extremely active social life, before taking a flat in Eaton Square. In 1958, he went into hospital for a minor operation where he died very suddenly from shock on 21 August at the age of fifty-six. Charles Johnston wrote in Lizzie's obituary: 'It was as if a vital source of light and warmth in our lives had been violently put out.'

Raymund de Trafford was released from Parkhurst Prison in 1941, having survived the air raids on the Isle of Wight during the Battle of Britain. He soon reported to his former regiment of the Coldstream Guards, hoping to rejoin, but he was turned down and his application for a commission with the Rifle Brigade was also refused. Eventually, in 1942, after having missed three years of service during the war, he was permitted to join the Pioneer Corps as a lieutenant. Raymund was posted to

Morocco where he worked conscientiously as the commander of a platoon of engineer workers, digging drains and building bridges. He remained in North Africa until 1945 when he was honourably discharged, having attained the rank of Captain. After the war, Raymund was awarded two medals. He also resumed his previous lifestyle, hunting, gambling, womanizing and visiting friends, including the writers Evelyn Waugh, Maurice Baring and Robert Graves. (When Baring died at the end of 1945, Raymund was named as his literary executor.) In 1950, he met Eve Drummond, whom he married the following year. The day after the couple's wedding announcement appeared in *The Times* on 21 May 1951, congratulatory telegrams arrived along with demands from six separate bookmakers. Raymund and Eve went to live in Ireland, but the marriage did not last long. Raymund used his asthma and worsening emphysema as an excuse to visit Robert Graves in Majorca, leaving Eve behind. Robert, who was very fond of Raymund, took him in almost permanently at his house in Deià on the Spanish island. In May of 1971, Raymund was visiting London when he suffered a fatal stroke. He was seventy-one years old. He is buried in the Catholic cemetery in Monks Kirby, Warwickshire. On his headstone is written 'Liber Scriptus Proferetur in quo totum continetur', a verse from the Catholic requiem mass which translates as 'The written book will be brought in which all is contained'. Dermot de Trafford, the sixth baronet and Raymund's nephew, has said of his uncle, 'He behaved badly, but he knew how to behave well.' Raymund left an estate worth £212.02.

Jock Delves Broughton sailed to Ceylon and India after the end of his trial for Joss's murder, staying until later that year. Diana was at his side. On their return to Kenya in 1942, they rented Joss's former home, Oserian, for a time: Diana said that it brought her solace to be surrounded by a place Joss had loved. The Delves Broughton marriage lasted until the end of the year, at which point Jock returned to England. Despite his acquittal, he had continued to be dogged by speculation and ignominy. Soon after his return he took a fatal overdose of morphine at the Adelphi Hotel in Liverpool, dying on 5 December 1942, a little more than a year after Alice's suicide.

Diana Delves Broughton stayed on in Nairobi, where she was more or less completely ostracized by the settlers, many of whom had come to blame her for Joss's death. Undeterred, she proceeded to marry one of the wealthiest men in Kenya, Gilbert Colvile, in 1943 (a month after Jock's suicide). Gilbert bought Oserian for Diana, and the couple went on living there until their divorce in 1955. At this point, Diana had already met and fallen in love with Thomas Pitt Hamilton Cholmondeley, fourth Baron Delamere, the son of the famed highland settler and third Baron Delamere, Alice's old friend D. Tom and Diana married in 1955. Despite Gilbert's divorce from Diana, he still left her his entire estate on his death, making her a very wealthy woman. When Tom died of heart failure in 1979, Diana was sixty-six years old, at which point she took an apartment behind the Ritz Hotel in London, staying there for a few months each year. The rest of her time was spent in Kenya, attending Nairobi races or fishing at Kilifi where she acquired a home called Villa Buzza. She died of a stroke on 7 September 1987 at the age of seventy-four. Her body was flown back to Nairobi and buried at Ndabibi between the graves of Gilbert and Tom. The inscription on her grave reads 'Surrounded by all I love'.

Alice's great friend Paula Long, née Gellibrand, also maintained her ties to Kenya. She and her husband, Boy, lived on their ranch, Nderit, at Elmenteita, where they farmed cattle, close to the lake whose shores are fringed with pink flamingos. It was an appropriately dramatic setting for this flamboyant couple: in the hills above the house is a place called Eburu, where hot steam emerges from splits in the rocks. After Boy's death in 1955, Paula left Elmenteita and returned home to England, where she lived at Henley-on-Thames, in Oxfordshire. Late in her life, she began to suffer with dementia and she died at the Priory, a private psychiatric hospital in London, in 1986 at the age of eighty-eight. She is buried in the small Oxfordshire village of Nettlebed.

After Alice's death, Idina went on living and farming at Clouds. Until the end of the war, Phyllis Filmer lived there too and Idina was evidently glad of the company – her husband of the time was the fighter pilot Vincent Soltau, and he was almost permanently away. What's more, during the course of the war she suffered the losses of her first and third husbands (Euan and Joss) and her two sons from her first marriage, David and Gee. By 1945, she had a nervous breakdown, brought on by grief. Her doctors advised her to seek relief from living continuously at so many thousands of feet above sea level and she left

Clouds for a time for her bungalow at Mtapwa Creek. Mtapwa is about ten miles north of Mombasa, on the banks of a long sea inlet. Here she planted a lushly beautiful tropical garden. After divorcing her fighter-pilot husband, Idina reverted to her maiden name, Sackville, promising never to marry again. In 1950, she met James Bird, known as Jimmy Bird or James the Sixth in honour of his position as the sixth 'husband' in Idina's life, although the pair were never officially married. He became her constant companion, despite the fact that he was something of a drunk and known to prefer men to women. 'I've worn out five husbands and the sixth is on his last legs,' Idina was often heard to say. In 1952 she had a hysterectomy, due to having been diagnosed with uterine cancer. Despite the operation, her cancer returned. After refusing to go back to the hospital Idina fell into a coma, dying at Mtapwa in 1955 at the age of sixty-two. Idina had once told her neighbour there, the essayist Edward Rodwell, that she knew the identity of Joss's killer and that she would tell Rodwell the name before she died. She never did.

And so one by one, the protagonists in the Erroll saga passed away, taking what they knew of the mystery of his murder to their graves.

Epilogue

The Missing Letter and the Great Beyond

In 1998 I had begun to cast around for information on Alice de Janzé, in the hope that I might write her biography. I was keen to track down Alice's former housekeeper Noel Case, who had helped run Wanjohi Farm after Alice's return to Kenya in 1933. I felt she must have great insight into Alice's life there, and that she could well prove essential to my research. By now, I had begun to suspect that Alice was responsible for the Erroll murder, but I needed to know more about her psychology and movements in order to be sure. I was already in contact with the writer Errol Trzebinski, who was at that time hard at work on her biography of Joss Erroll, *The Life and Death of Lord Erroll*. It was Trzebinski who put me in contact with a woman named Alice Boyle. Alice Boyle was the daughter of Dr

William Boyle, the physician who had raced to Alice de Janzé's bedside after her fatal suicide attempt. Trzebinski told me that Alice Boyle was in close contact with Noel Case and could perhaps put us in touch. Even so, Trzebinski warned me, I should not hold out too much hope of an interview. Apparently Noel was refusing to talk to anyone (even her own nephew) about her days with Alice de Janzé at Wanjohi Farm.

I obtained a telephone number for Alice Boyle (now Mrs Alice Fleet) and invited her to lunch at my house in London. I was met by an attractive woman in her fifties, with dark hair and a lively and capable air. As we began to speak – firstly about Noel Case and then about Dr Boyle – I realized that this Alice was shy and even a little defensive, especially when it came to talking about her father. Over lunch, she revealed to me that she was still in possession of the blue oil painting that Alice de Janzé had left to Dr Boyle at the time of her death. Later I learned that Alice Boyle was certain her father must have had some kind of an affair with Alice – who was his favourite patient – possibly before his marriage in 1936. It was only after our fifth or sixth meeting that Alice Boyle revealed information to me that cast the story I was researching in a startling new light.

'You know, my mother told me all about Alice's confession letter,' said Alice Boyle, obliquely, one day over lunch in London. She seemed to assume that I already knew about the existence of such a letter. I began to question her further, trying to suppress the true degree of my curiosity, in case it should disturb the telling of her story.

When Alice Boyle was eleven, she informed me, her mother, Ethnie, had told her that Alice de Janzé had left a confession letter addressed to the police before her death along with her suicide notes. Dr Boyle had shown his wife these letters before submitting them to the coroner's office. Ethnie Boyle had seen the confession letter with her own eyes and had told her daughter all about it. Alice Boyle continues to stand by the clear memory of her mother's words: Alice de Janzé confessed to shooting Lord Erroll in a letter. When I went back to my copy of James Fox's *White Mischief*, I even found a reference to this vital piece of evidence: 'She [Alice] left several notes. One was to the Police – its contents were never released,' wrote Fox.

So, if a confession did indeed exist, whatever happened to this missing letter? It is true that its contents were never released and the Kenya Police deny that there is any record of the note existing in their archives. Although Dr Boyle definitely submitted the note at the original coroner's inquest, the letter has since disappeared. Certainly, its contents were not disclosed at the inquest. What happened to the missing note? It is possible that the confession letter never reached the Kenya Police in the first place. It is my guess that the coroner was so shocked at the implications of Alice's confession that he directed the note to the personal attention of the Attorney General, Sir Walter Harrigan K.C. Harrigan was the Attorney General from 1933 to 1944, and prosecutor for the Crown at the trial of Jock Delves Broughton. Harrigan would doubtless have been extremely alarmed by the letter's contents. He would have weighed the implications carefully, bearing in mind that the Crown's case against Jock had failed and that numerous suggestions had been made both during and after the trial (some in writing) that the murder had been carried out by a discarded mistress. Rather than open up a can of worms, Harrigan could easily have decided to suppress the confession, justifying his decision on the grounds that he was stabilizing speculation about a controversial murder. To protect himself, he could have sent the confession out of the country in the diplomatic bag to London for safe keeping with a memorandum explaining his actions.

I soon discovered that I was not the only one to have learned of Alice's confession letter. Alice Boyle had recently revealed her story to Gordon Fergusson. At the time, Fergusson was in the process of writing a history of the Tarporley Hunt Club, entitled *The Green Collars*. Tarpoley, founded in 1762, is the oldest hunt club in England and once counted Jock Delves Broughton amongst its members (in fact he was the only member of the club ever to have been tried for murder). As a result, Fergusson was familiar with the Erroll case. When he met Alice Boyle socially in 1993, she told him the story about her mother and the confession letter. Fergusson felt he had information that would finally and definitively clear Jock's name and so he published his findings in *The Green Collars* in 1993. When Fergusson's book came out, the Peterborough column in the *Daily Telegraph* picked up the story, publishing it under the headline: 'Tarporley Man Puts the Finger on Alice'. This led to a little flurry of correspondence in the paper. 'No!'

replied J.N.P. Watson, a cousin of Dickie Pembroke. 'Alice was deeply in love with Pembroke and was in bed with him at the time of the murder.' Watson went on to argue that, apart from her alibi, it would have been 'quite out of character for Alice to have hidden in the back of Erroll's car in order to shoot him, or to have killed him up on the road'. But there is no doubt that Alice had the 'motive, means, and mentality for murder', wrote Fergusson, adding that her alibi was 'one that any woman could have arranged'.

During my investigations, I came across other clues further implicating Alice. In *White Mischief* James Fox wrote that after the trip to the morgue on the morning of Joss's death, Lizzie Lezard always suspected Alice as 'the murder fitted in with her morbid preoccupations'. Fox even went so far as to suggest that Alice might have confessed the murder to Lizzie. 'In later years Lezard was untypically evasive on the subject,' Fox wrote. Then there was Betty Leslie-Melville's memoir about her time in Kenya, *The Giraffe Lady*, published in 1997. Betty's mother-in-law, Mary Leslie-Melville, was once Alice's neighbour in the Wanjohi Valley. In *The Giraffe Lady*, Betty recounts the time she asked her mother-in-law who she thought had shot Lord Erroll. Mary replied without hesitation: 'My Dear, I do not *think* who may have killed him, I *know*.'

It was Mary's firm belief that Alice had shot Lord Erroll. Betty wrote:

> Alice knew that Erroll was due to have dinner at Muthaiga Club on the fateful night. Mary also knew that Alice was aware of the road Lord Erroll would

take to drive back from Karen afterwards. So Mary's theory was that Alice had waited at the cross road where the murder took place. The sight of her on the road would have stopped him. She would then have walked up to the car and shot him in the head. Afterwards she drove home.

And Mary claimed to have actual proof. A few years after Erroll's killing, Mary's headman was fishing rocks out of the little river that separated Mary's property from Alice's Wanjohi Farm in order to repair the road. Here he found a gun buried under one of the rocks. He took it to Mary. According to Mary, this gun was the exact make and calibre of the missing revolver used to shoot Joss. Mary concluded that Alice must have thrown it there after returning from shooting Joss on the night of his murder.

'What did you do then?' Betty asked, astonished.

'Nothing,' Mary replied. 'Erroll was dead. Alice was dead. What good would it have done to tell anyone?'

Mary led Betty to the hall cupboard in her Nairobi house, unlocked the door and showed her the revolver in question, just hanging there. By the time I read these words, Mary Leslie-Melville had long since died and the whereabouts of this supposed murder weapon was unknown. But its existence, as described by Betty, added further fuel to my theories.

With the clues provided by Alice Boyle and by Mary's story, I became convinced that it was Alice who had murdered Joss. Still, several questions remained in my mind.

Why would Alice have killed the man she loved? Wouldn't it have made more sense to kill her rival, Diana?

In 1998, I finally succeeded in calling on Alice's former housekeeper, Noel Case (then Mrs Eaton-Evans). Noel was white-haired by this time, in her eighties and living with her husband, Tom, at Diss in Norfolk. I had already sent various questions to her through Alice Boyle, and contrary to all my expectations, I was received hospitably by both Noel and her husband. We talked at length that day, exchanged letters, and when I called on her again a year later she offered me photographs of her time at Wanjohi Farm along with various letters pertaining to Alice's life there.

During my first interview with Noel I asked her if she thought it was Alice who had murdered Lord Erroll.

'It could have been Alice who shot Erroll,' Noel replied thoughtfully. 'Why she would want to do this is a mystery because she was madly in love with Erroll and surely it would have been more motivating to kill Diana and not Erroll. But, on the other hand, with her belief in the occult and her firm belief about the other side, it is possible that she thought that if she could send Erroll to heaven, where he might just have qualified for entry, she could join him there.'

In the French courts, when Alice was being tried for attempted murder, she had told the judge that she had shot Raymund because she wanted to join him in the 'Great Beyond'. If she did kill Joss then this desperate act must be seen in the same context. Alice had always believed in an afterlife. She had been brought up in the

Presbyterian faith. She took as gospel that when you die, your soul goes to be with God, where it enjoys God's glory and awaits the final judgement. The Presbyterian Scots Confession states: 'The chosen departed are in peace, and rest from their labours . . . they are delivered from all fear and torment . . .' Alice took for granted that after her death, she would be reunited with her loved ones, and that all her pain would be washed away. 'Now you are mine for ever,' she told Joss in the mortuary.

By killing herself, Alice completed what she had begun on the night of Joss's murder. Hence her strange words to Patsy Bowles just days before her death: 'If you have an obsession or a very deep wish, or even two wishes which you dream about and want – they often happen. The first of my wishes has happened. I wonder if the second one will occur?'

Her first wish was to kill Joss. Her second wish was to kill herself so that she could be reunited with him in the Great Beyond. Her own suicide had always been part of the plan, and yet she held off, unable to finish the job. Perhaps it was Dickie's devotion that kept Alice alive for the subsequent eight months after the murder. It was only after Dickie left for Cairo that she could no longer put off the inevitable.

As Alice's fatal dose of Nembutal took hold just a few months later, what were her final thoughts? Had she forgiven Joss for forsaking her? Had she forgiven herself for his murder? Did she think only of Joss as she approached her own death or also of her long-lost mother and estranged father, both waiting for her, she believed, on the other side? She had even ensured that her beloved dog Minnie would be there too. The revolver lay on her heavily bandaged bosom, its muzzle pointed at her heart. One squeeze of the trigger and she would finally be free. This time, she did not falter.

Author's Note

There was a set of compelling reasons and coincidences for writing about Alice de Janzé.

One of my first encounters with Alice's story was through her erstwhile husband, Raymund de Trafford. I was a schoolboy, living with my family at Yarmouth, on the Isle of Wight. It was wartime, shortly after the Battle of Britain, the famous aerial conflict between British and German air forces that took place in the skies above the south-east of England during 1940. One of the UK's largest radar stations was located on the Isle of Wight at Ventnor, and as a result, many thousands of tons of bombs had been dropped on the surrounding area during the conflict. On one occasion, a stick of bombs narrowly missed our home, destroying the house next door. Later,

I witnessed a German ME109 shot down on the farm opposite and I bicycled to the scene. The German pilot survived and was taken to nearby Parkhurst Prison.

Parkhurst was where Raymund was incarcerated throughout 1940. When he was released the following August – his sentence had been reduced due to good behaviour – he made immediately for our home at Yarmouth, where he knew he would be welcomed by my mother, his friend Margaret Spicer. It was six in the morning when he arrived at our door. My father had sent a car for him. The cook and maid were up early and gave him a very good breakfast of toast, eggs and bacon and coffee. I was at home from school for the summer. I remember Raymund's grey-looking, badly shaven face. He talked and talked. He spoke as if delivering a monologue: rattling off the names of numerous people from his Kenya days; describing his prison life; complaining about being left out of the war. He also spoke about Alice. This was a name that was familiar to me because it often came up in family conversation – my mother and Alice being friends from their Kenya days. Although Raymund was divorced from Alice by the time of his release, he was evidently still in contact with her because I distinctly remember him describing Alice's fury at the entry of Diana Delves Broughton into the tight-knit Happy Valley circle.

Before his departure at around eleven that morning my mother asked him, 'What are you going to do now?'

'I have written 4,500 words about my life in Parkhurst Prison,' Raymund replied. 'And I shall offer it to the *Sunday Dispatch*. But my family will pay me more not to publish. So that will set me up for a bit.' Even as a young boy, I could detect Raymund's aggression and toughness. He did not take much notice of me and concentrated such charm as he had on my mother. I do not think he liked my father.

As can be imagined, the appearance of an ex-convict at the breakfast table was extremely exciting for a young boy and I can still picture Raymund puffing out his cheeks before exhaling his cigarette smoke. After breakfast, he announced he was off to nearby Cowes where he would stay with his old friend Poppy Baring, the banking heiress, at her family's country seat. It was Cowes Week on the Isle of Wight and the annual yachting regatta was taking place despite the war. Raymund would doubtless have enjoyed the magnificent vantage of the Barings' Nubia House, with its views on to the silvery waters of the Solent, where, even in wartime, hundreds of boats had gathered for the regatta. Many years later, while researching this book, I met Raymund's nephew, Sir Dermot de Trafford, who told me that after Cowes Week, Raymund had travelled to London, returning to his club, White's, to see if he could locate any familiar faces. Raymund's contemporaries, however, had all been called up for the war and the club's venerable elder members refused to acknowledge this recently released prisoner. The story goes that Raymund went up to an elderly and extremely bald senior member of White's, who was sunk deep in his chair with his *Times* held high in the air. When the man refused to as much as look at him, Raymund smacked him on his bald pate, and declared, 'Hoity toity!' The room broke up with laughter.

Although I remained fascinated with Raymund, it was his appearance at my family's home that marked the point when my mind became concentrated on Alice's existence. Later, as a young man, I had my own first-hand glimpse into her world. It was 1950, and I was stationed in Kenya for two years to work for the British oil company Shell. The Erroll murder was almost a decade old but it was still a subject of fascination for those I encountered and I became intrigued. One day, I decided to motor up to Kipipiri on the peak beside Wanjohi Valley to see if I could find Idina Sackville at Clouds. I had already heard tales of Idina's infamous house parties in those early days of Happy Valley so I approached with a degree of curiosity mixed with trepidation. When Idina opened the door I introduced myself. She was then in her late fifties and had a strong upper-class English accent and an impressively girlish figure. She greeted me with great enthusiasm and questioned me closely about my mother and my father, whom she remembered. She also wanted to know whether I was related to the Spicers of Spye Park in Wiltshire into whose family her sister, Avice, had married (in fact, we are distantly connected). When Idina invited me to stay the night I accepted.

That evening, the moon was serving as an overhead lamp; a cool breeze swept down from the Aberdare Mountains behind the house and dinner was served at 11 p.m., as was customary in the carefree world that Idina had created for herself. After dinner was over, my hostess then turned to me and said, 'After I go to my bedroom, I shall wait ten minutes and then switch off the generator.

So that is all the time you have in which to undress and go to bed.' In my room I found a new pair of silk pyjamas laid out on my pillow, together with a bottle of brandy, a glass and a lighted candle on the bedside table. I lay in bed and watched for the electric lights to dim. Ten minutes later, as I was dozing off, I heard the door handle turn. Who could want to enter my room at such a time? Was it to be Idina herself? I pulled up the sheet to my neck and waited in dread anticipation. It was not Idina but Jimmy Bird, Idina's live-in companion. That evening he was obviously the worse the wear for drink and had possibly mistaken my bedroom for his own; I told him to leave, which he did quickly, and I locked my door. That night, I learned that when in Happy Valley, a locked door is a valuable defence against late-night intruders.

Later that month, I visited Thomson's Falls and went to the hotel there for lunch. (Thomson's Falls is not far from the road entrance to the Wanjohi Valley.) While waiting in the lobby, I was approached by a man of medium stature whose faded fair hair, almost orange in colour, was brushed to both sides over his ears in elegant quiffs. He introduced himself as Fabian Wallace and asked if I happened to be Paul Spicer. He said he had heard from Idina that I was in the area and asked if I were free for lunch. I gladly accepted and followed him in my car to his nearby house, which was set in a well-kept garden. There was a river at the end of the lawn, swept by weeping willow trees and bamboo. I sat on his verandah sofa, which was covered in newly laundered white linen, eagerly awaiting the luncheon. I was very hungry. I remember the menu because the first course was a hot consommé with a superb flavour. A servant wearing white gloves and dressed in a long white kanzu or robe, topped by a tall red hat called a 'tarboosh', served us. The second course was blue trout cooked in the French style, the fish having been caught from the stream below. After lunch, we sat back on the verandah sofa and drank coffee. Fabian produced a thick white carton of cigarettes with a 'By Appointment' insignia on the lid: inside were one hundred perfect hand-rolled cigarettes imported from St James's Street, London, each unusually fat cigarette containing Fabian's favourite blend of Virginia tobacco. I was young, earning very little money and readily impressed by the delightful comfort of the surroundings in which I found myself, if a little concerned that Fabian might make advances towards me (in fact, he did not). Unfortunately, we did not speak of Alice during that memorable lunch, although Fabian had been Alice's neighbour and had known her well in the years immediately preceding her death.

The world that Fabian and Idina inhabited would change irrevocably in the course of the 1950s. Land disputes had already become a source of increasingly bitter conflict among the local Kikuyu and white settler farmers. While a small number of Kikuyu landowners consolidated their farms and ingratiated themselves with the colonial administration, by the early 1950s almost half of all Kikuyus had no land claims at all. Such glaring disparity led to division among the Kikuyu and extreme resentment towards the settlers. Oath-swearing ceremonies took place throughout Kenya: those participating believed that if they broke with their promises, they would be killed by supernatural forces. In the beginning, tribe members swore to acts of civil disobedience but as time went on their rituals demanded that they fight and kill the Europeans. In 1952, the Mau Mau rebellion began in earnest and the British administration declared a State of Emergency. Settlers took to carrying loaded revolvers wherever they went and placing them on the table at dinner, the time of day when many attacks took place. Spurred on by reports of extreme violence and brutality, the British government sent troops to assist the colonists, although by the end of the conflict, the number of native Kenyans killed far exceeded that of the European casualties. When the core Mau Mau leader, Dedan Kimathi, was captured in 1956, it signalled the end of the rebellion and victory for the British. The brief era of Happy Valley, however, was most definitively over. What's more, the days of British rule in Kenya were also drawing to a close. The first elections for Africans to the Legislative Council took place in 1957 and when the Kenya African National Union led by Jomo Kenyatta formed a government in 1963, the stage was set for Kenyan independence.

During the Mau Mau period, which coincided with my first visit to Kenya, I also got to know Derek Erskine and his family. Derek was a neighbour of Jock and Diana Delves Broughton in Nairobi. I met Derek through his son, Francis, who befriended me on my arrival in Kenya and who was later awarded a Military Cross for his bravery while fighting the Mau Mau rebellion in the forests of the Aberdares. Derek was a businessman and his grocery firm, Erskine & Duncan Ltd, handled several exclusive accounts from the UK including Marmite and Bronco toilet paper. I remember the daily teatime assembly at Derek's house, Riverside, where toast and Marmite were the preferred fare. After tea, Derek and I would ride out across the Kikuyu Reserve on the same route that Jock Broughton had once taken on his hacking sessions. I had purchased an Arab polo pony called Rashid el Haroun from Juanita Carberry (in 1999 Juanita would publish a memoir of her childhood in Wanjohi Valley entitled *Child of Happy Valley*). During these evening rides, Derek talked much about life and business, explaining the difference between capital and income, how to embark on investment, and the workings of the gilt markets in London. Much to my fascination, he also spoke at length about Alice de Janzé. He remembered Alice's hatred for Diana Broughton. He recalled that despite Diana's infidelity, Jock and Joss were the best of friends: the two men would josh each other about 'whose turn it was to dry Diana today' when she went swimming nude in the pool at the Broughtons' house in Marula Lane. It was Derek's opinion that Jock had been a very good sport when it came to Diana's affair with Joss.

A man of strong opinions in general, Derek was determined to promote a multiracial society in Kenya, which sadly made him extremely unpopular amongst the white settlers at the time. When I arrived in Kenya, Derek had recently befriended Jomo Kenyatta, a Kikuyu-born schoolmaster who would be arrested by the British authorities and unfairly charged with 'managing and being a member' of the Mau Mau Society. Derek fought passionately for Kenyatta's release and, in 1960, he travelled to London where he joined the African delegates at Lancaster House to demand Kenyatta's freedom and Kenya's independence from the British. On Derek's return to Nairobi he was met by a group of angry settlers at the airport and one threw thirty pieces of silver at him for his 'treason'. Such opposition only strengthened Derek's certainty about the rightness of the cause of African independence. In 1963, when Kenyatta became Kenya's first president, the story goes he wanted to pass two laws: the first law was to stop all beating in schools; the second was to 'Make Derek Erskine a Lord!' Derek was later knighted by the Queen at Kenyatta's request. I make these digressions to give a sense of Derek's integrity and the likelihood that his recollections and opinions of Alice, Joss, Jock and Diana were especially reliable.

It was through Derek Erskine's daughter Petal – a Royal Academy of Dramatic Arts-trained actress – that I met Danièle Waterpark, wife of Lord Waterpark, who lived at Equator Farm in Subukia, Kenya. (I once went to stay there and acted as bodyguard to Lord Waterpark's mother Countess Enid Kenmare during a Mau Mau skirmish in the district.) Many years later, in 1990, it was Danièle, a Parisienne, who became a great provider of contacts in Paris as I undertook research into Alice's life. Danièle introduced me to Alice's grandson, Frédéric Armand-Delille, who is the owner of Parfondeval, the Normandy château where Alice spent much of her early married life. By coincidence, Petal had her own link to the Erroll case.

She was married to Lee Harrigan, son of Walter Harrigan, the former Attorney General of Kenya, prosecutor of Jock Delves Broughton for the murder of Lord Erroll, and possibly the man who had suppressed Alice's confession note.

Later, in 1970, with Kenyatta still presiding, I would find myself living in Kenya for a second time. I had been asked to travel to Kenya to become Managing Director for an international group's holding in East Africa. On this trip I was accompanied by my wife, June, and our two children. The house provided for me by the company was in Marula Lane. It was the same house that Jock Delves Broughton had secured after his new marriage to Diana in 1940 and where they were living at the time of Joss's murder. My wife and I immediately dubbed the place 'Murder House'. A Swiss couple devoted to chamber music had originally built the house. The black cotton soil underlying the cement foundation was unstable and therefore the whole structure was given to slippage, causing cracks at one end that had to be continually patched up. Much of the decor had been influenced by Diana whose bedroom had an en suite bathroom done up with the pink tiles that had last been fashionable in the 1930s. My wife and I called it the 'Brighton bathroom', as it looked to us like the kind of thing you might see at the famously salubrious Brighton Metropole Hotel in England. (The Metropole was where errant husbands would go to stay with a prostitute, thereby giving 'evidence' of adultery for divorce proceedings.) Jock's bedroom was next door to Diana's – it has been said that they never slept in the same room during their brief marriage. This room also had its own peculiar bathroom: the bath was surrounded on three sides by mirrors and there was also one on the ceiling above the bath. The reasons for such self-imposed voyeurism must be left to the imagination. Downstairs were three main rooms and a cloakroom near the entrance. The sitting room was long and dominated at one end by a fireplace. It was here that Joss and Diana had had their last conversation before he was shot. Across the hall were two front rooms, a dining room and an extra sitting room. One dining-room window looked out over the small round pool where Diana used to go skinny-dipping and which we filled with sand to provide a play pit for the children. At the back of the house were servants' quarters and a deep well, which provided fresh water for the house and was driven by a compression pump or ram; as well as the stables, one of whose loose boxes was once used to accommodate Pantaloon, a piebald polo pony. The stairs in the house did indeed creak – as the police investigation had revealed – but only halfway down.

When I first took up residence at Murder House, almost thirty years had passed since Alice's and Joss's deaths, but there were aspects of life in Nairobi that both would have found familiar. The Muthaiga Club was still a centre of social life for expatriates. Polo clubs were in full swing (I played in Nairobi, Gilgil and Nanyuki). Race days in Nairobi were still very popular occasions. And people still spoke about the Erroll case. It was during this trip that I first met Dickie Pembroke, who was Alice's last lover. I had heard much about him from my colleague, Colin Mackenzie, a professional cattleman from Rhodesia who was a director of the company I worked for at that time. One day in 1971, Colin came to visit me at Marula Lane, bringing Dickie with him. Dickie had returned to Kenya to retrace all the places he had lived with Alice and to remember their times there. The meeting was brief. Dickie gazed about him in a nostalgic sort of way and wandered around the garden, musing about the time some thirty years before when he had spent every day for five months with Alice before rejoining his regiment in North Africa to fight the Afrika Korps all the way back to Tunisia during the Second World War.

There is one more character in Alice's story to whom I am also closely connected: Geoffrey Buxton, Alice's Wanjohi neighbour and the man who had introduced Alice and Raymund in 1926. My mother got to know Geoffrey very well in 1928, which was how I became his godson. I still possess a King Charles II silver tankard he gave me. Engraved on its base are these words: 'For Paul Spicer from his Godfather G. Buxton.' Sadly, I never met Geoffrey.

All these coincidences and connections led me to the creation of this book. After I retired from business in 1994, I began to follow Alice's path around the world. I visited her house and farm in Kenya and her grave there. I met Dave Allen, a local bush pilot, and Senior Chief William Kinuthia, who helped me to identify her burial place. (The spot lies somewhere beside the banks of the Wanjohi River, close to a deep pool and near to where she had buried her dog Minnie in the iris beds.) I discovered Alice's Nairobi cottage, now a massage spa, and her 'golden' beach house at Tiwi on Kenya's south coast. I lunched with her grandson at Château de Parfondeval in Normandy. I trailed her story to Chicago, and to London and Paris as well. Over a period of ten years I gained first-hand impressions of Alice from those who knew her. In my portrait of her I have relied heavily on the reminiscences of her housekeeper for many years, Noel Eaton-Evans (née Case, now deceased). Other vital evidence came from Alice's close friend Patsy Chilton (formerly Bowles), who survives. I was fortunate to have in my possession the written recollections of my mother. I also interviewed Alice's then surviving daughter, Paola, as well as her half-sister Pat Silverthorne and her cousin Harry Hartshorne. I was lucky enough to speak to her grandchildren, Frédéric Armand-Delille, Guillaume de Rougemont, and Angélique Fiedler. Other vital insights came from Alice Boyle. Her revelation about Alice's confession letter assured me that I had a story to tell. Vi Case, Errol Trzebinski, Juanita Carberry, and Lee Harrigan also contributed enormously. My thanks go to all these people for helping me make this portrait of Alice as detailed and as conclusive as possible.

Cast of Characters

William (Bill) Allen
Married Paula Gellibrand in 1930 after her divorce from Marquis de Casa Maury. Eventually became head of British Secret Service in Ankara.

Lolita Armour
Daughter of J. Ogden Armour and Alice's second cousin. She introduced Alice to Chicago socially and was the matron of honour at her wedding to Frédéric de Janzé on 21 September 1921.

Poppy Baring
Daughter of Sir Godfrey Baring of Nubia House, Cowes, Isle of Wight. She became a mistress of the Duke of Kent

for several years. Raymund de Trafford knew her well – he went to stay with her soon after his release from prison.

Mr Barrat

Alice's lawyer in Kenya, he was a principal of the firm Shapley, Schwartze and Barrat. He processed the acquisition of Wanjohi Farm from Sir John Ramsden, who had agreed to sell to the de Janzés.

Karen Blixen

Author of *Out of Africa*. Born Karen Dinesen, she married Baron Blor Blixen. She became Denys Finch Hatton's closest friend and lover in Africa. Her original house in Karen, Kenya, has been restored and opened to the public as the Karen Blixen Museum.

Patsy Bowles

Married to Dr Roger Bowles, Alice's physician. She befriended Alice in 1938.

Roger Bowles

Alice's sometime physician, although not her main doctor.

Phyllis Boyd

Alice's sister-in-law. Married to Henri de Janzé, Frédéric's younger brother. She studied at the Slade School of Art in London and a direct descendant of Mrs Jordan and King William IV.

Alice Boyle

Only daughter of Dr William Boyle, Alice's main physician. She was told by her mother, Ethnie, about Alice de Janzé's letter in which Alice confessed to the shooting of Joss Erroll.

William Boyle

Studied at Cambridge and the London Hospital before arriving in Kenya. He married Ethnie Byrne, daughter of Sir Joseph Byrne, Governor of Kenya (1931–1937). He was Alice's favourite doctor and he attended the scene of her death, where he collected her last letters on 27 September 1941.

Diana Delves Broughton

Arrived in Kenya in November 1940, newly married to Sir Henry John ('Jock') Delves Broughton. She had become Jock's mistress at the age of twenty-two, when he was fifty-one. Her maiden name was Caldwell. Diana began her affair with Joss Erroll within a month of her arrival in Kenya, at which point she decided to leave her husband. Diana went on to marry Gilbert Colvile and then Thomas Cholmondeley, the fourth Baron Delamere.

Sir Henry John ('Jock') Delves Broughton (the eleventh baronet of Doddington)

Known as Jock, he arrived in Kenya in 1940 and became the prime suspect in the murder of Lord Erroll. He was married to Diana Delves Broughton, who left him after beginning an affair with Lord Erroll. Jock was tried and acquitted of the murder. He committed suicide in December 1942 at the Aldephi Hotel in Liverpool.

R.W. Burkitt
Famous Irish surgeon renowned for his rough treatment of malarial patients. He diagnosed Frédéric de Janzé when he contracted blackwater fever.

Geoffrey Buxton
Arrived in Kenya in 1910. Born in Norwich and brought up at the Buxton family home, Dunston. He acquired 2,500 acres in the Wanjohi Valley and was the first settler to own land there. In 1926 he introduced Raymund de Trafford to Alice de Janzé at a dinner party at his Tudor-style house.

Sir Joseph Byrne
Governor and Commander-in-Chief of Kenya (1931 to 1937). He readmitted Alice to Kenya and permitted her renewed residence there in 1933. His daughter Ethnie married Dr William Boyle, Alice's doctor.

Marquis de Casa Maury
A Cuban-Castilian Count (full name Pedro José Isidiro Manuel Ricardo Mones Maury). He married Alice's great friend Paula Gellibrand in 1923 in London. Divorced in 1928, he married Freda Dudley Ward, former mistress of Edward, Prince of Wales, in 1937.

Noel Case

At age twenty, she visited the Wanjohi Valley and located Alice's farm, which was for rent. After Alice's departure due to an expulsion order, Noel moved into the farm with her parents. Noel became Alice's housekeeper in 1933 when the latter returned from exile. She later married Tom Eaton-Evans.

Father Casey

The priest in Chicago who initiated Alice into the Catholic faith before her marriage to Frédéric de Janzé on 21 September 1921.

Emery David Chapin

Married Marietta Armour, daughter of Danforth Armour. The two daughters from this marriage were Juliabelle (mother of Alice) and Alice 'Tattie' Chapin, aunt of Alice and guardian of Nolwen and Paola.

Simeon B. Chapin (Uncle Sim)

Successful financier and stockbroker on Wall Street and Alice's uncle. Took the lead in making Alice a ward of court.

Hugh Cholmondeley (the third Baron Delamere)

Lord Delamere, better known as 'D', was a pioneer Kenyan settler who developed cattle ranching and wheat growing in the Rift Valley. Made close friends with Alice de Janzé in 1925.

Flo Crofton

Became Alice's housekeeper after Noel Case retired to get married. She was the daughter of General Northey, a previous Governor of Kenya. She married Dick Crofton, a white hunter living near Gilgil.

Bill and Bubbles Delap

Owners of 'Rayetta' farm in the Wanjohi Valley and neighbours of Alice and Frédéric.

Gaston Doumergue

President of France in 1927. Alice's sentence for the attempted killing of Raymund de Trafford was six months in prison (suspended sentence) but a total pardon was granted by President Doumergue in 1929.

Edward

Sent to France by Alice's Aunt Tattie, he served as butler to the de Janzés at Parfondeval. A skilled photographer and conjuror.

Derek Erskine

Friends with Alice, Joss Erroll, and Jock and Diana Delves Broughton. Successful grocer and entrepreneur in Kenya. Firm advocate of multiracialism. Knighted by Queen Elizabeth II at the request of Jomo Kenyatta (first President of Kenya).

Phyllis Filmer

Occasional mistress of Joss Erroll and wife of Percy

Filmer, the managing director of Shell in East Africa. Lived with Idina at Clouds after Lord Erroll's death in 1941.

Monsieur Fredin
Alice's examiner in the 12th Chamber of the Police Correctional Court on 23 December 1927 during her trial for the attempted killing of Raymund de Trafford.

Monsieur Gandel
One of two attorneys representing Alice at her trial. He pleaded for Alice 'indulgently'.

Paula Gellibrand
Close friends with Alice in Paris. Fashion icon in the 1920s. Photographed by Cecil Beaton and often described as the most beautiful woman in Europe. She married the Marquis de Casa Maury and then William Allen. Later she went to Kenya where she married 'Boy' Long.

Prince George (Duke of Kent)
Fourth son of King George V. He made friends with Alice at the Embassy Club in London in the late 1920s. His black and white bulldog mated with Alice's bulldog 'Jimmy' in Paris.

Robert Graves
Author of numerous books including *Good-bye to All That* and *I Claudius*. Befriended Raymund de Trafford who went to live with him in Deià, Majorca after his second marriage collapsed.

Sir Edward Grigg
Governor of Kenya (1924–1931). Responsible for Alice's expulsion from Kenya in 1928.

Lady Joan Grigg
Wife of Sir Edward. Strong advocate of marital stability within the Kenya European community. Believed Alice was a threat to married society and so persuaded her husband to issue a prohibited immigrant order against her in February 1928.

Monsieur Guinon
The owner of the gun shop in avenue l'Opéra, Paris, where Alice bought the pearl-handled Colt revolver with which she shot Raymund de Trafford.

Sir Walter Harrigan
Attorney General in Kenya from 1933 to 1944. His prosecution of Jock Delves Broughton for the murder of Lord Erroll failed. He may have suppressed Alice's letter of confession which stated that she had killed Lord Erroll.

Josslyn Victor (Joss) Hay, Lord Erroll
Married Lady Idina Gordon (née Sackville) in 1923 and went to live with her in Kenya. Upon the death of his father, he became the twenty-second Earl of Erroll in 1928. Married Mary Ramsay-Hill in 1930. Alice's long-term lover after they met in 1925. Began affair with Diana Delves Broughton in 1940. Shot in mysterious circumstances in January 1941.

Alice de Janzé
Born Alice Silverthorne. Moved to Paris where she met her first husband, Count Frédéric de Janzé. Travelled to Kenya where she met and fell in love with Josslyn Hay and Raymund de Trafford. Married and divorced de Trafford after having attempted to shoot him in 1927 at the Gare du Nord. Committed suicide in September 1941, eight months after Joss's murder.

Count François Louis Léon de Janzé
Father of Frédéric and Henri. Married Moya Hennessy.

Frédéric de Janzé
Eldest son of Count François Louis Léon de Janzé. Married Alice Silverthorne in 1921. After his divorce he married Genevieve Willinger Ryan in 1930. Died suddenly while on assignment in the United States. Author of two books about Kenya, *Vertical Land* and *Tarred with the Same Brush*.

Henri de Janzé
Younger brother of Frédéric. Married to Phyllis Boyd.

Moya de Janzé
Married to Count François Louis Léon de Janzé. Mother of Frédéric and Henri. Her mother was a Mather of the United States. Her maiden name was Hennessy. Her sister Nora was godmother to Alice's first daughter, Nolwen, and married Lord Methuen of Corsham Court.

Nolwen de Janzé
Firstborn daughter of Frédéric and Alice de Janzé. She first married Lionel Armand-Delille, then Edward Rice, and then Baron Clark of Saltwood Castle, father of Alan Clark MP.

Paola de Janzé
Second daughter of Frédéric and Alice de Janzé. Married Walter Haydon and later John Ciechanowski. Paula Gellibrand was her godmother.

Lazarus Kaplan
Solicitor who helped Henry Harris 'Harry' Morris to defend Jock Delves Broughton during his trial for the murder of Lord Erroll.

Jomo Kenyatta
First President of Kenya. Supreme leader of Kenya's independent democracy and promoter of a multiracial society. Creator of the rallying cry of 'Harambee' meaning 'All pull together'. Close friend of Derek Erskine, whose knighthood he requested.

Betty Leslie-Melville
Author of *The Giraffe Lady*, about her life in Kenya. Married to 'Jock' Leslie-Melville whose mother, Mary Leslie-Melville, was an immediate neighbour to Alice in the Wanjohi Valley. Betty wrote in her autobiography that her mother-in-law was certain that Alice had shot Lord Erroll.

Mary Leslie-Melville

Farmed 5,000 acres in the Wanjohi Valley with her husband, the Honourable David Leslie-Melville. Neighbour to Alice. Assisted Alice in buying Wanjohi Farm from Sir John Ramsden. Found a gun that matched the missing Erroll murder weapon in a stream dividing her farm from Alice's.

Julian Joseph ('Lizzie') Lezard

Arrived in Kenya in 1940. Went to stay with Alice at Wanjohi Farm on Lord Erroll's instructions to conduct government surveillance work. Briefly Alice's main lover.

Edward Caswell ('Boy') Long

Invited by Lord Delamere to manage his cattle in the Rift Valley. Married Genesta Heath in 1924. Had brief affair with Idina Hay. Married Paula Gellibrand in 1938.

Marie

French maid and housekeeper to Idina Hay in 1925. Most helpful to Alice on her first arrival in Kenya.

Louise Mattocks

Alice's stepmother. Married William Silverthorne in Paris shortly after the death of Alice's mother, Juliabelle (Louise's cousin). She had several children by William, including Patricia, who was born in 1915.

Henry Harris ('Harry') Morris, KC

Well-known senior counsel based in South Africa. Hired by Diana Delves Broughton to defend her husband, Jock, at his trial (on Lazarus Kaplan's instruction). An expert on ballistics, he obtained an acquittal in the trial.

Alice May (Aunt Tattie)
Born Alice Chapin, she was the sister of Alice's mother, Juliabelle. Married Francis May of the Mays department store chain. Became joint guardian of Alice when Alice was made a ward of the court at the instigation of her brother, Simeon Chapin (Uncle Sim). Also served as long-term guardian of Alice's daughters, Nolwen and Paola.

René Mettetal
Alice's main lawyer in Paris and her defence counsel in her trial for the attempted murder of Raymund de Trafford. Procured her ultimate pardon from the President of France and put the case for her marriage annulment to Pope Pius XI.

Noreen Pearson
Friend of Alice in Nairobi. Had a daughter whom Alice admired – Alice stated in her will that her farm was to go to Noreen's daughter if her own children failed to take over Wanjohi Farm after her death.

Richard (Dickie) Pembroke
Alice's lover in 1940–1941. Testified in court that Alice had been with him on the night of Lord Erroll's murder. Carried Alice's letters with him in the desert campaign against the Afrika Korps in North Africa.

Pope Pius XI
Granted an annulment of Alice's marriage to Frédéric de Janzé in August 1928. Pope from 1922 to 1939.

Mary ('Molly') Ramsay-Hill
Divorced her husband, Cyril Ramsay-Hill, in order to marry Lord Erroll in 1930. Lived with Joss at Cyril's former home, Oserian, on the shores of Lake Naivasha. Her personal wealth was rumoured to have come from Boots, the chemist chain.

Sir John Frecheville 'Chops' Ramsden
Landowner and builder of settler-type houses in the Wanjohi area. Owned Wanjohi Farm prior to the de Janzés' purchase. Built their house for them under Alice's supervision.

Arap Ruta
Alice's chauffeur from 1933 onwards. Member of the Kalengin tribe. Remained with Alice until her death.

Lady Idina Sackville
Much-married founder of the Happy Valley set. Daughter of Albert Sackville, the eighth de la Warr. Married Josslyn Hay in 1923 and had four other husbands as well. Her house Clouds was the centre of Alice's social life after her return to Kenya in 1933.

Sir Francis Scott (the third baronet)
Pioneer settler based near Nanyuki. Made friends with Joss Hay.

Juliabelle Silverthorne
Alice's mother, who died when Alice was seven years old. She was the daughter of Emery David Chapin and Marietta Armour.

Patricia (Pat) Silverthorne
Alice's half-sister. Daughter of William Silverthorne by his second marriage to Louise Mattocks.

William Silverthorne
Alice's father, a businessman in Chicago, Buffalo and New York City. Married Juliabelle Chapin and then, shortly after Juliabelle's death, Louise Mattocks. All but disappeared from Alice's life after she was made ward of court by Juliabelle's family. Married for a third and fourth time late in life to Iris Cottell and Myrtle Plunkett.

Margaret Spicer
Friend to Alice. Mother of the author of this book. American-born and Swiss-educated. Married Roy Spicer in 1926 in Kenya. Died at Hampton Court in 1953 in the grace-and-favour apartment granted to her by Queen Elizabeth II.

Roy Spicer
Father of the author of this book. Son of Bullen Spicer and Adele von Besser. Scholar at St Paul's School, London. Fought in the First World War, wounded and gassed. Awarded the MC. Became Commissioner of Kenya Police

(1925–1931). Friends with Alice and Frédéric de Janzé. Later he was Inspector General of the Palestine Police (1931–1937). Joined the Allied Administration during the Second World War and as a full Colonel became Governor of Rome.

Sir Dermot de Trafford (the sixth baronet)
The current baronet is the son of Rudolph de Trafford and the nephew of Raymund.

Sir Humphrey de Trafford (the third baronet)
Father of Raymund de Trafford. Upon his death in January 1929, he was succeeded by his son Humphrey, who became the fourth baronet.

Raymund de Trafford
After arriving in Kenya, he became Alice's lover. He almost died when she shot him at the Gare du Nord in Paris in 1927. Went on to marry and divorce Alice. Later married Eve Drummond.

Sir Rudolph de Trafford (the fifth baronet)
Brother of Raymund and best man at Alice's marriage to Raymund in 1932. He became the fifth baronet upon the death of his brother Humphrey in 1971.

Fabian Wallace
Close friend of Alice's after her return to Kenya in 1933.

Evelyn Waugh
Renowned author who stayed with Raymund de Trafford in Kenya in 1931 and wrote about his visit in a travel book, *Remote People* (1931). Among his many other books are *Decline and Fall* and *Brideshead Revisited*.

Bibliography

Books

Aschan, Ulf. *The Man Whom Women Loved: The Life of Bror Blixen*. New York: St Martin's Press, 1987.

Brenan, Gerald. *Personal Record 1920–1972*. London: Jonathan Cape, 1974.

———. *Best of Friends: The Brenan-Partridge Letters*. London: Chatto & Windus, 1986.

Brinton, Christian. *The Ambrose McEvoy Exhibition*. New York: Redfield-Kendrick-Odell, 1920.

Cameron, Roderick. *Equator Farm*. London: William Heinemann, 1955.

Carberry, Juanita. *Child of Happy Valley: A Memoir*. London: William Heinemann, 1999.

Carrington, Noel, ed. *Mark Gertler: Selected Letters*. London: Rupert Hart-Davis, 1965.

The Church of Scotland Women's Guild of St. Andrew's. *Kenya Settlers Cookery Book and Household Guide.* Nairobi: East African Standard, 1928.

Connolly, Cyril. *Enemies of Promise.* London: Routledge & Kegan Paul, 1938.

Cooper, Artemis. *Cairo in the War: 1939–1945.* London: Hamish Hamilton, 1989.

Curtis, Arnold, ed. *Memories of Kenya: Stories from the Pioneers.* Nairobi: Evans Brothers, 1986.

Dinesen, Isak. *Letters from Africa 1914–1931.* Edited by Frans Larson; translated by Anne Born. London: Weidenfeld & Nicolson, 1981.

———. *Out of Africa.* London: Putnam, 1937.

Farrant, Leda. *Diana, Lady Delamere and the Lord Erroll Murder.* Nairobi: Publishers Distribution Services, 1997.

———. *The Legendary Grogan: The Only Man to Trek from Cape to Cairo: Kenya's Controversial Pioneer.* London: Hamish Hamilton, 1981.

Farwell, Byron. *The Great War in Africa: 1914–1918.* New York: W.W. Norton, 1987.

Fisher, Clive. *Cyril Connolly: A Nostalgic Life.* London: Macmillan, 1995.

Fox, James. *White Mischief.* London: Jonathan Cape, 1982.

Furneaux, Rupert. *The Murder of Lord Erroll.* London: Stevens & Sons, 1961.

Garnett, David, ed. *Carrington: Letters and Extracts from Her Diaries.* London: Jonathan Cape, 1970.

Gerzina, Gretchen. *Carrington: A Life of Dora Carrington, 1893–1932.* London: John Murray, 1989.

Goldsmith, Lady Annabel. *Annabel: An Unconventional Life.* London: Weidenfeld & Nicolson, 2004.

Graves, Robert. *Good-bye to All That.* London: Jonathan Cape, 1929.

Green, Johnnie. *The Legendary Hispano Suiza.* London: Dalton Watson, 1977.

Gregory, Joseph Richard. *Under the Sun: A Memoir of Dr. R. W. Burkitt, of Kenya.* Nairobi: English Press, 1952.

Grigg, E.W.M. *Kenya's Opportunity: Memories, Hopes and Ideas.* London: Faber & Faber, 1955.

Hamilton, Genesta. *A Stone's Throw: Travels from Africa in Six Decades.* London: Hutchinson, 1986.

Hartley, Aidan. *The Zanzibar Chest: A Memoir of Love and War.* London: HarperPerennial, 2004.

Hayes, Charles. *Oserian: Place of Peace.* Nairobi: Rima, 1997.

Hertz, Noreena. *The Silent Takeover: Global Capitalism and the Death of Democracy.* London: Arrow, 2002.

Hibbert, Christopher. *Africa Explored: Europeans in the Dark Continent.* London: Allen Lane, 1982.

Hill, Jane. *The Art of Dora Carrington.* London: Herbert Press, 1994.

Huxley, Elspeth. *The Flame Trees of Thika: Memories of an African Childhood.* London: Chatto & Windus, 1959.

———. *Nine Faces of Kenya.* London: Collins Harvill, 1990.

———. *Out in the Midday Sun: My Kenya.* London: Chatto & Windus, 1985.

———. *The Sorceror's Apprentice: A Journey Through East Africa.* London: Chatto & Windus, 1949.

———. *White Man's Country.* London: Macmillan, 1935.

Huxley, Elspeth, and Arnold Curtis, eds. *Pioneer's Scrapbook: Reminiscences of Kenya, 1890–1968.* Nairobi: Evans Brothers, 1980.

Jamison, Kay Redfield. *Touched with Fire: Manic Depressive Illness and the Artistic Temperament.* New York: Simon & Schuster, 1993.

Janzé, Frédéric de. *Tarred with the Same Brush.* London: Duckworth, 1929.

———. *Vertical Land.* London: Duckworth, 1928.

Jewell, J.H.A. *Mombasa and the Kenya Coast.* Nairobi: Evans Brothers, 1987.

Johnston, Charles. *Mo and Other Originals.* London: Hamish Hamilton, 1971.

Kenyatta, Jomo. *Facing Mount Kenya.* London: Mercury Books, 1938.

Kohler, Peter C. *Sea Safari.* Abergavenny, Wales: P.M. Heaton, 1995.

Leigh, Ione. *In the Shadow of the Mau Mau.* London: W.H. Allen, 1954.

Leslie-Melville, Betty. *The Giraffe Lady: The Autobiography of Betty Leslie-Melville.* Baltimore: Upland Publishing, 1997.

Lewis, Jeremy. *Cyril Connolly: A Life.* London: Jonathan Cape, 1977.

Lovell, Mary S. *Straight On Till Morning: The Biography of Beryl Markham.* London: Hutchinson, 1987.

Marco Africa (publisher). *Who's Who in East Africa.* 1968

Markham, Beryl. *The Splendid Outcast: The African Stories*

of Beryl Markham. Edited by Mary S. Lovell. London: Hutchinson, 1987.

Matheson, Alastair. *Land of Wide Horizons: An Illustrated Guide to East Africa*. London: MacDonald, 1962.

McEvoy, Ambrose. *Contemporary British Artists*. New York: Charles Scribner's Sons, 1924.

Miller, Charles. *Battle for the Bundu: The First World War in East Africa*. New York: Macmillan, 1974.

Mitford, Nancy. *The Pursuit of Love*. London: Hamish Hamilton, 1945.

Morton, James. *The Who's Who of Unsolved Murders*. London: Kyle Cathie, 1994.

Mosley, Nicholas. *Rules of the Game: Sir Oswald and Lady Cynthia Mosley, 1896–1933*. London: Secker & Warburg, 1982.

Nicholls, C. S. *Elspeth Huxley: A Biography*. London: HarperCollins, 2002.

O'Neill, Pat Cavendish. *The Lion in the Bedroom*. Sydney: Park Street Press, 2004.

Osborne, Frances. *The Bolter: Idina Sackville – the woman who scandalized 1920s society and became White Mischief's infamous seductress*. London: Virago, 2008.

Ostrovsky, Erika. *Eye of Dawn: The Rise and Fall of Mata Hari*. New York: Macmillam, 1978.

Pakenham, Thomas. *The Scramble for Africa*. London: Weidenfeld & Nicholson, 1992.

Pasley, Fred D. *Al Capone: The Biography of a Self-Made Man*. London: Faber & Faber, 1930.

Pavitt, Nigel. *Kenya: The First Explorers*. London: Aurum Press, 1989.

Pearson, John. *Wild Life and Safari in Kenya*. Nairobi: East African Publishing House, 1967.

Porter, Henry. *Remembrance Day*. London: Orion, 1999.

Ricciardi, Lorenzo, and Mirella Ricciardi. *African Rainbow: Across Africa by Boat*. London: Ebury Press, 1989.

Ridgeway, Rick. *The Shadow of Kilimanjaro: On Foot Across East Africa*. New York: Henry Holt, 2000.

Rodwell, Edward. *The Mombasa Club.* Nairobi: Rodwell Press, 1988.

Rutherston, Albert, ed. *Contemporary British Artists: Ambrose McEvoy.* New York: Charles Scribner's Sons, 1924.

Sandford, Christine. *Ethiopia Under Haile Selassie.* London: J.M. Dent, 1946.

Schoenberg, Robert J. *Mr. Capone.* New York: William Morrow, 1992.

Scott, Pamela. *A Nice Place to Live.* Salisbury, England: Michael Russell, 1991.

Taylorson, A. W. *Revolving Arms.* London: Herbert Jenkins 1967.

Thesiger, Wilfred. *My Kenya Days.* London: HarperCollins, 1994.

Tomalin, Claire. *Mrs Jordan's Profession: The Story of a Great Actress and a Future King.* London: Penguin, 1994.

Trench, Charles Chenevix. *Men Who Ruled Kenya: The Kenya Administration 1892–1963.* London: Radcliffe Press, 1993.

Trzebinski, Errol. *The Kenya Pioneers.* London: William Heinemann, 1991.

———. *The Life and Death of Lord Erroll: The Truth Behind*

the Happy Valley Murder. London: Fourth Estate, 2000.

———. *The Lives of Beryl Markham.* London: William Heinemann, 1993.

———. *Silence Will Speak.* London: Grafton Books, 1985.

Vatican Council. *Dignitas Connubii.* Vatican City: Libreria Editrice Vaticana, 2005.

Wagner, Rob L. *Classic Cars.* New York: MetroBooks, 1996.

Wahrman, Dror. *Michael's Jerusalem: The New Guide.* Edited by Michael Shichor. Tel Aviv: Inbal Travel Information, 1993.

Waugh, Evelyn. *Remote People: A Report from Ethiopia and British Africa, 1930–1931.* London: Duckworth, 1931.

Wheeler, Sara. *Too Close to the Sun: The Life and Times of Denys Finch Hatton.* London: Jonathan Cape, 2006.

Wills, Colin. *Who Killed Kenya?* London: Dennis Dobson, 1953.

Privately Published Sources

Cartland, Barbara. 'Firsts'. Last entry dated 1997.

Silverthorn Family Newsletter, 1986.

Newspapers and Periodicals

Baltimore Sun

Le Boulevardier

Bystander

Chicago Tribune

Daily Express

Daily Mail
Daily Mirror
Daily Sketch
East African Standard
L'Echo de Paris
New York Times
News of the World
Paris-Soir
People
Le Petit Parisien
Reynolds Illustrated News
Star
Sunday Express
Sunday Pictorial
Tatler
Telegraph
The Times

Acknowledgements

Dave Allen Exceptional bush pilot with superb skills in navigation and low flying. For discovering Wanjohi Farm from the air and then delivering me there.

Frédéric Armand Delille, son of Nolwen de Janzé and owner of Château de Parfondeval. For his hospitality at his country house in Normandy, for allowing me to inspect the family photograph albums in the Plum Room, and for the loan of two photographs of Alice on display in his main sitting room at Parfondeval.

Alice Boyle, daughter of Dr William Boyle, Alice de Janzé's doctor in the last years of her life and the key witness regarding the letter of confession left at Alice's bedside on her death. For her constant friendship and help on the story of Alice de Janzé.

Richard Britten-Long For all his help with photographs of Paula Gellibrand and Augustus John.

Dame Barbara Cartland For her correspondence and supply of 'Firsts' and for the details she provided about the Embassy Club and who went there on Thursday evenings.

Juliet Cassidy For six years of continuous research and help on rewrites, and for her visits to Paris, Normandy, and particularly Chicago, where she would discover details about Alice's early life. A meticulous researcher and scribe. But perhaps her greatest asset apart from her academic prowess is her splendid personality.

Causeway Resources For providing numerous press cuttings.

Eve Charles A very talented editor. For her mastery of the English written word and deep understanding of the subject, and for giving a high polish to the story I had crafted.

Patsy Chilton, former wife of Dr Roger Bowles. For detailed written notes about her meetings with Alice at the Muthaiga Club, Nairobi in 1939.

Paola Ciechanowski, Alice's younger daughter. For our

friendly meetings in Londinières and endless chats, for the memories she provided of her mother, and for our correspondence over five years.

Sir Toby Clarke For his introductions in Chicago.

Dick Crofton For his guidance regarding the military records of Dickie Pembroke and Raymund de Trafford (both Coldstream Guards officers).

Tom Eaton-Evans Husband of Noel Case. For providing help and acting as a liaison.

Sir Derek Erskine For his continuous friendship since 1950 and for many insights into life in Kenya in 1930.

Francis Erskine, Derek's son. For his hospitality on our visit to the Wanjohi Valley.

Patrizia Erskine, Francis Eskine's daughter-in-law. For being good enough to accompany me to Alice's home in the Wanjohi Valley.

Petal Erskine, Derek's daughter. For her many memories of her father.

Dr Peter Fenwick, neuropsychiatrist. For his detailed comments on Alice's probable mental state and his explanation of the difference between bipolar disorder and cyclothymia.

Captain Gordon Ferguson, the secretary of the Taporley Hunt Club and author of *The Green Collars*, a history of England's oldest hunt club. Gordon included an addendum in an edition of *The Green Collars* about Alice's confession to the shooting of Joss Erroll. He also recommended that I seek out Barbara Cartland about the Embassy Club.

Angélique Fiedler, Alice's granddaughter. For her heartfelt and protective interest in the de Janzé name; and for making letters from her mother (Nolwen) and Alice available to me.

Christy Fletcher and Grainne Fox My wonderful agents at Fletcher & Company, for their superlative precision and competence in bringing the Alice story to its completion.

William Gachanja For tracing the location of settlers' farms in the Wanjohi Valley.

Madame Genèvieve François-Poncet A great friend of Frédéric Armand Delille's father. For her help in arranging for me to meet Frédéric.

Michael Harley For acting as a liaison in Kenya.

Aidan Hartley, author of *The Zanzibar Chest* (2004). For his advice and well-chosen introduction to Emma Parry and with thanks to Claire, Aidan's wife, for her apt and perceptive comments.

Doreen Hartley, mother-in-law of the current owner of Giraffe Manor, formerly owned by the Leslie-Melvilles. For making me aware of *The Giraffe Lady* by Betty Leslie-Melville, with its revelation of Alice's possible culpability.

Harry Hartshorne Jr, the grandson of Simeon Chapin. For his help that resulted in the supply of several unique early photographs taken in the United States and for his welcoming hand on our visit to New York.

Margaret Hayes, the widow of the author of *Oserian*, Charles Hayes. For kindly obtaining four reels of tape recording every issue of the *Boulevardier* publication. Her husband's book *Oserian* covers a century of Kenya's social history including some details concerning Alice de Janzé.

Dr Noreena Hertz, author of *The Silent Takeover: Global Capitalism and the Death of Democracy*. For introducing me to Juliet Cassidy and for persuading me to write for two hours a day.

Robin Hollister For his insight into the making of *Out of Africa*, and for his enlightened comments on the making of *The Constant Gardener*, a film set in Kenya.

Joanne Grady Huskey, author, educator and wife of an American diplomat. For accompanying the author on his first visit to Alice's house in the Wanjohi Valley.

Senior Chief William Kinuthia, a resident of the Wanjohi Valley whose house is near Alice de Janze's former home there. He was kind enough to coordinate my visit.

Robin Long For his help and his many memories of his stepmother Paula Gellibrand Long.

Patricia McGuigan (neé Silverthorne), Alice's half-sister. For her extensive help and her memories of Alice while in London.

Lord Montagu of Beaulieu For identifying and describing Mr Silverthorne's enormous Stoddard-Dayton motor car.

Clare Naylor Vivacious and intelligent author of seven books. For her encouragement. It was her enthusiasm for the Alice story and her professionalism that led me into the world of writing.

Martha Nyman For discovering and bringing to my notice the sensational photograph of Alice in the Correctional Court in Paris.

Frances Osborne For her friendship and cooperation while writing her second book, *The Bolter*, a biography of her great-grandmother Lady Idina Sackville, who married Joss Hay, Earl of Erroll.

Emma Parry The most competent literary agent that

anyone could wish for. Inspirational and clever in her dealings with neurotic authors.

Henry Porter, author of the novel *Remembrance Day* and one-time London editor of *Vanity Fair*. For listening to the Alice story and for encouraging me to make the Gare du Nord event one of the key chapters in this book.

P.J. Ransley For enabling me to trace the original deed plan of Alice's home in the Wanjohi Valley.

Arnold Raphael For listening early on and lending his support in my research. It was he who made me aware of the crime documentary by Rupert Furneaux.

Guillaume de Rougement, Alice's grandson. For providing me with detailed notes that he wrote down at the bedside of his mother, Paola, in Londinières, Normandy. These notes contained information about Alice, and the de Janzé family. A very remarkable man with the finest collection of beetles (Coleopterus) in the world, and who speaks Aramaic (the language of Jesus Christ).

Kerri Sharp, my editor in the UK. For her inspiring enthusiasm about the Alice story and her essential role in producing this edition of the book.

Sir Sacheverell Reresby Sitwell For supplying a brilliant photograph of Lizzie Lezard, who had been a friend of his mother's, and frequently stayed at her country home.

Penny Smith, a secretary who has laboured mightily with six years of research correspondence and numerous drafts of the manuscript. For her aptitude and loyalty.

Yaniv Soha, Charles Spicer's editorial assistant. For his dedicated help and first-class capability in the art of bringing a book to completion.

Charles Spicer, my editor in the United States. For all his help and perceptive understanding of this biography; for his enthusiasm and wit, and for his in-depth knowledge of publishing.

Dermot de Trafford, Raymund de Trafford's nephew. For the loan of his uncle's personal photograph album compiled in Kenya in 1926, and for his help in describing Raymund's life after the war.

Errol Trzebinski, a great and well-known writer, who has made Kenya a special subject of study. Her biography of Joss Erroll, *The Life and Death of Lord Erroll: The Truth Behind the Happy Valley Murder* (2000), has proved to be invaluable. For her enthusiasm about this project, and for generously giving me both ideas and help.

Ronnie Ward of Lake Forest, near Chicago, for his liaison work in that part of the world.

Danièle Waterpark For being French, for taking me to the Bibliothèque Nationale in Paris, for finding French newspaper coverage of the Gare du Nord event, and for providing instant translations. I am also grateful to her for introducing me to Frédéric Armand Delille, the son of Nolwen de Janzé; for inviting me to stay at her daughter Caroline Goulding's house in Le Touquet and driving me to Normandy to visit the Château de Parfondeval and Paola in Londinières, and for introducing me to Angélique Fiedler, Alice's granddaughter.

Michael Watson For his enlightened comments about his cousin Dickie Pembroke.

Rupert Watson For his research in Kenya.

The Honourable Vicky Westrop For providing a family album showing pictures of Phyllis de Janzé (née Boyd) in later years.

Index

(key to initials: AJ = Alice de Janzé; DB = Diana Broughton; DH = Donald Haldeman; EL = Edward Long; FJ = Frédéric de Janzé; HDB = Henry Delves Broughton; JH = Josslyn Hay; MJ = Moya de Janzé; MRH = Mary Ramsay-Hill; RP = Richard Pembroke; RT = Raymund de Trafford)

Index

Index

Index

Index

Alice in a pony and trap, aged seven, Buffalo, New York, shortly before her mother Juliabelle died on 2 June, 1907. (From the collection of Harry Hartshorne Jr.)

Fred Silverthorne in his Stoddard-Knighton nine-litre motorcar with uniformed chauffeur. (From the collection of Harry Hartshorne Jr.)

Portrait photo of Alice, aged eighteen, before she met Frédéric de Janzé. (From the collections of Harry Hartshorne Jr. and Guillaume de Rougemont)

Wedding of Frédéric and Alice in Chicago on 21 September, 1921. (From the collections of Harry Hartshorne Jr., Guillaume de Rougemont, and Pat Silverthorne)

Hunting at Château Parfondeval in Normandy, France, where Alice spent long weekends and summers from 1922 to 1925. (From the collection of Guillaume de Rougemont)

Paula Gellibrand dressed as a mannequin in 'a coat of white rainproof cloth trimmed in black wool'. Paula was Alice's closest female friend in Paris and later in Kenya. (From Paula Gellibrand's scrapbook)

S.S. Gascon, *the ship of the Messageries Maritimes, on which Alice and Frédéric sailed from Marseilles to Mombasa, Kenya, on 17 September, 1925.* (Image provided by Iziko Museums of Cape Town)

Alice with Lord Delamere and Raymund de Trafford at Delamere's house, 'Loresho', Nairobi, Kenya, 1926. (Courtesy of Sir Dermot de Trafford Bart.)

Alice and Joss Erroll in 1926. (From the collection of Sir Dermot de Trafford Bart.)

Lapérouse restaurant where Alice and Raymund met for lunch on 17 March, 1927. They shopped in the afternoon, with Alice purchasing a revolver and six bullets. Alice shot Raymund and herself at 4:30 P.M. on that day.

Alice in the Paris Correctional Court awaiting a verdict on the attempted murder of Raymund de Trafford, 23 December, 1927.
(© Corbis)

Studio portrait of Alice with pearls, 1928, while in exile from Kenya. (From the collection of Frédéric Armand Delille)

Press photo of Alice with Raymund and bulldog Jimmy after their marriage in Paris on 22 February, 1932. The marriage lasted only three months.

Porto Luca Cottage in Muthaiga, Nairobi, rented by Alice. She slept here on the night of Joss Erroll's murder in January 1941. (Courtesy of the author)

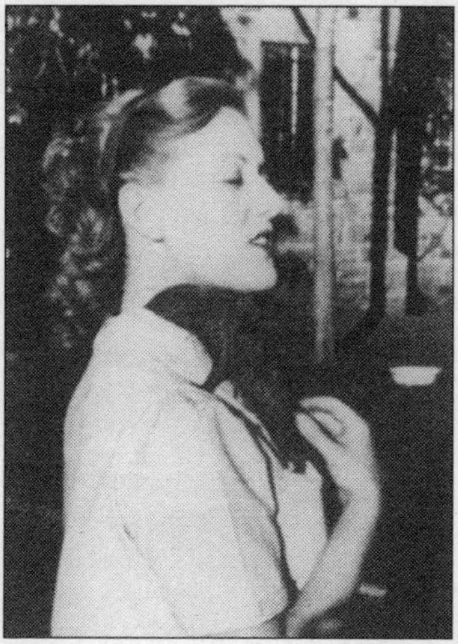

Lady Diana Delves Broughton, née Caldwell, with her pet mongoose at the Marula Lane House at Karen, Nairobi, 1941.

Marula Lane House at Karen, Nairobi. It was from this house that Joss Erroll departed on the night of 24 January, 1941, only to be murdered on his drive home. (Courtesy of the author)

Dickie Pembroke at Alice's house in Tiwi. This was a coastal property south of Mombasa. Dickie was Alice's last lover. (Courtesy of Noel Eaton-Evans)

The veranda side of Alice's house in Wanjohi Valley. This was where Alice died on Saturday, 27 September, 1941. (Courtesy of Noel Case)